Hawthorne and the Real

GW00645231

Hawthorne and the Real

Bicentennial Essays

Edited by Millicent Bell

The Ohio State University Press
Columbus

Library of Congress Cataloging-in-Publication Data

Hawthorne and the real : bicentennial essays / edited by Millicent Bell.
    p. cm.
   Includes bibliographical references and index.
   ISBN 0–8142–0986–6 (cloth : alk. paper) — ISBN 0-8142-9060-4 (cd
rom)
     1. Hawthorne, Nathaniel, 1804–1864—Criticism and interpretation. 2.
Literature and society—United States—History—19th century.   I. Bell,
Millicent.
   PS1888.H39 2005
   813'.3-dc22
                                  2004027320

   Paper (ISBN: 978-0-8142-5612-1)

   Cover design by Jay Bastian
   Type set in Minion

Contents

Preface

The essays collected in this volume owe their existence to the idea of a group of "Hawthornians" at a meeting of the Executive Council of the Nathaniel Hawthorne Society in the spring of 2002, that the bicentennial of this famous writer's birth, on July 4, 2004, was an occasion for a rediscovery as well as a celebration. Hawthorne's is a reputation that has never needed revival. Yet how still unsettled, we found ourselves exclaiming to one another, is the significance of even his greatest and best-known work, *The Scarlet Letter.* The staple of the schoolroom, it has also been pitched onto the dissecting table by critics in each generation since it was published, and the present one seems no exception.

At that 2002 meeting, the approaching bicentennial moment seemed appropriate for defining "our Hawthorne." That phrase, of course, reminded us all of a famous essay with such a title written by Lionel Trilling in 1964 for the *Centenary Essays,* published by the The Ohio State University Press to mark the anniversary of Hawthorne's death. That distinguished volume, the result of an impulse similar to our own, has been of enduring importance, even though most of the views it offers have since been disputed many times in many ways. What might strike one most was the fact that few who write about Hawthorne today would share their prevailing bias in favor of a portrait of the artist who was more the moral allegorist than the historian. We are not as ready as past interpreters to credit Hawthorne's own claim to have been a writer of romances little connected with the social subject matter of the "realist" novel. Might not a new commemorative volume define our later response?

Having undertaken, at the Executive Council's urging, the editing of such a collection, I began to solicit contributions among outstanding scholars and critics working on Hawthorne today. I did not propose any overall unitary thematic topic or common approach. Yet, as it turned out, most of the essays submitted hung together to a striking degree—confirming our sense that we had a Hawthorne to call particularly "ours." Almost all exhibited a common intent to explore, in one way or another, in one or another of Hawthorne's works, the relation of his imagination to "the real"—that is, to the social reality he sometimes claimed to find uninteresting or unrepresentable. They make an argument for the interpretation of Hawthorne's writings as more expressive of the objective common conditions and public issues of his day than has been conceded until quite recently. It is this viewpoint I have chosen to argue for in the essay I have myself contributed and it is the emphasis intended in its title, "Hawthorne and the Real," which I have borrowed for the book as a whole. But aside from this common interest, the reader of these essays will find a provocative spirit of controversy among the essays. Not all can be said to be in agreement, and no reader, perhaps, will equally concur with every one of the essayists, though, hopefully, all will provoke strong interest. The question of "Hawthorne and Politics" is deepened and complicated by a striking essay by Michael T. Gilmore which examines the relation of the mid-nineteenth century's sectional crisis to the agency of language and the reflection of this dissension in Hawthorne. Larry J. Reynolds then argues powerfully for what is still a controversial view of Hawthorne's response to the slavery issue, bringing out with particular pertinence his distrust of political terrorism and discovering a representation of this in his interest in the seventeenth-century witchcraft trials. Both Lawrence Buell and John Carlos Rowe challenge the traditional assumption of exclusive "Americanness" in Hawthorne's writing by new interpretations of *The Scarlet Letter* and other works. Nina Baym's essay, a retrospective survey of the response of "feminist" interpretation of Hawthorne over the past thirty years, also offers a reformulation of her own pioneer views, and Leland S. Person and David Leverenz contribute new studies of Hawthorne's complex responses to femininity. Hawthorne's late unfinished romances, often dismissed as of minor importance, are carefully reviewed in their sequence by Rita K. Gollin, who searches out particularly themes reflecting the quest for a national identity which preoccupied Hawthorne's countrymen and women. The final essay by Brenda Wineapple, testifies to the persisting elusiveness and strangeness along with his relation to real history that Hawthorne offers as a biographic subject.

My labors as editor have been supported in various ways by the members of the Hawthorne Society Executive Council, to whom I offer my thanks for encouragement and advice in the original conception of this collection, and in soliciting the essays or evaluating and editing them: Richard Millington, Rosemary Mims Fisk, Leland S. Person, Nancy Bentley, Samuel C. Coale, Michael T. Gilmore, Brenda Wineapple, Myra Jehlen,

Brigitte Bailey, and David B. Kesterson. Thanks are due also to Heather Lee Miller, Acquisitions Editor of the Ohio State University Press, who responded with warm interest to my original proposal for the book and who has guided me in putting it together. Above all, I am grateful to the gifted contributors who consented to join me in this effort by writing— and sometimes rewriting—these essays with interest and devotion.

Embedded references to Hawthorne's works are made throughout this volume by reference to the Centenary Edition, edited by William Charvat et al. (Columbus, Ohio: Ohio State University Press, 1962–1997), vols. I–XXIII. Each work will be cited by volume number in capitalized Roman numerals followed by the page number(s) in Arabic numerals.

Millicent Bell

1

Hawthorne and the Real

MILLICENT BELL

Hawthorne would always say that his writing offered an insufficient view of what most persons call "reality." In 1860, when all the fiction he would live to complete had already been written, he told his publisher, James T. Fields, that *The Marble Faun* was hardly a book he would have chosen to read if someone else had been the author:

> My own individual taste is for quite another class of works than those which I myself am able to write. Have you ever read the novels of Anthony Trollope? They precisely suit my taste; solid and substantial, written on the strength of beef and through the inspiration of ale, and just as real as if some giant had hewn a great lump out of the earth and put it under a glass case with all its inhabitants going about their daily business, and not suspecting they were being made a show of. (XVIII 229)

Hawthorne did not give a name to the "class" to which Trollope's books belonged. As Henry James later observed, Hawthorne "was not a man with a literary theory; he was guiltless of a system," and probably had not heard of realism, "this remarkable compound having (although it was invented some time earlier) come into general use only since his death" (*American Writers* 321).

In the 1830s and 1840s, when Hawthorne was writing most of his short stories and sketches, Balzac's *comédie humaine* completed its succession of dense representations of French society, and when Hawthorne was writing his longer works of fiction in the next decade, the French had already begun to label as "*réalisme*" not only the major novels of Balzac, but those of new writers like Turgenev, Maupassant, the Goncourts, Zola, and Flaubert, who was notoriously prosecuted for the supposed indecency of *Madame Bovary* in 1857. But it is doubtful if Hawthorne was familiar with this French new wave; indeed, it was not until 1853 that a review of Balzac's *comédie* in the *Westminster Review* employed the English word as a literary term (203, 212, 214). Hawthorne's influences remained chiefly British writers whose comprehensive verisimilitude was mixed with contrary effects. Scott had been his earliest enthusiasm, the inspiration not only of his romantic apprentice novel, *Fanshawe,* but of his undertaking to recover an authentic native past in *The Scarlet Letter.* In 1851, Hawthorne was reading *David Copperfield* to his children during winter evenings in Lenox. He had just finished *The House of the Seven Gables,* a work of Dickensian mingling of the grotesque with social fact though without Dickens's plenitude of reference. In 1859 he called Thackeray "the greatest living novelist" (Kendall 90); the author of *Vanity Fair* could be said, like Trollope, to have shown how to seize a lump of the world whole, and place it on view as though under glass. It was, however, too late for either Thackeray or Trollope to be his models.

For some of Hawthorne's greatest American contemporaries—Emerson, Thoreau, and even Melville (despite the whaling-voyage factuality mixed with the visionary in *Moby-Dick*)—the "real," in any case, was what might be thought, by less platonic minds, to be the *un*real. The "real," to the romantic transcendentalists, was the "ideal" of which physical facts were merely symbolic. Melville detected in Hawthorne a gloomy view of humanity that he might have inherited from his puritan ancestors. But this was something available without reference to that heritage, something to be felt by any deeply reflective person. It was an insight into the hidden cavern of changeless human nature. It was the poet's task to strike through the mask of the here and now and even of the there and then. Meville's Hawthorne was not concerned to know, for its own sake, the historic past, despite his use of American colonial materials. Nor was he interested in the mere appearances of the present. He had described himself accurately, Melville would have said, in his preface to *The Snow Image and Other Twice-told Tales,* published in 1851, as one "who has been burrowing, to his utmost ability, into the depths of our common nature, for the purposes of psychological romance, and who pursues his researches in that dusky region, as he needs must, as well by the tact of sympathy as by the light of observation" (XI 4).

Nevertheless, Hawthorne sometimes had a bad conscience about his apparent neglect of the outward world there to be believed in. Matter, understood in the "light of observation," was what mattered in a "materialist" society, and he felt at fault for slighting it. He blamed himself for his seclusive habits and meager interest in the observable. "I have seen so little of the world, that I have nothing but thin air to concoct my stories of, and it is not easy to give a lifelike semblance to such shadowy stuff," Hawthorne wrote his Bowdoin classmate, Longfellow, when, in 1837, he sent him a copy of his first book of stories, *Twice-told Tales.* It was a picture he painted also for Sophia Peabody—with whom he had fallen in love. He told her that for years he had spent a "long seclusion" spinning morbid fantasy out of his imagination in a "solitary chamber"(XV 494). Longfellow was moved by Hawthorne's letter and wrote a supportive review of his book. Sophia responded to his plea for rescue from the prison of solitariness and married him. There was, however, something quite literary—a resort to a familiar romantic convention of the melancholy poet-exile—in this description. It was already proving so effective in the creation of his narrative persona that he would be compelled to give warning in the second edition of *Twice-told Tales* that he had exaggerated. But this confession did not change the impression Hawthorne had made on many readers, and later critics and biographers would, with only a few exceptions, tend to ignore it. Arlin Turner, one of Hawthorne's best twentieth-century biographers, not only would call the letter to Longfellow "one of the most remarkable instances of self-revelation and self-analysis in our literary archive," but would declare it to be a key to the writer's lifelong artistic aims. It showed, says Turner, that "for Hawthorne, the author of moral romances and studies of human character, the important consideration was not what an event or a situation was, but rather what his creative imagination conceived it to be. To him, every object, act or person, including himself and his activities, was less significant in itself than what it could be taken to represent" (1980, 88–89). But Turner took too little account of Hawthorne's joke—his less than candidness—and deduced too much about his aesthetics from his suspect self-portrait.

In fact, the young Hawthorne had not really been the "owl" he described but a habitual daytime stroller about town and in the countryside, and he had regularly passed summer weeks in the deliberate exploration of New England, visiting rural communities, recording assiduously his encounters and observations. An active, outward-directed side to his personality was also revealed in a less often quoted part of the Longfellow letter when he added that he intended to shortly leave his "owl's nest" for a tour of New England and was trying to get employment either as an editor or as historian of the contemplated government expedition to the South Seas, "for though fixed so long to one spot, I have always had a desire [to] run round the world." The expedition, eventually led by Charles Wilkes, would be gone for four years and circumnavigate the globe, charting three hundred previously unknown islands and the coast of Antarctica. Hawthorne did not get the appointment (what a different life history his might have been if he had!). But his appetite for an untranscendental reality would persist. The man who had portrayed himself as a solitary who preferred to live withdrawn from common life found the group withdrawal of Brook Farm unacceptable. He felt that his stay had been "a dream" and he only "a spectre" there. He decided that he could "best attain the higher ends of [his] life by retaining the ordinary relation to society" (XV 237),

In the sketch "Old News," published in 1835, Hawthorne had already written of coming upon collections of old newspaper reports of colonial times showing the hardships of daily life among the first settlers. He was prompted to declare that "[a]ll philosophy that would abstract mankind from the present is no more than words" (XI 133). Even when he lived in Concord, while keeping himself at a certain distance from Emerson and his followers (Emerson he would call "that everlasting rejecter of all that is, and seeker for he knows not what"), Hawthorne found more interest in the rubbish of old newspapers and almanacs accumulated in the Old Manse than in the theological treatises left behind by resident clergymen. He wrote in his preface to *Mosses from an Old Manse,* "It was as if I had found bits of magic-looking glass with the images of a vanished century in them." The writers of the old books of theology had "been able to produce nothing half so real, as these newspaper scribblers and almanac makers had thrown off, in the effervescence of a moment" (X 20).

The preface to his *Mosses from an Old Manse* has not been read sufficiently for its ambiguity. The Manse itself Hawthorne describes as not having "quite the aspect of belonging to the material world." The sluggish Concord River that never occupies itself in turning a solitary mill spindle or grinding any corn, seems to him a representation of idleness he cannot afford, and a remove from the actual. But the Concord past sends other messages. There is the disturbing story told him by Lowell of a wounded British soldier's murder by a Concord Revolutionary. A "wilder interest" in primal American guilt is aroused when, led by Thoreau, Hawthorne finds Indian arrowheads near his door and imagines the vanished Indian village of chiefs and warriors, squaws, and children at play. He wonders if he feels joy or pain as he looks at the houses and stone fences of the white men who displaced them. Frightened of what his vision of the true past implies, the resident of the Manse somewhat frantically concludes: "But this is nonsense. The Old Manse is better than a thousand wigwams" (X 11).

Living among the better-incomed Concord intellectuals, Hawthorne's sense of the untranscendental had only increased. He could not keep up with the rent on the Manse, property belonging to the Emerson family, though he and Sophia sold apples that grew on the place. They moved with their new baby back to Salem to live with his mother's relatives, the same humiliating shelter he had accepted for years after college. He would feel, repeatedly, the common American shame of pecuniary failure when, after his expulsion from the Salem Custom House, he had had to accept a fund raised for him by friends. "Ill-success in life is really and justly a matter of shame," he said (XV 309). Not until he was forty-eight did Hawthorne enjoy near-solvency. After the critical success of *The Scarlet Letter* and then, in rapid succession, the publication of *The House of the Seven Gables* and *The Blithedale Romance,* he was able, at last, to buy a house of his own. But his life would continue to the end to be fraught with matter-of-fact realities that a propensity for dreaming could not obscure.

Hawthorne understood how the machinery of social power engaged the ambitious in the sleights and maneuvers by which a literary career might be promoted. During the public excitement over his dismissal as Surveyor of the Salem Custom House after the electoral victory of the Whigs over the Democrats, he was portrayed by his supporters as a man with no interest in politics and politicking—the owl-man image again attracting sympathy. Hawthorne himself asked a friend to tell the Whig party leader, Rufus Choate, that he was "an inoffensive man of letters—having obtained a pitiful little office on no other plea than his pitiful little literature"(XVI 264). But Hawthorne had been more "political" than he pretended. He had not, it is true, followed custom by firing all the Whig survivors who remained on his staff when he took office, although he had got his post in the first place through the efforts of friends among the Democrats. But he may really have been guilty of some party favoritism—the malfeasance of which he was accused by his enemies. He was hardly unworldly.

It is not surprising that Hawthorne's other friendships made in college with future politicians Jonathan Cilley, Horatio Bridge, and Franklin Pierce proved far closer than his relation with Longfellow, their class laureate. These less intellectual friends were active to secure him a government appointment even before he got his first job in the Boston Custom house in 1839, and they continued to assist him by such efforts thereafter. It has been held that his eventual literary fame was made possible by his contacts with the literary establishment—writers like Longfellow or Emerson and his circle (Tompkins 1985). But more useful than these had been the Democratic journalist and editor John O'Sullivan, who published two dozen of Hawthorne's tales and sketches in the *Democratic Review,* a party organ, between 1838 and 1845. Hawthorne's publisher, Fields, the canny literary entrepreneur who understood the literary *market* better than anyone, became his most reliable counselor, important to him to the end of his life. But dearest of all was Pierce, an intimate on every level. Hawthorne's final, most lucrative government post was that of U. S. Consul in Liverpool, the reward—which he must have expected (though he played innocent)—for writing the future president's campaign biography. Pierce was already odious to northern intellectuals—including members of Sophia's family—for his support of the Missouri compromise, and Emerson would call him the worst president the country had ever had. But he was a devoted supporter in a friend's times of difficulty. And with this "practical" man of the world's conservative temporizing, Hawthorne's own pessimism about human possibilities was ultimately in tune.

We are entitled, I want to urge, now, to read Hawthorne's own directions to readers with the same distrust due his descriptions of his personal character as that of someone remote from common reality. Hawthorne has misled critics who have so often begun discussion of his fiction by quoting the brief passage in *The House of the Seven Gables'* preface which offers a definition of the romance with its vague grant of "a certain latitude, both as to its fashion and material, which he would not have felt himself entitled to assume, had he professed to be writing a Novel"—that is, a work in which literal realism played a major part. Romancers, among whom Hawthorne numbered himself, were not, like the novelist, obliged to aim at "a very minute fidelity not merely to the possible, but to the probable and ordinary course of man's experience." But he may have been making his discrimination with some irresponsibility, as if he were not taking it as seriously as his critics since have done. It needs to be asked how much and what sort of latitude makes the difference in question. Where can the line be confidently drawn between the supposedly different genres? He goes on to allow, almost as an afterthought, that the romantic latitude he speaks of must be resorted to restrainedly. The writer should, preferably, "mingle the Marvelous rather as a slight delicate, and evanescent flavor than as any portion of the actual substance of the dish offered to the Public" (II 1). Hawthorne thus reduces the role of improbability or fantasy—an important aspect of his discrimination—to an inconsequence. Hawthorne must have known that there were few examples he could name that might be airily set apart with no admixture of each other. No master of the novel ever offered fuller and more direct observation of English commonplace life than Dickens, but no writer of romance indulged more audaciously than Dickens in sinuosities of improbable plot and the romantic grotesque.

Hawthorne may have been uncertain when he himself was writing romantically or realistically. *The Scarlet Letter* is strongly historical in detail, based on the germ of a true episode and framed in an exact calen-

dar of known historic events, a story plain and probable except for occasional moments disclaimed by the narrator as unverifiable (this, itself, a
realist gesture). Its subtitle, "A Romance," is Hawthorne's own, to be found
on the manuscript title page that is the sole surviving fragment of his book
in his own hand. This was something more generic than the "A Tale" set
beneath the title of *Fanshawe*. But, originally, he had wanted to include his
longer colonial tale in a collection to be called "Old time Legends: Together
with Sketches, experimental and ideal." "Experimental" is an unclear desig-
nation, perhaps suggesting "experiential" or dealing with reality in some
way; based on experience, as opposed to fanciful or ideal. The sketches
would have conditioned readers' response to the short stories and this
newer work also representing old New England. The narrator of *The Scarlet Letter* refers, in the book's final sentence, to the "concluded legend" just
retold—returning to the first proposed title of the collection, and suggesting a traditional tale with some claim to historicity. "A Romance" may have
been a last-minute decision. Fields had advertised the book as *The Scarlet
Letter: A Novel*.

The Custom House preface asserts, though only pretendingly, the historicity of what it introduces—the rewriting of a previous manuscript
derived from the verbal testimony of witnesses and confirmed by material
evidence, the actual letter once worn by Hester Prynne. And the
Hawthorne narrator offers to show Surveyor Pue's document and the
embroidered scrap of cloth to any skeptical inquirer. Of course, this claim
is an old novelistic device not meant to deceive. But on one level it succeeds
at least in asserting that the tale to be told has something *like* the authority
of historic record; it is in congruence with the frame of recorded colonial
history within which it is cunningly placed. Hawthorne also presents himself as a kind of witness from later time by invoking the participations of
his Puritan ancestors in persecutions of which Hester's ordeal is an example, and admitting that he is one of them in nature. Their views and acts,
their historic exclusions and executions, made them—and him—complicit
in the punishment of deviant persons like Hester.

In a passage too readily seen as a port of entry into Hawthorne's aesthetic, "The Custom House" preface does seem to declare, nevertheless,
that the writer's imagination was a dream realm which bore only indirect
relation to the obvious "true" of waking experience. But this, too, is less
forthright than has been supposed. The "familiar room," the deserted par-
lor where he sits, is no fantasy and has no romantic strangeness. The coal
fire and moonlight which are its only illumination make every object
"minutely visible"—as in realist description—rather than indefinite or dis-
torted. Around him are the ordinary objects of a "domestic scene"—the

table with its workbasket, the sofa and bookcase, the child's shoe and toys. Yet he claims it "suitable for a romance-writer to get acquainted with his illusive guests" (I 35), though we cannot be sure what kind of guests these are. Are the personages who people his tale *un*real or unlikely fantasies, romance silhouettes, or psychologically "rounded" novelistic characters? Does the romantically demonic Chillingworth—someone E. M. Forster called a "flat" character—inhabit the same generic atmosphere as Hester?

Hawthorne is insistent about the romance status of his later fiction. But in the preface to *The Marble Faun* he remarks upon the difficulty, for a foreign visitor, of composing "a portrait of Italian manners and character"— that is, a detailed and accurate novelistic presentation of a people in its society. He observed that he had "lived too long abroad not to be aware that a foreigner seldom acquires that knowledge of a country, at once flexible and profound, which may justify him in endeavoring to idealize its traits." Does this not imply that if he chose, *he* might have written realistically when his subject was his familiar homeland? He had, actually, declared that impossible when he wrote his three earlier books located in his native scene, all labeled outright romances by himself, and denied their status as portraits of American manners and character. To muddle the matter more, Hawthorne also declares, in this same *Marble Faun* preface, that the ideal materials for *romance* had been absent from that American scene where "actualities" were "so insisted upon." No author, without a trial," he writes, "can conceive of the difficulty of writing a Romance about a country where there is no shadow, no antiquity, no mystery, no picturesque and gloomy wrong, nor anything but a common-place prosperity, in broad and simple daylight, as is happily the case with my dear native land"—unlike Italy, which had all the requisite sites and props including especially ruins, Romance needed, "like ivy, lichens, and wall flowers . . . to make it grow" (IV 3). These supposed absences should have (but had not) prevented him from writing those three earlier books—if romances they were! How had Hawthorne managed to write them without those essentials? Or had he been writing more realistically than he admitted?

In 1879, when he wrote his book about Hawthorne from which I quoted at the beginning of this essay, Henry James took over Hawthorne's confusions and added his own to his account of an American writer's handicaps when he referred to the "large number of elements that were absent . . . for a romancer looking for subjects" in "Hawthorne's America" and went right on, as though his change of term were of no importance, to speak of the contrasting "fund of suggestion for a *novelist*" available in the "European spectacle." (emphasis added). His list is not Hawthorne's except for its syntactic rhythm of "no this . . . no that," though James has been assumed to be merely repeating and expanding his predecessor in an almost humorous fashion. But his augmentations make it a recipe no longer suited for romance as Hawthorne had defined it. Instead, they suggest the furnishings of its supposed contrary in the presumed world of social institutions like an aristocracy, church or army, and of palaces, castles, manors, country houses, parsonages, thatched cottages, cathedrals, abbeys, little Norman churches, universities and public schools, even race tracks—a heterogeneous rundown that includes, in addition to Hawthorne's ivied ruins, ingredients for a comédie humaine (*American Writers* 351–52). It was the *novel,* of course—as developed by Balzac and his followers, and by the English realists—that required this plenitude—and not, conventionally, the romance.

It seems likely that James's own struggles to redefine realism for his own use may have brought him to suspect that there was something disputable about the view that the novel had to "compete" with life by means of exact and full replication of exterior appearances, or that this replication was any more to be trusted than something more freely imagined—and he suspected, rightly, I think, Hawthorne's own suspicion of the terms he himself had used. He was seeking out ways of implying a verifiable social world by other means, including the development of the inner mirror of consciousness. James deplored what he called Hawthorne's penchant for allegory and the thinness of his depictions of persons and events. But he added a statement that reflects his judgment of the naturalists he had recently met in Paris—and redeems Hawthorne for the "real," after all. He declares that Hawthorne's writing

> testifies to the sentiments of the society in which he flourished, almost as pertinently (proportions observed) as Balzac and some of his descendants—MM. Flaubert and Zola—testify to the manners and morals of the French people. He had certainly not proposed to himself to give an account of the social idiosyncrasies of his fellow citizens, for his touch on such points is always light and vague, he has none of the apparatus of an historian, and his shadowy style of portraiture never suggests a rigid standard of accuracy. Nevertheless, he virtually offers the most vivid reflection of New England life that has found its way into our literature. (*American Writers* 321)

A few years later, in his "The Art of Fiction," James finds the novel/romance distinction sterile and arbitrary and calls these pigeon-holes of romantic and real "clumsy separations [that] appear . . . to have been made by critics and readers for their own convenience, and to help them out of their occasional queer predicaments, but to have little reality or interest for the producer." He adds, "I can think of no obligation to which the 'romancer' would not be held equally with the novelist" and deprecates a dull categorizer like Walter Besant, to whom his essay is responding, for his "habit of calling this or that work of one's fellow-artist a romance—unless it be, of course, simply for the pleasantness of the thing, as for instance when Hawthorne gave this heading to his story of *Blithedale*" (*American Writers* 55–56). James may be grasping at Hawthorne's idea of a mixed form to which the name neither of novel nor of Romance, in their traditional senses, is applicable. Much later, writing a preface to *The American* for its revision in the Scribner New York Edition in 1907—and feeling the need to justify this early work's violations of strict probability—James attempted once more to define "romance" but, recalling his dislike of this tag, he went on to admit that the great realists he admired had somehow achieved a higher art in which such a distinction became insignificant. "Men of large responding imagination before the human scene," like Scott or Balzac, even "the coarse, comprehensive prodigious Zola" were, he wrote, masters of fiction in which "the current remains therefore extraordinarily rich and mixed, washing us successively with the warm wave of the near and familiar and the tonic shock, as it may be, of the far and strange" (*European Writers* 1062–63).

Despite this wisdom of James's, which I have called upon for support at this later time in critical history, Hawthorne continued for many years to be taken not as a realist in any sense, but as the romantic fabulist or the transcendental symbolist Melville had hailed. Melville's idea that Hawthorne's historical fictions were illustrations of universal truths rather than exact reflections of a particular past had its most powerful re-statement in the mid-twentieth century, when F. O. Matthiessen (1941) also said, as Melville had, that Hawthorne's view of man's existence was simply an ancient tragic one—like Shakespeare's. Matthiessen also detected in Hawthorne the idea that human life could be read allegorically. It was an idea derived from a long tradition of which Puritanism was an early American expression and Emerson a later one. It seemed arguable that Hawthorne could have adapted from the Puritans just what Emerson, also, had inherited; that is, a way of reading history as a divinely written text, so subduing its resistant obscurities—the stuff of realism—to a scheme of universal meaning. Of course, neither Puritanism nor Emerson was the necessary origin of a post–World War II "new" critical penchant to which Matthiessen also responded, one that tended to detach literary works from immediate sociohistorical "context." Reacting against 1930s critical readings that reduced literature to evidence of historical determinism, some postwar critics preferred to see Hawthorne as a symbolist or allegorist whose meanings were related to the national experience only in the most abstract way. If he could be said to represent American life, it was because he represented its enduring myths. Along with Emerson, Thoreau, and Melville, the giants of Matthiessen's "American Renaissance," Hawthorne was thought by Henry Nash Smith (1950) and R. W. B. Lewis (1955) to express a pristine "Adamic" spirit at the heart of American culture, the product of its special origins in a "virgin land" empty of the fixed institutions and traditions of older nations. Richard Chase, in a widely influential book (1957), argued that Hawthorne had been a writer of romances rather than realist novels because romance was the *inevitable* literary genre for American writers from Brockden Brown to Faulkner, the ultimate expression of the frontier experience of persistingly unfurnished American conditions.

In the 1970s and 1980s these ideas were seen to be inadequate to account for the whole of American culture in the antebellum period as new scholars and critics discovered another American Renaissance of the uncanonized or marginalized, particularly writing by women and African Americans. It became obvious that the supposed American vacancy was filled with realities that had not been ignored by these previously less celebrated writers. But *had* these realities been as much ignored by Hawthorne and other "white, male" establishment writers as appeared? It now may seem that it is more accurate to say that evasion of history was really not possible even for those cultural icons who have been unnaturally separated from the general stream by a dubious critical elevation. Their supposed suppressions may be only apparent.

"Historical Romance" may be an especially misleading term in Hawthorne's case. It is true that his early stories incorporated only a few of the visibilities of persons and places gathered from his reading in historical colonial sources. He liked, sometimes, to elaborate an abstract moral paradox for which his historical tone barely provided a lightly indicated background. But the reader who has naively taken a literalist view of Hawthorne's sketches and stories about seventeenth-century New England and, above all, of *The Scarlet Letter,* is justified. These repeatedly incorporate some incident or description that is not merely the incidental product of Hawthorne's idle browsing in authentic record, not merely a way of distancing what transpires in the tale from the reader's sense of the real. Even when the tale told is imaginary, Hawthorne's stories of early New England are historically resonant. One of his best, "My Kinsman, Major Molyneux," was rediscovered and appreciated in the 1950s as it had not been before, but mostly as a psychological fable of youth's coming to manhood—though it is implicated in a complex vision of the antecedents of the American Revolution, as Q. D. Leavis (1951) finally pointed out. One critic of the day, Seymour Gross, wrote, "History as history had but very little meaning for Hawthorne artistically." The Gentle Boy," a story about Quakers in the Bay Colony at a precise moment in 1659, seemed to this interpreter "the clearest instance of how Hawthorne deliberately attempted to transmute an historical phenomenon into an elemental condition of existence" (Gross 99).

Hawthorne, however, appears to have undertaken, at an early stage, to conduct a deliberate inquiry into the historical meaning of his local past in projected collections with titles like "Seven Tales of My Native Land" and "Provincial Tales," as Michael Colacurcio (1984) has pointed out. *The Scarlet Letter* shows everywhere the traces of its origins in his regional and familial reality, based as it is not only on the true story of the woman condemned for adultery and forced to wear her "A" like a brand, but also locating the story in the enveloping reality of the Massachusetts colony. The choice between use of the fictionized past either as a setting for a gothic tale or, instead, as an encounter with historical reality is expressed precisely in Hawthorne's early story "Alice Doane's Appeal," when the authorial narrator describes his attempt to entertain two young ladies—his representative readers—during a walk to Salem's Gallows Hill. He offers, first, as illustration of his art, a "wondrous tale of old times"—of brother-sister love, "distempered jealousy," fratricidal murder, devilish malice—at which mélange of gothic romance his young auditors merely laugh. Only then does he undertake to "see whether truth were more powerful than fiction," and depicts the veritable horrors of Salem in 1692, the witchcraft trials, the zeal of Cotton Mather, the scaffold of executions—and makes his hearers shudder. At the end he calls for a "sadly commemorative" monument on the spot, as though he desires, himself, to make art out of historic memory

But as even Colacurcio has insuffiently noted, the shorter tales of the New England colonies, and even Hawthorne's masterpiece, *The Scarlet Letter,* conduct an inquiry into the nature of a past still active in the American present. Such commemorative recovery of the past can be said to participate in America's mounting need, in the antebellum period, to understand its early beginnings in order to determine what its unity in diversity was coming to mean. Orators like Daniel Webster celebrated the two hundredth anniversary of the Plymouth landing as an occasion for honoring "our attachment to the principles of civil and religious liberty for which [the pilgrims] encountered the dangers of the ocean, the storms of heaven, the violence of savages, disease, exile, and famine, to enjoy and establish" (Bell 1971, 9). But the persecutors of Roger Williams and Anne Hutchinson—not to speak of Salem's witches—represented, as well, a precedent of repression rather than liberty, and in 1850, as *The Scarlet Letter* was published, Webster supported the Fugitive Slave Act. "What to the American slave is your Fourth of July?" Frederick Douglass asked on Independence Day two years later (Zinn 182). Slavery was not only a contradiction discoverable in the past, but the source of mounting conflict while the antebellum years were riven by contesting ideas of nationality. As the United States encompassed greater diversities, it also aspired to a consolidated nationhood. In 1838, Hawthorne had already exhibited the predictive colonial contradiction with exquisite precision in "Endicott and the Red Cross." The sketch appears to conclude with unqualified praise of Endicott tearing the symbol of English domination from the colonial flag. His gesture is linked to the future Revolution: "We look back though the mist of ages, and recognize in the rending of the Red Cross from New England's banner, the first omen of that deliverance which our fathers consummated, after the bones of stern Puritans had lain more than a century in the dust" (IX 441). Yet this tribute is undercut by the reader's recollection of the narrator's description of other presences in that early scene—the Catholic in the stocks, the labeled "Wanton Gospeller" on the scaffold and his companion with her tongue cruelly held down by a cleft stick, and others suffering mutilation or, at least, symbolic branding, like the man condemned to wear a hangman's halter or the woman who wears an "A" signifying her adultery. This last victim of Puritan severity is already Hester Prynne. She not only wears her "A" for the same cause but anticipates Hester's reinterpretation of its meaning. Criminalized by Endicott, the woman of the Letter has embroidered her badge with gold thread "so that the capital A might have been thought to mean Admirable" (IX 435). Hawthorne draws in both cases upon the early American experience of justified revolt—even Anne Hutchinson's antinomianism—to which Hester refers herself.

One might take notice of the suggestive symbolic discovery of Hester's embroidered Letter *in* the Custom House rather than somewhere outside it. It was in the realm of recovered fact—that storage room of the past above the stagnant office where he spent his days—that the Surveyor found inspiration for the masterpiece to be written upon his forced exit. On the lower floor of the Custom House itself, he said, it had been "folly, with the materiality of this daily life pressing so intrusively upon me, to attempt to fling myself back into another age; or to insist on creating the semblance of a world out of airy matter"(I 37). But though a fictional world built entirely out of "airy matter" remained impossible even after his escape, Hawthorne would, very soon, fling himself back into another age perceived through veracious history. "The past was not dead" (I 27).

It was not dead because it was refigured in the present. In the fullness of character Hawthorne awards her, Hester is, after all, incongruous in colonial Boston. She is a nineteenth-century woman imagined as inhabiting a seventeenth-century world. Her growth into an exponent of new freedoms is the center of her story, her originating sexual transgression not being even worth naming within the narrative. Hawthorne's narrator tries to account for her anachronistic character by the fact that she is someone whose exceptional mind, provoked by sufferings and loneliness, is able to anticipate ideas not conceivable by others in the New World: "In her lonesome cottage, by the sea shore, thoughts visited her, such as dared to enter no other dwelling in New England" (I 164). But her views are only explicable as those of a radical American woman of the year 1850. Hester thinks of her love affair with Dimmesdale like a nineteenth-century romantic when she tells him it had a "consecration of its own." (I 195). As though she is already Hawthorne's feminist contemporary, Margaret Fuller, she conceives of a time when the relation of the sexes will be changed. Extending the implications of her dissidence further, one may even be ready to suspect her adherence to other revolutionary ideas of the modern era. Her feminism suggests other nineteenth-century American causes embraced along with their own by feminist militants in Hawthorne's later life.

Without mentioning slavery directly, *The Scarlet Letter* evokes the earliest American polity to discover the presumption. that sustained it in Hawthorne's day in a land that had been supposed providentially voided for the white man. Still on the American conscience were the excluded Native Americans glimpsed at the edge of the gathered populace of Hester's Boston. They seem to arouse some interest in Hawthorne's narrator, who remarks upon the Indians in their deerskin robes. They watch the ceremony of the Puritan Election Day as they also had watched Endicott's flag-tearing in Hawthorne's description. They "stood apart with countenances of inflexible gravity, beyond what even the Puritan aspect could attain" (I 232). We are invited to wonder about the meaning of their gravity. We can also recall the remarkable passage already referred to in the sketch prefacing *Mosses from an Old Manse*. in which Hawthorne expresses his mixed feeling about the genocide of the Native American.

More absolutely suppressed from the text of *The Scarlet Letter* is the witness of the Africans who formed a part of the first immigrant settlements, as Hawthorne knew, for their descendants were still living in his Salem as well as in Boston. The history of slavery since colonial times could not have been invisible from the vantage of such slave-trade outposts as Salem, Boston, and Liverpool. Writing *The Scarlet Letter* only a decade before the Civil War, Hawthorne understood already the consequences of a long social pretense of their non-presence. Later, in his ambiguous Civil War essay, "Chiefly About War Matters," he drew attention to an apt symbol in the coincidence that the same ship that had brought early white settlers to Boston, had, soon after, come again with a cargo of African slaves, white and black thus linked in commitment to the New World. Slavery was an ancient gloomy wrong too grave to be called "picturesque," though Hawthorne had outrageously declared, in *The Marble Faun* preface, his regret that America was a country with "no picturesque and gloomy wrong" for Romance to feed on. He did not forget the crimes against witches and dissidents in which his ancestors had participated. Nor could he have been unaware of the history of slavery, the long perpetrated wrong that had become the burning issue of his day.

If black men or women are absent from the scene of *The Scarlet Letter,* their condition *is* shadowed in Hester's. Her figurative chains recall the slave's literal ones. After her condemnation, Hester is thought by Hawthorne's Puritans to have become their "life-long bond-slave" (I 227). It is no accident that the image Hawthorne uses to represent her situation is that of the chains that bind the slave: "The chain that bound her was of iron links and galling to her inmost soul" (I 80). Her desire for a greater freedom is thought to resemble the literal condition of the black slave fleeing his enslavement when she throws away "the fragments of a broken chain" (I 164). When *The Scarlet Letter* was being written, American feminists had already begun to use the word "bondage" to describe the state of women, to liken their unfreedom to the slave's. Hester on her scaffold in the book's opening scene is even represented in Howard Roberts's 1872 sculpture as leaning her hand upon a post from which a fragment of linked chain still hangs even though she no longer bears the shackle on her wrist or ankle. As Jean Fagan Yellin (1989) has shown, a rhetorical feminist tradition identified the slave's condition with that of all women. There was, also, an evolving popular iconography which transmuted the plea of a kneeling, fettered slave to a white *man*—"I am a man and your brother"—to the appeal of a fettered black woman to a white woman, "I am a woman and your sister." As the "free" white woman's sister, the slave reminds the other woman not only of her right to be free but also of the white woman's own bondage. She implies that the woman she addresses might also be reminding men of her sibling equality to *them.* The standing white woman to whom the appeal is made has herself become, like Roberts's Hester, a chained victim of a master's will. Early agitators for female liberation like Sophia Hawthorne's two sisters, Elizabeth Peabody and Mary Mann, committed themselves to the anti-slavery cause with some sense of this identification. *The Scarlet Letter* is thus the biography of a feminist whose wider sense of the meaning of human equality can be presumed.

Hawthorne professed to dislike female propagandists for reform, but in *The Scarlet Letter* as well as in *The Blithedale Romance* and *The Marble Faun,* a feminist woman is the magnetic center of his story, irresistible to others despite her odor of transgression. These books express Hawthorne's distaste for female reformers who campaigned for the rights of political self-expression as well as for the abolitionist cause by raising their voices from public platforms. But he cannot help his own responsive fascination even if he compels Hester, Zenobia, and Miriam to surrender any hope of the immediate fulfillment of their missions. Zenobia and Miriam do not address themselves to public audiences in our hearing, actually. Hester, especially, is a silent woman whose insurrectionary thoughts are unheard almost until the end. She finally cannot—though she would have wished it—become an orating prophetess of personal independence, like Anne Hutchinson. But when she returns to resume her marginal place in the Boston community, it is not because she accepts the old judgment upon her but because she does, after all, have a prophecy to leave to her sisters, though personally and privately conveyed. The prophecy is melioristic—and seems evasive in its rejection of feminist urgency. "[A]t some brighter period, when the world should have grown ripe for it, in Heaven's own time, a new truth would be revealed, in order to establish the whole relation of man and woman on a surer ground"(I 263). This is precisely the way Hawthorne wanted to be able to think about the withering away of slavery—"one of those evils which divine Providence does not leave to be remedied by human contrivances but which, in its own good time . . . it causes to vanish like a dream" (V 416–17), as he said in the campaign biography he wrote for Pierce. Hawthorne's language analogizes the causes of abolition and female liberation—both causes whose exigence seemed obvious to others in his day.

In the light of such implicit reference to Hawthorne's own present reality as well as to that of past history, we may allow ourselves some skepticism concerning his claim, in introducing the historic otherness of *The Scarlet Letter,* that he had been unable to "diffuse thought and imagination through the opaque substance of today" (I 37). But he makes this assertion even concerning the two novel/romances he wrote promptly after, though his recognition of the reality of his contemporary America is openly evident in them. When he writes about his own modern Salem in *The House of the Seven Gables,* Hawthorne warns the reader unconvincingly that his story should be read as "having a great deal more to do with the clouds overhead than with any portion of the actual soil of the County of Essex"(II 3). He would insist that in writing *The Blithedale Romance*, his "concern with the Socialist Community [was] merely to establish a theatre, a little removed from the highway of ordinary travel, where the creatures of his brain may play their phantasmagoric antics, without exposing them to too close a comparison with the actual events of real lives" (III 1). But he admitted that he had stayed a while at Brook Farm and, as everyone knew, he had been a friend of Margaret Fuller, who resembled his fictional Zenobia. But these were more than the customary disclaimers to avoid suit. They were a deliberate denial of an art of reference that he was disinclined to confess to. Even the literally identifiable if dead Roman landscape of art objects and ruins replicated in *The Marble Faun*, had, he said, been serviceable only as a "fairy precinct, where actualities are not terribly insisted upon as they are or must be, in America" (IV 3). But his American scene cannot be dismissed as a "fairy precinct." Hawthorne's constant claim was that he aimed to escape that American insistence upon actuality, but we may have taken him too readily at his word.

In the two fictions set in the America of his own time, Hawthorne no longer reads the present in the past, but faces the reality of the present directly. The sense of this in *The House of the Seven Gables* is undeniable, despite its gothic features—ancestral curse, decaying old mansion, hidden document, mysterious painting, and the rest. All of these blow away in the end, routed by everyday sunshine, that daylight which is also nineteenth-century positivism and optimism. Hawthorne strove to insert in this book what he called in its preface "the realities of the moment." He gave significant importance to such new phenomena as the railroad and the daguerreotype. Both technical innovations enforced new modes of consciousness—an awareness of simultaneously merged experiences acquired by Clifford in his flight from the ancient house of the Pyncheons and a new literal vision, threateningly percipient, possessed by Holgrave with his camera.

But the corrupt politics Hawthorne knew all about is represented in the career of Jaffrey Pyncheon. And the presence of mesmerism in the book is not merely for its gothic effect but because it represents the subjugation of weaker wills, especially those of women, but also of the subject wills of workers, to the powerful. Ancient crime persisting in its effects into the living present is the governing motif of *The House of the Seven Gables*, though its author struggles, along with his characters, to escape such continuities and to break into a more democratic world. And Holgrave, the enthusiast of the latest fads and minor reform movements, is a critic also of the fundamental curse of inherited "real" property. His is the

ultimate radicalism of a socialist-communist theory of social equaliza-
tion. The "romance" plot structure by which the descendant of the Maules
triumphs over long-privileged authority and revenges an ancient appropriation is profoundly social and political. But we are compelled by the
book to ask at what cost a mere storyteller and "idler" (as Hawthorne's
own ancestors would have called Holgrave as well as Hawthorne) might
achieve a place in the modern world. The modern world no less than the
Puritan would really have regarded such a person as no more than negli-
gible. There may be more pessimism and irony than we have supposed in
the fact that the erstwhile revolutionary and artist does not so much surrender his old views as submit to what he has vanquished. He accepts the
uses of those powers over others his mesmerist talents had represented,
even though these have been renounced. The descendant of a carpen-
ter/house builder moves into another old house, albeit in the unpolluted
country, though he had once believed that every generation should
destroy the structures elevated by its predecessors and build anew. The
curse of inherited wealth is not to be forgotten in the transfer from the
House of the Seven Gables to this alternate Pyncheon property. Masculin-
ist hegemony is doubtfully corrected by the domestic fairy influence of a
Pyncheon country cousin.

The Blithedale Romance is still less committed to romance formula. A
suspicion of utopian expectation—itself a romantic idea of escape from the
social world—operates in the book. Blithedale may be a mythical Happy
Place where the refugees from reality discover reality again. But it is also the
latest instance of utopian delusion. Hawthorne is distrustful of the contemporary reformer personality as instanced either by Hollingsworth or
even the passionate Zenobia. As in *The House of the Seven Gables*, mesmerism suggests social as well as personal appropriation of the wills of others. Priscilla knits little purses by hand but looks like a mill girl from
Lowell. As a hypnotic medium she is a representative of the new slavery of
the factory which bound thousands like her to mechanized needlework
under the rule of a the male factory manager. This darkest of Hawthorne's
books ends not only with the humiliation of Hollingsworth, but with
Zenobia's drowning, a reflection of Hawthorne's feeling about Fuller, from
whose writings her speeches are borrowed. Her stiffened body being pulled
from the water in which she drowned seems a nightmare imagining of
Fuller, whose body was never recovered after the shipwreck in which she
died on her voyage home from revolutionary Rome. Finally, in this only
one of Hawthorne's longer fictions written in the first person, Coverdale,
perhaps speaking for Hawthorne, admits that he had a "decided tendency
toward the actual." Reviewing *The Blithedale Romance* in the *Westminster*

Review, the anonymous reviewer (perhaps George Eliot) protested the author's expectation that his community could be passed off as a mere convenience of romantic framing. "Would he paint an ideal slave-plantation merely for the beauty of the thing, without pretending to elicit a conclusion, favorable or otherwise, to slavery?" (Crowley 1970, 263). For whatever complex personal reasons, Hawthorne seemed always to want to deny the thrust of his own representations.

As I have been saying, one feels inclined with James to dispense with the realism/romance classification in studying Hawthorne's fiction. It certainly proves an obstacle to a full response to him. We may even find grounds in a more thoroughgoing materialism than his own for rejecting his unconfident sense that an impermeable barrier divides the real from the fantastic. We may want to say that nothing the writer writes escapes the taint of reference, that the realities of literal history speak even through the figurations of fantasy. On the other hand, considering that Hawthorne put himself so insistently in the anti-realist camp, we may, in quite another way, be tempted to find in him an anticipation of a recent skepticism. He claimed to have "read and reread Montaigne in early youth" when his sister borrowed the *Essais* from the Salem Athenaeum on his behalf. Somehow he foresaw a "postmodern" way of thinking that "reality" is a word always to be set in quotation marks as a part of the mind's figuration. It is remarkable—though not generally remarked upon—how Hawthorne expresses the suspicion that the "real" cannot be confidently distinguished from the imaginary because all we can claim to know in either case is the problematic world of our ideas. James, despite his admirations for Balzac, initiated a realism that was above all, relativist, the register of how we *take* what we see—and so ushered in the modernism of Joyce and Woolf. If this too, was still mimesis, as Eric Auerbach believed, it was no longer that classic Realism that was the mode of a vision of life as not only confidently recognizable in its details, but confidently interpretable.

Hawthorne himself sometimes seems to make an ironic mockery of our search for stable meanings. How faithful to our experience of reading his stories or novels are the morals he sometimes announces? "Be true, be true . . ." may be only "one of many meanings that press upon us from the poor minister's miserable experience," the Hawthorne narrator concedes as he concludes *The Scarlet Letter.* Hawthorne's notorious cultivation of ambiguity in his stories seems to mean that he, like ourselves, longed vainly for the classic realist's confidence in the singularity and accessibility of meaning, the structures of story that lead to an indisputable consequence like the outcome of natural law, the solidity of a world which is not undermined by doubt of our perceptions. But his fiction does not grant to our perceptions an indissoluble bond with unquestionable reality. What *really* happened to Young Goodman Brown in the forest? Was Beatrice Rappaccini corrupt or innocent? Had Robin betrayed his kinsman Major Molyneux or risen to an adult vision of the necessary historical future? Was Owen Warland's worship of the Beautiful a failure to accommodate to life as it was or the triumph of art and idealism? Such questions remain unanswered at the conclusion of some of Hawthorne's finest tales. The open-endedness of his plots is a denial of classic realism—and where his art faltered, as in *The Marble Faun,* the open end looked only like irresolution, and readers—to Hawthorne's annoyance—protested because he had not "cleared everything up" and told what happened further to Donatello and Miriam. Hawthorne was even forced by popular demand—against his own inclination—to add a clarifying "postscript" to the second printing of *The Marble Faun.*

In his masterpiece, *The Scarlet Letter,* however, it was precisely this suspension of conclusion and explanation that makes final judgment impossible in the case of Hester, who fails and triumphs, is censured or vindicated from moment to moment as we read Hawthorne's book. Perhaps Hawthorne's denials of his own referentiality were rooted in his personal habit of distrust and misgiving in an age of conflicted certainties. Realist reality—at least as it was understood in the nineteenth-century novel—was felt to be something knowable, just as nature had become knowable through science; hence, the general preference for an omniscient narrator whose observation can be relied upon. But Hawthorne's third-person narrator (not to speak of that self-doubting autobiographical voice that governs *The Blithedale Romance* and Hawthorne's sketches) is no such reliable observer. Even the almost anonymous narrator of *The Scarlet Letter* continually protests his inability to determine things, the inaccessibility of the indisputable. Concerning the appearance of the letter exposed at last to public view on the bosom of Dimmesdale, he offers the contrary theories of supposed witnesses, and says "the reader may choose"—a coy evasion of narrational responsibility which Hawthorne had already practiced in such early stories as "Young Goodman Brown."

The modern reader is likely to feel at home with such indeterminism. Hawthorne's open endings can seem to enrich our sense of the complexity of life, its irreducibility to linear plot. But Hawthorne may have been distressed by his own reluctance to simplify. It is, of course, impossible to tell how much his skepticism contributed to the near-surrender of his literary vocation when, after the swift succession of publication of three of his published long fictions between 1850 and 1853, he went into government harness again. In accepting his Liverpool consulship, Hawthorne knew that he was not the kind of writer to turn books out in off hours from a grueling job—and did not publish his next work of fiction, *The Marble Faun,* until 1860. He seems to have found it more and more difficult to compose the mixed form that had proved successful in his American novels. Remote from his familiar native scene, his descriptive faculty was lavished on the antiquities instead of the living present of Rome, and the thinness of his characterization in the depiction of his Americans removed from their explanatory American world, represented a failure. His late unfinished romances were never-to-be completed efforts to achieve a vision uniting past and present, fantasy and fact. He had kept his notebooks up, recorded numerous observations during his travels, and made a book of his English impressions. It is difficult to say how much failing health contributed to something like the collapse of Hawthorne's confidence, but the war he had dreaded yet came to see was inevitable and to which he acknowledged his commitment, seems to have profoundly depressed him. "The Present, the Immediate, the Actual has proved too potent for me. It takes away not only my scanty faculty, but even my desire for imaginative composition," Hawthorne wrote (V 4) only months before he died in 1864.

2

Hawthorne and Politics (Again): Words and Deeds in the 1850s

MICHAEL T. GILMORE

The consensus on Hawthorne and politics goes something like this: unlike Emerson and Thoreau, unlike Douglass and Stowe, activists all, he was an *inactivist* who fetishized deferral. His campaign biography of Franklin Pierce is said to provide a retroactive template for his fiction. Only a consummate trimmer could have championed that Doughface Democrat, a New Hampshire man so morally obtuse that as president he did the South's bidding on the Fugitive Slave Law. (Pierce proved so unpopular in the North that his party refused to support him for a second term.) Hawthorne the artist contemplated subversion—most notably, in the person of Hester Prynne—only in order to break its spirit, and he regarded idealistic political action, whether against slavery or any other injustice, as a wrongful arrogation of God's power to dispose of human affairs when and how He saw fit. *The Scarlet Letter, The House of the Seven Gables, The Blithedale Romance*—Hawthorne's three "American" novels— gave fictional form to the age's ethical and legislative impasse, the Compromise of 1850.[1]

In this essay, I do not so much want to overturn this consensus as to deepen and complicate our understanding of what was motivating Hawthorne, and, in so doing, to revise our picture of the American Renaissance. I have gone into some detail in my opening paragraph, highlighting the importance of the sectional crisis to Hawthorne's politics, because it is precisely the worsening conflict over slavery that holds the key to my two objectives. A crucial point about that conflict—*the* crucial point for literature—is that it reanimated the agency of language. Verbal anti-slavery agitation was seen by Southerners, and by many Northerners, too, as an "incendiary" (the preferred adjective) intervention in the polity that had to be suppressed at any cost, even, if necessary, by destroying civil liberties. The security of the "peculiar institution," and, so Southern fire-eaters threatened, the preservation of the Union itself, required nothing less. Utterance, unless checked, would plunge the Republic into chaos. Thus were discourse and the circulation of ideas, the very stuff of the literary sensibility, invested with a power that they had not enjoyed in American culture since the Revolution, when the oratory and pamphlets of the Founders had aroused an entire people to throw off the British yoke.

Repeated assaults on free speech spanned the decades of Romanticism's flowering. In the 1830s, just as Emerson was forsaking the ministry for a career as a writer and lecturer, Southern postmasters began to seize and burn abolitionist documents sent through the mails. Andrew Jackson, the highest official in the land, reacted by denouncing the written materials and not their interdiction as unconstitutional. Eighteen thirty-six brought the petition controversy. Slaveholders in Congress, in a flagrant violation of the First Amendment, refused to receive appeals to outlaw involuntary servitude in the District of Columbia. They rammed through the so-called "gag rule" tabling all such petitions without a hearing. Former president John Quincy Adams, now a congressman from Massachusetts, fought for eight years to repeal this ban on the discussion of slavery in the nation's capital, tirelessly insisting that the right to petition was a cornerstone of the whole edifice of liberty. Meanwhile, riots against anti-slavery advocates erupted across the country. One mob dragged William Lloyd Garrison through the streets of Boston at the end of a rope; a second shot dead Elijah Lovejoy in Alton, Illinois while he was defending his printing press. Lawless acts of violence against dissent subsided above the Mason-Dixon line, but continued unabated in the South right up to the firing on Fort Sumter. People could be tarred and feathered and, in some cases, hanged, for the "crime" of voicing opinions or reading books critical of slavery. The lynched were typically white people, not blacks: slaves were illiterate and, as property, worth too much money to be disposed of so cavalierly.[2]

I emphasize the race of these victims because their fate underlined a grim reality about the antebellum United States: wherever slavery existed, and blacks were in chains, freedom was extinguished for whites as well. W. J. Cash, in his famous study of *The Mind of the South,* published in 1941, went so far as to compare the slave regime to the totalitarian states of Soviet Russia and Nazi Germany (Cash 1941, 88–89, 134–35). (With this difference, it should be noted: the force of public opinion took the place of the secret police in imposing ideological conformism.) And the decade of the 1840s left little doubt that the South intended to spread its system. The War with Mexico was not just a struggle over land: annexing Texas meant adding a slave state to the Union and, more than that, reestablishing bondage in an area where the more enlightened Mexicans had abolished it. The Compromise of 1850, cited earlier, provoked the widespread outrage that it did because the Fugitive Slave Act extended Southern contempt for basic rights into the North. The Act commanded all citizens, regardless of their views, to assist federal agents in detaining fugitives, and it overruled state personal liberty laws by explicitly denying suspected runaways the writ of habeas corpus and the right to trial by jury. No wonder that the emergent anti-slavery coalition took as its motto the slogan "Free Soil, *Free Speech*, Free Labor, and Free Men" (McPherson 62 [emphasis added]).[3]

The campaign against intellectual freedom reached its apogee in the 1850s. The Kansas-Nebraska Act of 1854 revoked the Missouri Compromise and opened the unsettled continent to the depredations of the Slave Power. What this might portend for the free states was made clear by the slave code adopted by the Kansas legislature in 1855. That document provided for two years at hard labor for all individuals who should "print, publish, write, circulate, or cause to be introduced in this Territory" any opinion hostile to the "right of persons to hold slaves." Bleeding Kansas spawned Bleeding Sumner: for the offense of speaking his mind on the Senate floor, the radical Republican Charles Sumner was beaten senseless by a South Carolinian named Preston Brooks. It would be hard to imagine a more symbolic encounter: Brooks attacked his victim with a cane while the unarmed Massachusetts senator was sitting at his desk writing, and the South rose as one to express its approbation of this "heroic" action. Expansionism accelerated as the war neared: the Dred Scott Decision, from a Supreme Court with a Southern majority, apparently setting the stage for the legalization of slavery nationwide; attempts to purchase Cuba as a slave territory; and demands to reopen the African slave trade. I have said that the South resembled a twentieth-century dictatorship, but only the most ruthless of modern states have been as efficient in proscribing unwelcome ideas. Consider that in 1860, the outer limit of the American Romantic period, Lincoln's name was not allowed on the ballot in the Deep South, and even in the slaveholding border states, the Republican candidate for president received a bare 3 percent of the total votes.[4]

The American Romantics were only too aware of these developments.[5] Every one of them, from Emerson through Margaret Fuller to Walt Whitman, shared the recognition that in the crucible of the slavery crisis language had acquired the potency of deeds. They may have regarded the verbal with suspicion, or simultaneously feared and celebrated it, or sought to mobilize it for liberty, but they never doubted its influence. In the compass of a brief essay, there is obviously not room to make this case in detail, so I will confine myself to a handful of illustrations. Emerson's *Nature*, issued in the year of the gag rule, deplores second-handedness and calls for a revival of the linguistic immediacy interred in the "sepulchres of the fathers." Emerson's essay launched the American Renaissance, and its opening sentences capture that term's double significance: "Renaissance" understood as art of stellar quality, and as a renewal of the word-act unity of the Revolutionary generation. (The last surviving "Father," James Madison, died in 1836.) Thoreau, in "Civil Disobedience" (published by Hawthorne's sister-in-law, Elizabeth Peabody), imagines a speaker-legislator from outside the government whose eloquence would be "capable of settling the much-vexed questions of the day." It need hardly be added that the charismatic wordsmith Thoreau had in mind, igniting reform from the sanctuary of Walden Pond, was himself.

Or take a writer from far outside the Transcendentalist circle at Concord: Frederick Douglass. His account of his life as a bondman first appeared in 1845, a year after the congressional gag rule was rescinded and as an aggressive South was pressing for the annexation of Texas. Slavery, of course, was a permanent gag rule for the enslaved, and Douglass's memoir documents an array of restrictions on literacy and speech. The slave narrative, established in this era as a distinctive American genre, broke the white man's monopoly on language and became an important weapon in the struggle for emancipation. And then there is a nonactivist like Melville, whose greatest creation, Captain Ahab, commandeers the ship of state through a combination of demagogic oratory and "tricks of the stage." What "incendiary" abolitionist could equal the *Pequod*'s leader in harnessing words to apocalyptic devastation? Ahab's spellbinding verbal skills have a counterpoint in Melville's work in those characters, such as Bartleby the Scrivener and the ringleader Babo from "Benito Cereno," who seem to exist under a ban on articulation, whether self-imposed or enforced from without. Babo's refusal to testify before the Lima tribunal, a facsimile of the actual legal speechlessness of American slaves, memorializes the futility of utterance under a regime of censorship.

Hawthorne was out of the country during much of the 1850s, as Pierce's consul in Liverpool and then as a resident in Italy; but during his creative heyday, from 1850 to 1852, he was acutely conscious of the mounting pressures on free speech. Indeed, his book on Pierce placed him at the center of those pressures. He hoped the prohibitions would prevail and stifle the seditious ferment of anti-slavery oratory. His "little biography" (XXIII 273), as he disparagingly calls it, concludes with a frank endorsement of the end of partisan debate—almost, one might say, the end of politics. Hawthorne reports that the two national parties, Whigs and Democrats, have ceased to differ over principles. They have put aside their disagreements to unite "in one common purpose—that of preserving our sacred Union, as the immovable basis from which the destinies, not of America alone, but of mankind at large, may be carried upward and consummated." The result, greeted by the text with relief, is "unwonted quiet and harmony," a blanket of stillness happily descending on all regions of the country (XXIII 369–70).

Hawthorne's position, to put it mildly, is highly anomalous: he is himself a storyteller, a man of words, and yet the performative power of speech menaces the societal stasis he cherishes. One way to circumvent the anomaly, perhaps, would be to purge discourse of deceptive artifice. A reclusive type with no competence in politics, Hawthorne contends that his sole qualification for writing about Pierce is that he knows the general personally and will "tell the truth" about him (XXIII 274). The campaign biography bristles with antipathy toward verbal cleverness, a revulsion from the mastery of language possessed by so many characters in Hawthorne's fiction. Pierce emerges from his portrait as a kind of anti-Dimmesdale. Unlike *The Scarlet Letter*'s adulterous pastor, whose intoxicating oratory catapults him ahead of his seniors as the foremost preacher of Puritan Boston, Pierce scrupulously avoids pushing himself forward in debate. He will not open his mouth to say anything if some "other and older man could perform the same duty as well as himself" (XXIII 289). Nor, when he does bring himself to address the people, does the Democratic candidate resort to manipulation and half-truths—again, the special province of Arthur Dimmesdale. Pierce "never yet was guilty of an effort to cajole his fellow citizens, to operate upon their credulity, or to trick them even into what was right" (XXIII 349–50). Hawthorne goes so far as to compare his old college friend to the representatives of the Continental Congress, paragons of moral probity whose earnestness supposedly trumped their linguistic polish. Today, he adds, eloquence has degenerated into something other than a medium of truth; it has become "a knack, a thing valued in itself" (XXIII 298).

But it would be a mistake to construe Hawthorne's quarrel in *The Life of Franklin Pierce* as being directed exclusively against verbal glitter or the use of language to beguile and mislead. Language itself is the object of his strictures, and he praises Pierce, not simply for eschewing rhetorical excess, but for having "no fluency of words" whatever (XXIII 289). As we have seen, the general is reputed to be a speaker of rare integrity. Yet the extraordinary fact about the biography is how infrequently it quotes from its subject's public pronouncements—perhaps a score of paragraphs in all, most not from addresses but from two relatively minor sources, a letter declining President Polk's offer of the attorney generalship and a brief communication accepting the Democratic nomination. Hawthorne offers no direct testimony of his own, in that age of oratory, to Pierce's linguistic prowess. He confesses that he has none to offer:

> It has never been the writer's good fortune to listen to one of Franklin Pierce's public speeches, whether at the bar or elsewhere; nor, by diligent inquiry, has he been able to gain a very definite idea of the mode in which he produces his effects. To me, therefore, his forensic displays are in the same category with those of Patrick Henry, or any other orator whose tongue, beyond the memory of man, has mouldered into dust. (XXIII 305–6)

Several individuals are summoned as eyewitnesses to Pierce's exploits at the bar and in the forum. One, a Professor Edwin D. Sanborn of Dartmouth College, relates that during the revision of the New Hampshire state constitution, Pierce conducted himself with "eloquence" and "magnanimity" (XXIII 359). The reader has to take the declaration on trust, however, because nothing is quoted as corroborating evidence. As for his famous rallying behind the Compromise of 1850, Pierce's support was consistent with his long-held convictions. From the time of his first election to Congress, Hawthorne tells us, again without illustration, his friend always "raised his voice against agitation" (XXIII 351).

Hawthorne's reticence projects an image of Pierce as "a man of deeds, not words" (XXIII 290), a legislator so disgusted by contemporaneous "agitation" that he would rather wrap himself in silence than condescend to utterance. It is as though language has been so debased by anti-slavery militancy that it has no proper place in politics at all. A political biography rightly honors this separation by relegating glibness to the margins or, better yet, expunging it from the text almost completely. Indeed, Hawthorne's preface suspends judgment on the accuracy of his rendition of Pierce's sentiments. So few of the candidate's actual words and ideas appear in the book that Hawthorne's speculations "may, or may not, be in accordance" with his subject's opinions. The reader can best glean Pierce's views, not from the author's sketch of them, but from his "straight-forward and consistent deeds," which are superior to any public statement as a register of what he thinks (XXIII 273–74). Thus does Hawthorne invert the word/deed dynamic of the antebellum years; he presents the Democratic nominee for president as a verbal lightweight whose acts do his talking for him, and who expressly refrains from deranging the culture's equilibrium with flights of oratory.

It is true, though, that Hawthorne inserts a long selection from the private journal Pierce kept while he was serving with the Ninth Regiment in Mexico, "hasty jottings-down in camp" that allegedly reveal more about him than "any narrative which we could substitute" (XXIII 319). (Chapter IV of the biography is titled "The Mexican War.—His Journal of the March from Vera Cruz.") But here, once again, the journal entries—more copious than any extracted speech—subordinate rhetoric to action. They consist of a tedious chronicle of events: we proceeded with eighty wagons, we encountered enemy fire, so-and-so's horse was shot from under him, we bivouacked near the river, we broke camp at dawn, and so on. The compiler of Pierce's war journal records no memorable ideas or insights, and he puts on display no talent for language. In this, as in so much else, the Doughface Democrat was the opposite of the Republican standard bearer who followed him eight years later into the White House. Abraham Lincoln wrote and spoke his way into the hearts of his countrymen; Pierce, Hawthorne implies, should be elevated to the presidency because he grasps the aversion of patriotism to empty phrase making.

Let us, following critical fashion, take the campaign book as our template. The imperative that Hawthorne's text urges most forcefully is the quarantining of discursive agility from the practical realm of politics. Ostensibly, the two domains, the verbal/aesthetic and the worldly/civic, share little and fare best in isolation from each other. Hawthorne, as a well-known novelist and "the Author of this Memoir," disavows any connection to politics and makes much of his unfitness to represent a "public man" to the electorate, that being a "species of writing too remote from his occupations—and, he may add, from his tastes"—for him to carry out satisfactorily (XXIII 273). He acknowledges, moreover, that there have been large gaps in his intercourse with Pierce. Their "modes of life" have simply been too different, their "culture and labor" too unlike. "[T]here was hardly a single object or aspiration in common between us" (XXIII 302). Yet this seemingly natural division between the man of words and the man of action masks a fearful recognition that on some deeper level they are not only entangled with each other—after all, Hawthorne, for all his protests of unsuitability, compiled *The Life of Franklin Pierce*—but that the literary possesses an anarchic energy dangerous to civic peace. The pose of linguistic/artistic innocence or impotence is just that, a pose, one founded on the mid-nineteenth-century reality that abolitionist agitation, and Southern efforts to crush it, were hurtling the nation toward internecine warfare.

To turn to Hawthorne's longer fiction at this point—to approach it, as he invites us, through the entryway of "The Custom House"—is to reencounter the segregation of the aesthetic from the functional, and from the arena of politics in particular. The man who would become Pierce's biographer began his career as a novelist, at the very moment the 1850 Compromise was being cobbled together in Congress, by positing an absolute breach between literature and public life. In the introduction to *The Scarlet Letter* (1850), he comes before the reader as a representative of "Uncle Sam's government" (I 5), a political appointee to the Salem customhouse. (President Polk, the annexationist Southerner who fomented the War with Mexico, named him to the post.) But as a romancer turned Surveyor of the Revenue, Hawthorne is a fish out of water, gasping for survival in an element thoroughly inhospitable to the creative imagination. His fellowship once included intellects of the caliber of Emerson, Thoreau, Alcott, Ellery Channing, and Longfellow; it now consists of aging public functionaries, former military officers, and an unnamed "man of business," few of whom have read or even heard of his literary accomplishments. The effect on his productivity is disastrous. Even after he discovers the packet belonging to Surveyor Pue, with its dozen or so yellowed pages on Hester Prynne and its moth-eaten scarlet letter, Hawthorne cannot reanimate his powers of invention. His imagination is "a tarnished mirror" (I 34). Employment by the United States government has extinguished his ability to write.

It must be among the oddest introductions on record to a major work of art, a narrative of the author's failure to compose the very text we are holding in our hands. The paradox of American literary culture in the age of slavery's expansion is that it almost expires in a writer's block. Hawthorne details the paralysis that gripped his mind while he was pocketing Uncle Sam's wages, and he recounts the miraculous dissolving of that obstruction as soon as he escaped from his position with the state. Verbal fluency and politics, we are instructed, do not mix. "So little adapted is the atmosphere of a Custom-House," Hawthorne says, "to the delicate harvest of fancy and sensibility, that, had I remained there through ten Presidencies yet to come, I doubt whether the tale of 'The Scarlet Letter' would ever have been brought before the public eye" (I 34). Only expulsion from office—a figurative beheading, as he conceives it—liberates him from his protracted silence. Restored to his customary occupation of man of letters, Hawthorne regains his voice and dashes off the novel in a blaze of creativity.

The ensuing tale reconstitutes the introduction's polarities with a significant variation. The wrinkle, which recurs in *The House of the Seven Gables* and *The Blithedale Romance,* is the presence of a tertium quid, a wielder of words whose morally problematic or dissident speech hovers on the margins of the language/politics rupture, and whose eventual acquiescence leaves a residue of discontent. For the moment, I want to defer discussion of these figures who disconcertingly evoke their creator, Nathaniel Hawthorne, in order to concentrate on the pattern familiar from the Pierce book. The speaker in *The Scarlet Letter* is the narrator or author of the introduction, finally rid of his customhouse duties and able to set his words down on paper. We are constantly aware of him addressing us. He offers reflections on the contrast between Puritan New England and the nineteenth century, muses about the motivations of his characters, and calls attention to his verbal mannerisms. These last include an addiction to asking questions ("Could it be true?" [I 59]; "What imagination would have been irreverent enough to surmise that the same scorching stigma was on them both?" [I 247]), and a habit of announcing when he is about tell us something ("We have as yet hardly spoken of the infant . . ." [I 89]; "we have a matter of business to communicate to the reader" [I 261]).

At the opposite extreme from this voluble and highly articulate figure are the ruling elders of Boston, leaders who orate or preach before the multitude but fail to do so with distinction. Like Pierce, they have "no fluency of words." Hawthorne reiterates that while the community's eminent men possess dignity and respectability, they lack the gift of imagination. "They would have vainly sought—had they ever dreamed of seeking—to express the highest truths through the humblest medium of familiar words and images" (I 143). When their senior member, the Reverend John Wilson, delivers his sermon on Hester's sin, we are provided only a summary and not permitted to eavesdrop on his actual disquisition.

Also on the side of taciturnity is Hester Prynne. The heroine is a subverter of societal norms, an apostate from the Puritan state, but, unlike the abolitionist protesters of the antebellum era, she lives under a sentence of virtual silence. Practically her first words in the text are "I will not speak!" (I 68), and although we have access to her thoughts, she seldom gets to enunciate them aloud. Except for one or two scenes—the meeting with Dimmesdale in the forest, for instance—Hester says about as little as any protagonist in American fiction. And when she does attain utterance, the setting is invariably a confidential location distant from the public sphere, such as a prison cell or the primeval woods. She relies on Dimmesdale, her former pastor, to argue her case for retaining Pearl to the Puritan magistrates. Her credo, as she cautions her daughter, is, "We must not always talk in the market-place of what happens to us in the forest" (I 240).

One could reasonably suggest that the invention of the American psychological novel was the corollary to an historical epoch when aroused Southerners and conservatives anathematized provocative speech. The author of *The Scarlet Letter* shared the suspicion of the discursive, and in his book he deals with the taboo by denying impolitic public statement to his characters, especially Hester Prynne; he then accesses the characters' proscribed thoughts and feelings by digging deeply into their interiors. For antebellum reviewers, the novelty of Hawthorne's story of the Puritan past was its relentless (some felt morbid) dissection of guilt, vengeance, and forbidden passion. The critics sensed that they were witnesses to a seismic change in the technique and matter of fiction. Chapters like "The Interior of a Heart" and "Another View of Hester" investigate consciousness, not assertion or action. The heroine wandering "in the dark labyrinth of mind" (I 166), neither speaking her thoughts nor putting her ideas into practice, is the signature activity of these soundings. Creative resurrection and the culture's campaign to trammel speech combined to produce Hawthorne the novelist of inward exploration, precursor of Henry James.

The split between politics and the aesthetic continues in *The House of the Seven Gables* (1851). The two positions are embodied in Clifford Pyncheon and Judge Jaffrey Pyncheon, the first a lover of the beautiful, the second a prominent jurist and prospective candidate for governor of Massachusetts. (The consanguinity between these adversaries hints at unacknowledged affinities.) Clifford has returned to Salem after serving a thirty-year jail term for a murder he did not commit. He is a shattered spirit who nevertheless possesses a hyperactive imagination and "an exquisite taste" (II 108). When he and Hepzibah flee their ancestral home, he delivers a tirade against convention to a "gimlet-eyed old gentleman" on the train, who dismisses his "wild talk" of social upheaval as "All a humbug!" (II 259, 262–63). As in his previous romance, Hawthorne would banish such indecent speech from the public concourse. Unflattering "stories," "fables," "traditions," and "gossip" about the community's eminent citizens circulate in chimney corners and byways, but this "hidden stream of private talk" never makes its way into print (II 122–24, 310). Like Clifford's questioning of the status quo, it is quite without consequence, a muffled whispering that leaves those in power unaffected.

Clifford's nemesis, the Judge, is a figure of solidity whose smiling exterior conceals a "hot fellness of purpose, which annihilated everything but

itself" (II 129). Two objectives drive Jaffrey: he wants to be the chief magistrate of the commonwealth, and he wants to coax or bully his cousin into
revealing the secret of the Pyncheons' missing wealth. When he tries to
force an entrance into the house to confront Clifford, the latter cries out for
mercy in an "enfeebled voice," his "murmur of entreaty" no more capable
of dissuading the hard-hearted Judge than the wail of a "frightened infant"
(II 129). Jaffrey's political ambitions were to be realized on the evening he
dies from the family's inherited liability. He had planned to dine with the
"little knot" of influential schemers who regularly "steal from the people"
the right of selecting their rulers (II 274). Hawthorne sums up the dispro-
portionate strength of his two characters, and, by implication, of the literary sensibility and the world of politics, by observing that Clifford could
never have survived a face-to-face encounter with the Judge: "It would be
like flinging a porcelain vase, with already a crack in it, against a granite
column" (II 242).

The Blithedale Romance (1852), Hawthorne's third and last novel occur-
ring in America, takes as its inspiration the socialist experiment at Brook
Farm. Literature and politics are once again sharply differentiated.
Hawthorne's preface finds "the author" (as he repeatedly calls himself) dis-
avowing any intention, "favorable or otherwise, in respect to Socialism."
The setting is nothing more than a "theatre . . . where the creatures of his
brain may play their phantasmagorical antics" (III 1). Hawthorne erects a
barrier between his own voice—the voice of the apolitical artist—and
those of the activists at Blithedale. The minor poet Miles Coverdale relates
the adventures of the community and thus, for the first time in the fiction
we have been examining, displaces Hawthorne himself as the narrator. So,
too, the various proposals for political change can be traced back, not to the
name on the title page, but to the zealots who assemble at the would-be
utopia. Besides Coverdale, two other major characters dream of reform
and traffic in language. They are the feminist and writer Zenobia, who
declaims against woman's oppression with the eloquence of "a stump-ora-
tress," and the former blacksmith Hollingsworth (III 44). Zenobia frames
female victimization as an act of physical silencing: "Thus far, no woman
in the world has ever once spoken out her whole heart and her whole mind.
The mistrust and disapproval of the vast bulk of society throttles us, as
with two gigantic hands at our throats" (III 120). Hollingsworth has come
to Blithedale to recruit disciples for his project of prison reform. He is constantly exhorting his fellow philanthropists at the boulder-pulpit where
John Eliot preached to the Indians. "No other speech of man," comments
Coverdale of his friend's performances, "has ever moved me like some of
those discourses" (III 119).

All three characters end up dead or defeated, and it is hard not to read their unfortunate outcomes as Hawthorne's vengeance on his utopians for daring to advocate societal renovation. For all her feminist rhetoric, Zenobia proves to be another dependent woman; she kills herself when Hollingsworth rejects her. The prison reformer is overwhelmed by guilt and abandons his ambitious plans to focus on a single criminal, himself. And Coverdale, soured by his experience at Blithedale, renounces political ideals altogether. He would be ready to join the struggle for Hungarian rights, he confides to the reader, only if Kossuth pitched the battlefield "within an easy ride of my abode" and arranged the conflict for "a mild, sunny morning, after breakfast. . . . Further than that, I should be loth to pledge myself" (III 247). If Coverdale does eventually write the romance we have just finished reading, the preface's tone of authorial fastidiousness should not surprise us. The erstwhile radical has, in his disaffection from activism, become one with his creator.

The problem with these readings of Hawthorne's fiction should be evident. In every case, a charismatic speaker or linguistic rebellion has been omitted. This is the complicating factor persistently slighted by the current consensus: Hawthorne's politics of pacification always contain an unpacified dimension. Even though the potent wordsmith is discredited or subdued, and the dissident rhetoric muted, "the power of words" (to filch the title of one of Poe's stories) haunts Hawthorne's narratives as a resilient and unruly force. Furthermore, the watertight compartmentalization between the imagination and politics keeps springing leaks. The aesthetic exercises authority over practical areas that seem to be immune from its effects.

Perhaps the most obvious example of this intersecting is the introduction to *The Scarlet Letter*. Hawthorne may be speechless in the custom-house, but he discovers there, preserved by his "official ancestor," Surveyor Pue (I 33), the ancient documents that fertilize his fancy after his expulsion. The brick building flying "the banner of the republic" (I 5) *originates* the story that follows; structurally, the political sphere serves as the anteroom to the opening of the verbal floodgates, much as, in mid-nineteenth-century culture at large, the polity's attempted suppression of "agitation" gives rise to the American Renaissance. An embargo on discourse, either external or internally generated (and for Hawthorne, the distinction is blurred), is in both cases the necessary precondition for artistic prodigality.

As for the oppositions of the romance, they are eroded by the very existence of the Reverend Dimmesdale. His singular standing as at once a brilliant orator and a leader of the settlement folds into one individual the seemingly antithetical principles of linguistic ingenuity and worldly influence. The young divine has the gift "of addressing the whole human brotherhood in the heart's native language," the "Tongue of Flame" denied his elders (I 142); and his skill in the pulpit deconstructs the speaker/ruler divide. Hawthorne has emphasized all along that the Puritan magistrates lack literary or intellectual distinction. None of those officials can preach effectively. Dimmesdale, on the other hand, is a man of eloquence who could also be a man of action:

> His was the profession, at that era, in which intellectual ability displayed itself far more than in political life; for—leaving a higher motive out of the question—it offered inducements powerful enough, in the almost worshipping respect of the community, to win the most aspiring ambition into its service. Even political power—as in the case of Increase Mather—was within the grasp of a successful priest. (I 238)

Of course, Dimmesdale is a morally compromised character whose boundary transgressions might be taken to vindicate the lesson: words and deeds overlap at their peril. His parishioners receive the minister's oratory with rapture, but his speeches are exercises in equivocation. Cunning delivery turns his vague confessions in church into falsehoods; his "revelation of the scarlet letter" in the final scaffold scene is similarly evasive and ambiguous, and the Puritans disagree about its meaning. Are we to conclude, then, that when verbal fluency crosses into public space, it automatically mutates into verbal treachery? Is the Pierce biography, Hawthorne's own venture into political speech, another example of linguistic turpitude, or is it the exception that proves the rule? Certainly Dimmesdale's inspired tongue refutes the idea that the literary sensibility is dysfunctional when it colludes with power. And what of the minister's election sermon? That discourse, which owes its "deep, sad undertone of pathos" to Dimmesdale's guilt, culminates in a prophecy that has to count as truthful because it is realized in history. Though we are not permitted to hear the sermon—an indication of Hawthorne's continuing uneasiness with language as power—we learn that the preacher's mission was "to foretell a high and glorious destiny for the newly gathered people of the Lord" (I 249). Hawthorne, speaking of the United States two centuries after Dimmesdale's death, declares in the Pierce book that on the welfare of the Union rest the destinies of all mankind.

Prophecy is performative utterance at its most dramatic. The "old prophets of Israel" (I 249) cited by Hawthorne did not deal in feckless sentences; their judgments, backed by the omnipotence of the Deity, summoned events into being. Dimmesdale's announcement of the future is the first of a number of such predictions in Hawthorne's work, some positive, others much more ominous, all marked by a deed-like impact on the actual. The minister's flair for prophetic speech passes on to Hester. The two characters have ventriloquized each other before: Dimmesdale at Governor Bellingham's mansion, where he pleaded with the colony's leaders to let Hester keep Pearl; and Hester in the forest scene, where the emotionally and physically drained pastor implored her to "Think for me. . . . Thou art strong. Resolve for me!" (I 196). (Hester's counsel to her lover, "Preach! Write! Act!" [I 198], suggests her stake in articulation as intervention.)

In the novel's "Conclusion," the heroine picks up the mantle of seer that Dimmesdale has left behind—or half picks it up. The final pages are a study in ambiguity. Hawthorne explicitly states that Hester will *not* be the prophetess of a new truth about gender roles. But he also says that the wearer of the scarlet letter firmly assures her listeners of a "coming revelation" in which "the whole relation of man and woman" will be placed "on a surer ground of mutual happiness" (I 263). He has her publicize that belief in precisely the kind of marginalized but quasi-open forum favored by emergent political movements, such as the antebellum struggle for emancipation. Hester, until this moment, has done all her speaking in clandestine or solitary spaces; now she addresses a gathering or, perhaps, a succession of women in her cottage near the settlement, at meetings that could not possibly escape the notice of the governing elders. As with Dimmesdale's election sermon, Hawthorne does not provide us access to Hester's conversations (which recall his contemporary Margaret Fuller as much or more than Anne Hutchinson). He gives us only a digest. Is his restraint another attempt to muzzle the voice of dissent—whose intuition of the future has arguably come true, in our day if not in his? Or does Hawthorne's second-hand account paradoxically betray an awareness of his own lack of distance from the age's polemical tumult, his inevitable implication as a writer in the transformative power of speech?

What is undeniable is that the motif of prophecy moves to center stage in Hawthorne's fiction, and that it acquires ever greater ascendancy over the real. In *The House of the Seven Gables,* the young boarder in the Pyncheon house, Holgrave, is a writer, lecturer, daguerreotypist, and reformer whose "lawless" (II 85) words bend others to his will. More generally, the members of the Maule family, from whom the pseudonymous Holgrave is descended, have always known how to use language as a weapon. The tradition dates back to Matthew Maule, the progenitor of the line. Maule was wrongly convicted of witchcraft and pronounced a "prophecy" against his persecutor, Colonel Pyncheon. "God will give him blood to drink!" (II 8), the condemned man cried on the scaffold; his prediction was fulfilled in the manner of the Colonel's sudden death, with his beard and ruff drenched in blood. The Maule family medium, in short, is the curse, the dark twin of oracular utterance.

The inheritance has taken a slightly less lethal turn in Holgrave. The "artist" or "author," as Hawthorne calls him, rails in Emersonian fashion against the past's hold on the present. After haranguing Phoebe Pyncheon about "Dead Men's houses" such as that of the seven gables (II 183), he proceeds to read aloud to her one of his magazine contributions entitled "Alice Pyncheon." The story revisits the "chimney-corner legend" (II 197) of the curse and has the grandson of the original wizard, also named Matthew Maule, assert hypnotic sovereignty over the haughty Alice. This venture into subterranean discourse, into the sort of scandalous "superstition" the novel as a whole relegates to the domestic sphere, casts a spell over Phoebe similar to the one that subjugated Alice. While Holgrave toys with the thought of "empire over the human spirit," Hawthorne adverts to his real target in this scene, the specter of political speech. In an otherwise mysterious aside, he mentions the moon melting into the dusk, "like an ambitious demagogue, who hides his aspiring purpose by assuming the prevalent hue of popular sentiment" (II 212–13). The "artist" catches himself in time to waken the half-conscious girl and refuse the mastery conferred by his narrative.

Hawthorne, another artist averse to verbal power, brings Holgrave to heel in the remainder of the novel, just as he returned the wearer of the scarlet letter to Puritan Boston and a life of penitence. Holgrave's renunciation can no more cleanse the text of disruptive discourse than Hester's could, however. The descendant of the Maules recants his radicalism and proposes marriage to the utterly conventional Phoebe, promising her that he "will conform [himself] to laws, and the peaceful practice of society" (II 307). Yet this apostasy, which presumably means that Holgrave will also abandon authorship, could not have happened without the reassertion of linguistic dominion. The two young people bond with each other, and declare their love, over the corpse of Judge Pyncheon; and that grasping hypocrite, like his forebear the Colonel, was felled by Maule's curse. (According to Holgrave, the Judge's "mode of death has been an idiosyncrasy with his family, for generations past" [II 304]). Not even departure from the family mansion can quell the "legendary." After the lovers drive off into the sunset, the Pyncheon elm is heard to whisper "unintelligible prophecies" (II 319). As in *The Scarlet Letter,* the oracular voice hovers unconciliated over the novel's final pages, and conservatism triumphs without getting the better of verbal agency.

The Blithedale Romance transfers the imperialism of the curse to Zenobia; and Hawthorne, as I have suggested, retaliates against his "dark lady" by sentencing her to a histrionic death. Not only that, the entire novel exposes clairvoyance as a humbug. The subplot of the Veiled Lady, the "Sibylline" (III 6) medium concealed behind a strip of white cloth, brings out the close link between mesmeric soothsaying and the "cold and dead materialism" of Professor Westervelt (III 200). Zenobia is tainted by her collusion with this mountebank, and Priscilla's supposed second sight draws a blank outside the contrived setting of the public stage: she is quite stumped by Coverdale's inquiry, "what is about to happen" at Blithedale? (III 143). Hawthorne would have us believe that prophetic intimations, conveyed through speech, are fraudulent when they are not positively evil.

But it is a nice question as to who gets the last word in the narrative, the author or the female character he tries so hard to confound. Hawthorne's final statement is Miles Coverdale's weariness with political activism, as well as his equivocal confession of his love for Priscilla—equivocal (and Dimmesdale-like) because Coverdale has seemed completely obsessed with Zenobia. The storytelling and fiery speeches of the anti-heroine, who, though not an accomplished writer, possesses a voice both "living" (III 120) and "inimitable" (III 107), prove much more efficacious. Chapter XIII, significantly called "Zenobia's Legend," takes up *The House of the Seven Gables'* theme of disreputable but potent speech. Zenobia relates a "wild, spectral" tale (III 107) about "Theodore" and the Veiled Lady that in one possible interpretation predicts Coverdale's pining for Priscilla and so "certainly accorded with the event" (III 6). (The quoted phrase is the poet's own formulation, from the first time he watched Priscilla perform.)

Zenobia's presentiments, scattered throughout the text, escalate in the final pages and assume an unerring authority. She foretells her death—a bit cryptically, perhaps, but such is the nature of oracles—when she announces to Coverdale that he will next see her face "behind the black-veil" (III 228). The river in which she drowns during the night is a "broad, black, inscrutable depth" (III 232); and Zenobia, one might say, has donned the prophetic veil that formerly covered her sister's countenance, in the process altering its color from silver to the darkness of the curse. (Interestingly, Zenobia's gift for forecasting seems to be contagious; following the confrontation at Eliot's Pulpit, no less a character than Coverdale has a dream-premonition in which he correctly divines her suicide.) The clairvoyant-oratress herself waxes bolder and more imperious. After Hollingsworth jilts her for Priscilla (and Priscilla's money), she exclaims to Coverdale, "Tell him he has murdered me! Tell him that I'll haunt him!" According to our narrator, Zenobia "spoke these words with the wildest energy" (III 226); it is not long before they achieve their purpose. We next encounter Hollingsworth several years later near the retired cottage where he dwells with Priscilla. Suffering has reduced him to childlike dependency on his wife, and when he tells Coverdale that he has been busy with but "a single murderer," the poet instantly recalls Zenobia's imprecation: "I knew what murderer he meant, and whose vindictive shadow dogged the side where Priscilla was not" (III 243). In the Hawthorne universe, otherwise so dismissive of human action, "mere" words outlive their speaker and prostrate the object of their spite.

A much-quoted passage from *The House of the Seven Gables*—quoted, rightly, as evidence of Hawthorne's conservative recoil from human schemes of improvement—urges resignation to the principle that "God is the sole worker of realities" (II 180). But all three of Hawthorne's American novels qualify that Pierce-like hostility to reform. The not-so-hidden message of the novels, culminating in Zenobia's curse, is that language rivals God as an engine of transformation. The Deity, Hawthorne would no doubt prefer us to forget, is the model for this conception of speech. The first chapter of the Book of Genesis is the touchstone: "And God said, Let there be light: and there was light. . . . And God said. . . . And God said . . . and it was so."

Toward the end of *The Blithedale Romance,* Hawthorne has Zenobia liken herself to "an hereditary bond-slave" (III 217). The comparison reverberates. Is it nothing more than coincidence, a topical reference with no subtext? Or does the analogy amount to an equivocal confession on Hawthorne's part that the prophetic voice he most feared, heralding the Civil War within a decade, was that raised on behalf of the enslaved?[6]

NOTES

1. On Hawthorne's politics, influential work has been done by Jonathan Arac (Bercovitch and Jehlen 1986, 247–66), Sacvan Bercovitch (1991), and Lauren Berlant (1991). Studies of Hawthorne and slavery include Walter Benn Michaels (Michaels and Pease 1985, 156–82), Jennifer Fleischner (1991), and Teresa A. Goddu (2001).

2. The best study of the anti-slavery petitions is by William Lee Miller (1996). On riots, the reader should consult David Grimsted (1998). Still useful on lynching

(which originally meant any act of extralegal "justice," not just hanging) is Cutler (1905).

3. Eric Foner misleadingly omits "Free Speech" from the title of his otherwise magisterial *Free Soil, Free Labor, Free Men: The Ideology of the Republican Party before the Civil War* (1970).

4. The laws banning anti-slavery discourse can be found in *The Border Ruffian Code in Kansas* (1855), 1–2. For the 1860 election, see Ollinger Crenshaw (1945).

5. Some important treatments of the American romantics and the struggle over slavery are Len Gougeon (1990), Gregg D. Crane (2002), and Martin Klammer (1995).

6. Although the topic of feminism is beyond the scope of this essay, one cannot ignore the fact that Hawthorne's "anti-slavery" prophet is a woman. Margaret Fuller, the probable inspiration for Zenobia, repeatedly analogized between the plight of women and that of African slaves. Fuller writes of abolitionists in *Woman in the Nineteenth Century* (1845): "And this band it is, which, partly from a natural following out of principles, partly because many women have been prominent in that cause, makes, just now, the warmest appeal in behalf of woman" (15).

3

"Strangely Ajar with the Human Race": Hawthorne, Slavery, and the Question of Moral Responsibility

LARRY J. REYNOLDS

In the midst of the Civil War, Nathaniel Hawthorne wrote his friend Horatio Bridge, thanking him "for a shaded map of Negrodom, which you sent me a little while ago. What a terrible amount of trouble and expense, in washing that sheet white!—and, after all, I am afraid we shall only variegate it with blood and dirt" (XVIII 428). The map Hawthorne refers to most likely resembled the "Moral Map of U.S." (see Figure 1), which Northern abolitionists had used to illustrate the white moral purity of the free states compared to the black evil of the Southern slave states. The map's linking the putative color of slaves with the evils of slavery was an injustice so ingrained in the American political unconscious that it remained invisible, even to abolitionists. Embedded within Hawthorne's comments on the map are two features of his political thought that would earn him condemnation in his own times and ours. The first is his skepticism, called by one of his English critics "the most immoral kind of political fatalism."[1] The second is his racism (implicit in the term "Negrodom"), which has become more noticeable and objectionable with each passing year.

Hawthorne's skepticism about purifying the country by eliminating slavery arose not from any proslavery sentiments (he hated slavery, calling it a "foul scurf" [XXIII 431] upon the South); but rather, from his deep-seated belief that attempts to rid a village, region, or nation of evil could

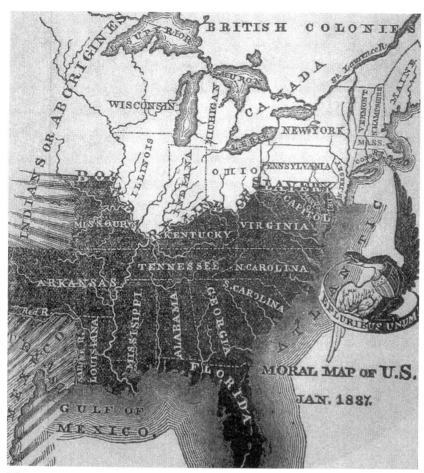

Figure 1. "Moral Map of U.S." Frontispiece of *The Legion of Liberty! And Force of Truth.* 2nd ed. New York: American Anti-Slavery Society, 1843.

produce results just the opposite of those desired, especially if the means used were violent. As a student of history and lifelong observer of human nature, he considered almost all people and causes as irrevocably "variegated," a mixture of moral qualities resistant to purification and cleansing. In tales such as "The Birth-Mark" (1843) and "Earth's Holocaust" (1844), he made this point explicitly, and it also informed his attitude toward the abolitionist movement. In 1857 Hawthorne responded to an abolitionist pamphlet by his sister-in-law Elizabeth Peabody by telling her that "vengeance and beneficence are things that God claims for Himself. His instruments have no consciousness of His purpose; if they imagine they have, it is a pretty sure token that they are *not* His instruments. The good of others, like our own happiness, is not to be attained by direct effort, but incidentally" (XVIII 116).[2]

Because of this conviction, Hawthorne found himself during the 1850s and 1860s more and more at odds with his absolutist contemporaries, who professed to have direct access to the will of God. After he brought his skeptical outlook to bear upon the issues of slavery and the Civil War publicly, he became the object of sanctimonious denigration among New England writers and reformers. William Lloyd Garrison's *Liberator* called his "Chiefly About War-Matters" (1862) "flippant and heartless" and accused Hawthorne of writing "automatically, as though his veins were bloodless" (June 27, 1862: 2). *Harper's Weekly* found the "tone of doubt and indifference" toward the Civil War in *Our Old Home* (1863) repellent, like that of "the most charming companion who should prove to have no objection to infanticide" (November 21, 1863: 739). After Hawthorne's death, Emerson lamented in his journal that Hawthorne had "removed" himself "by the indignation his perverse politics & unfortunate friendship for that paltry Franklin Pierce awaked,—though it rather moved pity for Hawthorne, & the assured belief that he would outlive it, & come right at last" (*JMN* 15: 60).[3] Hawthorne's movement that Emerson speaks of was relative to his own position, of course, to his own sense of "right."[4] The most severe condemnation of this kind came in a long memorial review on Hawthorne in 1864 by the editor George William Curtis, who had been a friend of Hawthorne's at Brook Farm and later Concord. Unable to suppress his outrage at Hawthorne's lack of commitment to the Northern cause, Curtis characterized him as "hard, cold, and perverse" and claimed "he cared little for man; and the high tides of collective emotion among his fellows left him dry and untouched" (551). Curtis concluded by declaring, "his own times and their people and their affairs were just as shadowy to him as those of any of his stories," and asserted that the reader's "heart, bewildered, asks and asks again, 'Is he human? Is he a man?'" (555).[5]

This moralistic approach to Hawthorne's political thought has persisted into the present day, and he continues to be charged with the sins of blindness, cowardice, and escapism.[6] Because he shared the racism of his white middle-class society, this feature of his vision, rather than his political "perversity," has become the focus of recent judgments directed at him.[7] The opprobrium cast upon Hawthorne in his time and ours holds considerable interest for anyone seeking a fuller understanding of the difficulties faced by a person of imagination and integrity in times of political strife, but to measure the depth and value of Hawthorne's political views, we must go beyond the discourse of the New England antislavery movement, which persists in American cultural and literary criticism, and explore his own historically informed, albeit still partial, imaginative world. In this essay, I want to extend previous studies of Hawthorne's responses to slavery and abolitionism by examining two psychohistorical images that shaped his political and moral vision: revolutionary violence and witchcraft, both of which emerged from his deeply felt knowledge of American and European history.

A number of scholars have discussed the ways in which *The Scarlet Letter* (1850) incorporates Hawthorne's stance toward the issues of slavery at mid-century and how an "Africanist presence" (Morrison 46) underlies the imagery and themes of the work.[8] The romance Hawthorne tried to write some twelve years later in the midst of the Civil War, "Septimius Felton," has received little critical attention, yet it reveals even more clearly the relationship between his political views and his imaginative thought. It also points to fears of revolutionary violence, witchcraft, and racial mixing as compelling sources of the "immoral" detachment that isolated him from his fellow New Englanders. The plans and notes Hawthorne wrote to himself in his manuscripts are especially revealing about the links between his personal views and the writing of his fiction. Before a long account of the mixture of Indian and white blood his protagonist has inherited, for example, Hawthorne in a marginal note reminds himself of the following: "The mixture of race a crime against nature, therefore pernicious" (XIII 256), which applies not only to Septimius personally, but also to racial relations in New England and the country over the course of several centuries. Although Hawthorne never completed "Septimius" nor sorted out the attitude he expected the reader to have toward its subject, it "promised to be the best thing of its kind Hawthorne had ever done" (Baym 26). With great effort, and intermittent confidence, he sought to resolve fears about the dissolution of his life and that of his nation, especially the latter's bloody way of addressing the problem of variegated racial identities within the house divided.

Hawthorne began working on "Septimius" in the summer of 1861, several months after the firing on Fort Sumter, and by setting it in Concord in 1775 at the beginning of the American Revolution, he was able to draw upon his own ambivalence about the war fever surrounding him. His protagonist, Septimius, lives in a house modeled on the Wayside, and when the farmers and neighbors start assembling for battle, he, like his creator, finds that his meditative cast of mind sets him apart from their excited patriotism: he

> went into his house, and sat there, in his study, for some hours, in that unpleasant state of feeling, which a man of brooding thought is apt to experience when the world around him is in a state of intense motion, which he

finds it impossible to chord with. There seemed to be a stream rushing past him, which, even if he plunged into the midst of it, he could not be wet by it. He felt himself strangely ajar with the human race, and would have given much, either to be in full accord with it, or to be separated from it forever. (XIII 22–23)

In "The Old Manse" (1846), Hawthorne had contrasted his "circle of repose" at the Manse with the social activism at the other end of Concord, where "bats and owls, and the whole host of night-birds" flap around the "intellectual fire" (X 31) there (Emerson), and in "Septimius" he sets up a similar polarity by creating the character of Robert Hagburn, an activist eager to join the fight. Hagburn's name connects him, I believe, to witch-hunting, and the kinds of men willing to forsake reason and moderation in order to rid the land of what they consider evil. As the British troops retreat from Concord, the trailing colonists shoot at them from hiding, and as one redcoat staggers and falls, Septimius shudders because "it was so like murder that he really could not tell the difference." Revealing his own sense of quietism, Hawthorne writes, "how strange, how strange it is, this deep, wild passion that nature has implanted in us, to be the death of our fellow-creatures and which co-exists at the same time with horror" (XIII 24).

After Septimius kills one of these British soldiers himself, not by shooting at him from hiding, but in a face-to-face confrontation on the hillside behind his house, Hawthorne brings issues of race and amalgamation into the plot, making Septimius's Indian blood account for a repressed savageness in his behavior. He lives with his Aunt Keziah, who works as his housekeeper, and they trace their mutual ancestry to a Puritan who married the daughter of an Indian Sagamore. Among later descendants are a half-breed woman executed "during the prevalence of the witchcraft delusion." The injustice of her fate and its link to false witnessing is explained by Hawthorne, yet also attributed to this person herself: "the wild traits of her heathen ancestry overpowered those of the civilized race with which her blood was mingled; she was said, too, to have had a very dark skin, the straight black hair, and that Indian form of the face, and Indian eye, lineaments which are said to be harder to eradicate . . . than those of the negro race. Something, also, perhaps of the fierce and cruel Indian temper, and generally, a cast of character that made her disliked by her neighbors" (XIII 265–66). Aunt Keziah (later renamed Aunt Nashoba) whose darkness endows her with mysterious knowledge, seems based in part upon Tituba, an Indian slave from Barbados who became the first accused witch in the Salem trials presided over by Judge Hathorne. (Tituba became half Indian-half black and then all black in nineteenth- and twentieth-century histories.)[9] According to the Hawthornes' daughter Rose, there was another person who "no doubt stood for a suggestion of Aunt Keziah," Mrs. Peters, the Hawthornes' black servant while they lived in the Berkshires. Rose describes her as

> an invaluable tyrant, an unloaded weapon, a creature who seemed to say, "Forget my qualities if you dare—there is one of them which is fatal!" As my parents possessed the capacity to pay respect where it could be earned, the qualities of Mrs. Peters were respected, and she found herself in a sort of heaven of courteous tolerance. (Lathrop 1897, 161–62)

The aunt-nephew relationship Hawthorne establishes in "Septimius" suggests he may have felt some familial tie with Mrs. Peters, if only because, like Poe, his troubled lineage made him identify with and feel revulsion toward blacks, as alienated Others. As in *The House of the Seven Gables* where the blood lines of Maules and Pyncheons converge and unite, in "Septimius" Hawthorne combines Puritan witch-hunter and Indian witch within the same house or family line. Secluded in his study, Septimius, student of theology, contends not only with the enemy of all humankind, Death (seeking the elixir of life by deciphering a torn manuscript the dying soldier gave him), but also his own racial heritage, and, by extension, the dark and bloody presence within the emergent nation itself. When a red flower grows from the grave of the British redcoat, Septimius plucks it to make a trial effort at creating the elixir of immortality, but when he gives the elixir to Aunt Keziah, who has become critically ill, the drink kills rather than saves her. Hawthone thus thematizes the destructive effects of good intentions, especially the harm inflicted upon racial others by those (such as Puritan divines, British redcoats, and New England scholars) deluded into thinking they are their more civilized saviors. In one of his plans for the romance, Hawthorne told himself, "Perhaps the moral will turn out to be, the folly of man in thinking that he can ever be of any importance to the welfare of the world; or that any settled plan of his, to be carried on through a length of time, could be successful" (XIII 529).

The sources of Hawthorne's pessimistic political vision, which thus appears so strikingly in "Septimius," can be traced, as I have suggested, to images of revolutionary violence and witchcraft that had long haunted his imagination. A crucial overlooked fact about life in antebellum American society is the nearness in time to the Reign of Terror, which gave terms such as "jacobinical," "bloody," and "revolutionary" such powerful associations, now lost to us by the passage of time. Sensational reports about the horrors of the Santo Domingo slave revolts between 1791 and 1804 also provided terrifying images for those like Hawthorne who pondered the relation between abolitionist exhortation and slave violence.[10] Today we tend to regard abolitionists as heroic moral leaders of their age, but for a number of years they were viewed as dangerous fanatics, even by those who would later join their ranks. Initially, the antislavery movement took a number of forms, including colonization, philosophical abolitionism, and immediate emancipation gradually accomplished (that is, the conferring of civil and political rights in stages following emancipation); however, it was the immediate and unqualified emancipation advocated by William Lloyd Garrison and his followers that galvanized public attention, inspired the most violent reactions, and eventually "usurped" the field of antislavery thought.[11]

Many progressive supporters of the antislavery movement feared the consequences of immediate emancipation, especially the prospect of large numbers of ex-slaves joining Northern society and its labor force.[12] Like his white contemporaries, Hawthorne believed that amalgamation between whites and people of color would degrade American civilization and lead to various social ills, such as "strange pursuits, ill-temper, passionateness, secret grudges" (XIII 266). As everyone knew, "the horrors of San Domingo" began with a mulatto revolt, inspired by the Jacobins in France.[13] Anxiety about such consequences, expressed by Thomas Jefferson among others, led to the establishment of the American Colonization Society in 1817, whose goal was to deport free Negroes to Liberia. In the 1820s and 30s the threat of amalgamation inspired mob action against people of color in a number of northern cities, and it soon surfaced in the writings of even those devoted to the antislavery cause. In an 1851 essay on slavery for the *North American Review,* Elizabeth Peabody argued that "if the two races, after the slaves are set free, remain together at the South, we can foresee nothing but evil. If amalgamation should take place, it would create a third race, certainly inferior to the white, and probably inferior to the negro." "Of specific remedies," she concluded, "we know only one, and that is colonization" (363). Similarly, at the end of *Uncle Tom's Cabin* (1852), Stowe calls for first educating the emancipated slaves "until they have attained to somewhat of a moral and intellectual maturity, and then assist them in their passage to those shores [of Africa], where they may put in practice the lessons they have learned in America" (626). Less explicitly, but with some conviction, Hawthorne supported the activities of the American Colonization Society with his editing of the *Journal of An African Cruiser* (1845), written by his friend Horatio Bridge, telling about a recent cruise on the West Coast of Africa to protect American trade and stop slavers.[14] Hawthorne's own interest in the mysteries and dangers of amalgamation (later termed miscegenation) has been discerned in any number of his writings, specifically "Rappaccini's Daughter" (1844), *The Scarlet Letter* (1850), *The House of the Seven Gables* (1851), and *The Marble Faun* (1860).[15]

Hawthorne's racial and political anxieties interlocked with one another and, though displaced onto his fiction, they were periodically stirred by abolitionist activity. Garrison, whose fanaticism was most visible, dominated the movement in its early stages. After he founded the *Liberator* in 1831, he became an inspiration to slaves like Frederick Douglass and used the paper and public assemblies to provoke and inflame. His odium fell upon the heads not only of slave-owners, but also of ministers, politicians, and even members of other anti-slavery groups that questioned his positions. Filled with a sense of anger and rage, Garrison burned the Constitution in public, calling it "a compact with Satan," and spoke in the most passionate rhetoric. In his 1832 pamphlet criticizing the colonization movement, for example, he declared that if "the glorious day of universal emancipation" did not arrive,

> woe to the safety of this people! . . . A cry of horror, a cry of revenge, will go up to heaven in the darkness of midnight, and re-echo from every cloud. Blood will flow like water—the blood of guilty men, and of innocent women and children. Then will be heard lamentations and weeping, such as will blot out the remembrance of the horrors of St. Domingo. (59)

Although Garrison believed in nonresistance, claiming "We advocate no jacobinical doctrines" (75), his cause became associated with Nat Turner's notorious Southampton slave insurrection of 1831, during which Turner and his band killed over sixty white men, women, and children. Though Turner's only reading material had been the Bible, Garrison and the *Liberator* were widely perceived as instigators of the rebellion. Garrison received assassination threats from the South and New England both,[16] and in 1835, at a meeting of the Boston Female Anti-Slavery Society, a mob dragged him through the streets with a rope around his neck, before he was rescued and put in jail for protection.

Hawthorne's negative attitude toward abolitionism was shared by practically all his contemporaries during the late 1830s and early 1840s, due to its radicalism. Even Emerson, Thoreau, and Margaret Fuller—later its ardent supporters—found the movement objectionable.[17] Though often critical of the Transcendentalists, because he rejected their belief in the innate moral goodness of the individual, Hawthorne shared their early political quietism, built on a belief in an innate moral sense and the presence of a beneficent

tendency at work in the world. The commitment to moderation and compromise that scholars have discerned in Hawthorne's politics at mid-century,
yoking *The Scarlet Letter* (1850) to the *Life of Franklin Pierce* (1852), became
part of his social and moral outlook years before.[18] In a poem from his youth,
entitled "Moderate Views" and dated February 13, 1817 (when Hawthorne
was twelve!), he writes, "With passions unruffled untainted by pride/ By reason my life let me square" (XXIII 3). In a number of ways, Emerson and
Thoreau in the 1840s articulated this optimistic moral vision, but unlike
them, Hawthorne did not forsake it when faced with "the impending crisis."[19] Despite their commitment to contemplative idealism, almost all the
Transcendentalists, were "forced," as Stanley Elkins puts it, into more radical
views by Southern intransigence. Eventually, they sanctified John Brown and
beat the drums of war. Hawthorne, of course, did not. As the insightful
Emerson disciple Moncure Conway observed, "He had not the flexibility of
principle displayed by so many in those days. He thus had no party,—then
nearly equivalent to having no country" (206).

Throughout his adult life, Hawthorne shied away from partisan political activism not because it jarred with his artistic sensibilities, as he sometimes feigned, but because he feared the untamed passions of radical
action. Like Edmund Burke, he associated revolution with images of a
breakdown in the familial order—murder of the father, distress for mother
and children. In one of his early pieces, "Old News" (1835), he observes, "A
revolution, or anything, that interrupts social order, may afford opportunities for the individual display of eminent virtue; but, its effects are pernicious to general morality" (XI 159). In 1840, Hawthorne described Burke
as "one of the wisest men and greatest orators that ever the world produced" (VI 176), and one finds a consistent Burkean conservatism underlying Hawthorne's settings, symbols, and themes. His most striking early
treatment of radical sociopolitical behavior appears in "My Kinsman
Major Molineux" (1831), first entitled "My Uncle Major Molineux," where
a "temporary inflammation of the popular mind" (XI 209) in the mid-seventeenth century causes angry colonists to tar and feather (and thus presumably murder) the royal governor. At the end of the tale, as the boy
Robin watches the mob and their victim (his kinsman) pass, Hawthorne
writes, "On they went, like fiends that throng in mockery round some dead
potentate, mighty no more, but majestic still in his agony" (XI 230).[20] A
comparable scene appears in Hawthorne's story for children, "The
Hutchinson Mob" (1841), an account of the attack on Lieutenant Governor Hutchinson's house by colonists in 1765. Hutchinson's daughter alerts
her father that they are coming "as wild as so many tigers," yet, "He was an
old lawyer; and he could not realize that the people would do anything so

utterly lawless as to assault him in his peaceful home" (VI 157). But they do enter, like an "enraged wild beast" and a "tempestuous flood" and destroy tables, hearths, volumes of his library, family portraits, and mirrors. At the end of the account, Grandfather tells the children who are his auditors that this "was a most unjustifiable act. . . . But we must not decide against the justice of the people's cause, merely because an excited mob was guilty of outrageous violence" (VI 159). As with "My Kinsman," the imagery of this violence, rather than its justification, predominates in the telling.

Throughout Hawthorne's works, revolutionary mobs engage in forms of symbolic emasculation, and it seems likely they are linked to the radical change that occurred in his life upon the death of his father when Hawthorne was a boy. One need not subscribe to Frederick Crews's theory that Hawthorne suffered from unresolved filial hatred to believe that after he, his mother, and sisters moved in with the Mannings out of necessity, the boy experienced a sense of upheaval and victimization that stayed with him throughout his life.[21] Despite his adult Jacksonianism, Hawthorne clearly identified with a number of his more refined characters when they were assailed by their social inferiors (Hester being the most obvious example), and even those characters who suffer from the "absurd delusion of family importance" (II 19) (such as the Pyncheons) receive the benefit of his nostalgia for a lost aristocratic past, even if he has to wrench a plot to provide it.[22] His joke in "The Custom-House" sketch about having been beheaded by bloodthirsty Whigs reveals a deep-seated anxiety about revolutionary violence,[23] and his notorious outburst about the "d——d mob of scribbling women" (XVII 304) also suggests an aristocratic sense of persecution. Like Burke, Hawthorne empathized with the royal family, and in a letter to his fiancée, Sophia Peabody, in 1840, he told her about a nightmare of his:

> Dearest, thou didst not come into my dreams, last night; but, on the contrary, I was engaged in assisting the escape of Louis XVI and Marie Antoinette from Paris, during the French revolution. And sometimes, by an unaccountable metamorphosis, it seemed as if my mother and sisters were in the place of the King and Queen. (XV 427–28).

The king and queen were subsequently decapitated, of course. In the fall of 1849, after the death of his actual mother and his own firing or "decapitation," Hawthorne refreshed his memory of the 1789 French Revolution by reading Alphonse de Lamartine's *History of the Girondins* (1847), which had just inspired the 1848 revolution in France and the tragic "Bloody June Days" that followed. At the same time, he started writing *The Scarlet Letter*, using a scaffold as his central setting.[24]

If we keep these revolutionary images in mind, it becomes easier to understand why Hawthorne, who had no first-hand knowledge of the horrors of slavery, would resist the growing agitation over the issue, even though he felt drawn to the more liberal wing of the Democratic Party. In an 1851 letter to Zachariah Burchmore, Hawthorne specifies where he stood in the wake of the Fugitive Slave Act and the Compromise of 1850:

> I have not, as you suggest, the slightest sympathy for the slaves; or, at least, not half so much as for the laboring whites, who, I believe, as a general thing, are ten times worse off than the Southern negros [*sic*]. Still, whenever I am absolutely cornered, I shall go for New England rather than the South;—and this Fugitive Law cornered me. Of course, I knew what I was doing when I signed that Free-Soil document, and bade farewell to all ideas of foreign consulships, or other official stations. (XVI 456)

Within a year of writing this letter, Hawthorne found a means to position himself for another government appointment, however, by writing the campaign biography of his friend Pierce, a conservative "Hunker" Democrat nominated by Southerners. In the biography, Hawthorne's commitment to moderation informs his notorious statement about the future of slavery. After discussing the abolitionist position, he adds,

> but there is still another view, and probably as wise a one. It looks at slavery as one of those evils which divine Providence does not leave to be remedied by human contrivances, but which, in its own good time, by some means impossible to be anticipated, but of the simplest and easiest operation, when all its uses shall have been fulfilled, it causes to vanish like a dream. (XXIII 416–17)

Hawthorne knew, of course, that political passions had been inflamed by the Fugitive Slave Law, and before writing the biography he told Pierce, who had supported the Compromise, that the slavery question involved "knotty points," and though he did not yet know how to handle it, the subject was "not to be shirked nor blinked" but dealt with in such a way as to situate Pierce "on the broadest ground possible, as a man for the whole country" (XVI 561).

Hawthorne would later claim he had lost "hundreds of friends, here at the north, . . . in consequence of what I say on the slavery question" (XVI 605). These friends, some of the most educated and intelligent people in New England, were becoming more willing to condone the use of violence to achieve their political ends, and this key fact explains the growing divergence between their political and moral visions and those of Hawthorne. The annexation of Texas (1845), the Mexican War (1846–48), the revolutions in Europe (1848–49), and the Compromise (1850) stimulated their growing radicalism and opposition to slavery. As Hawthorne was writing *The Scarlet Letter* in 1849, Thoreau in "Resistance to Civil Government" and Fuller in her Italian dispatches were defending murder and assassination on behalf of liberty. In Thoreau's essay, often misread as an argument for passive resistance, he asserts, "But even suppose blood should flow. Is there not a sort of blood shed when the conscience is wounded? Through this wound a man's real manhood and immortality flow out, and he bleeds to an everlasting death" (235–36). Thoreau's later defense of John Brown, in "A Plea for John Brown," proceeds logically from such thinking and allows him to repress his knowledge of the Pottawatomie Creek massacre, when Brown and seven other men dragged five settlers from their homes on the night of May 24–25, 1856, and split open their skulls with broadswords.[25] Similarly, in Rome, after Count Pellegrino Rossi, the new prime minister of the Papal States, was stabbed in the throat on November 15, 1848, as he entered the Chamber of Deputies, Fuller reported that soldiers and citizens joined in singing "Blessed the hand that rids the earth of a tyrant," and she added, "Certainly, the manner *was* grandiose" (*SGD* 240[26]). In a private letter, she told her mother, "For me, I never thought to have heard of a violent death with satisfaction, but this act affected me as one of terrible justice" (*Letters* 5: 147).

Even members of the New England ministry in the 1850s began accepting the belief, put forward by Frederick Douglass and his followers, that the murder of oppressors was justified. Encouraged by the European revolutions, they came to believe, as Theodore Parker asserted, that "All the great charters of humanity have been *writ in blood,* and must continue to be so for some centuries" (qtd. Demos 519; emphasis in original). In his 1850 sermon "The Function and Place of Conscience in Relation to the Laws of Men" (1850), Parker told his congregation, "if I were a fugitive, and could escape in no other way, I would kill him [the slave-catcher] with as little compunction as I would drive a mosquito from my face. It is high time this was said" (277–78). Prominent abolitionists Angelina Grimké Weld, Samuel May, Wendell Phillips, Henry Wright, and Parker Pilsbury all abandoned their "peace principles" in the 1850s, and Pilsbury even told the Massachusetts Anti-Slavery Society that "he longed to see the time come when Boston should run with blood from Beacon Hill to the foot of Broad Street" (qtd. Demos 523).

Hawthorne's response to the growing commitment to violence surrounding him may be found in *The Blithedale Romance* (1852), where he portrays Hollingsworth as a fierce, cold-hearted reformer and Zenobia (obviously modeled on Fuller) as an activist who seems capable of plunging a dagger into her rival, an act of passion more appropriate "in Italy, instead of New England" (III 78). (Some eight years later, in *The Marble Faun,* he again drew upon his knowledge of Fuller's political activities in Rome to have Miriam and Donatello, after the murder of the model, pass by Pompey's forum, where Miriam proclaims, "there was a great deed done here! . . . a deed of blood, like ours! Who knows, but we may meet the high and ever-sad fraternity of Caesar's murderers, and exchange a salutation?'" (IV 176). [27] In *Blithedale,* Hawthorne also exaggerates his own quietism by describing Coverdale's unwillingness to stir himself on behalf of the Hungarian revolution, led by the famous Louis Kossuth. "Were there any cause, in this whole chaos of human struggle, worth a sane man's dying for," Coverdale says,

> and which my death would benefit, then—provided, however, the effort did not involve an unreasonable amount of trouble—methinks I might be bold to offer up my life. If Kossuth, for example, would pitch the battle-field of Hungarian rights within an easy ride of my abode, and choose a mild, sunny morning, after breakfast, for the conflict, Miles Coverdale would gladly be his man, for one brave rush upon the leveled bayonets. Farther than that, I should be loth to pledge myself. (3: 246–47)

Several critics have linked Coverdale's attitude with Hawthorne's own, emphasizing the irony he directed at the prospect of becoming politically engaged.[28] Yet, the sense of loss and enervation he attributes to his characters as a result of their detachment describes only a portion of his attitude. (While in England, he privately criticized Kossuth for failing to speak out against slavery in the United States.)[29] Unlike Coverdale, he had steel in his character; as a public intellectual, he earnestly and consistently adhered to his political quietism, displaying a boldness (or stubbornness, if you will) that his self-effacing humor veils from his readers. What has been called Hawthorne's "retreat" or "escape" into fantasy, then, can also be seen as his means of securing and maintaining a detached and complex understanding of current events.

While Hawthorne was abroad during 1853–1860, he read about the growing controversy over slavery in the United States and reacted negatively to the partisan rhetoric he encountered in the papers.[30] The Kansas-Nebraska Act, the arrest and trial of Anthony Burns, the beating of Charles Sumner on the floor of the Senate, and the attack on Harpers Ferry by John Brown inspired an impassioned thirst for revenge among Northerners and

Southerners alike that repelled Hawthorne.[31] In the summer of 1854 he found it "impossible to read American papers (of whatever political party) without being ashamed of my country" (XVII 237), and two years later, he declared to William Ticknor, "I sympathize with no party, but hate them all—free-soilers, pro-slavery men, and whatever else—all alike" (XVII 559). As consul Hawthorne spent his time assisting wronged Americans who came to his office and attending to case after case of brutal treatment of sailors by shipmasters. At first he followed policy, but "by the end of his term," as editor Bill Ellis points out, " . . . he acted more decisively, siding, for instance, with the black seaman William Valentine of the *Vanguard,* who, threatened and goaded by his white superiors, finally turned on one of his oppressors with a knife and was in return beaten senseless" (XIX 28). Hawthorne defended Valentine and sought prosecution of the officers, who he told the U.S. Secretary of State had been "very tyrannical, and had grossly illtreated the men" (XX 154). In an attempt to alleviate the suffering he witnessed, Hawthorne appealed for help to Charles Sumner of Massachusetts, the leading abolitionist in the Senate, telling him that "no slave-drivers are so wicked" as the shipping masters, "and there is nothing in slavery so bad as the system with which they are connected" (XVII 345). Sumner never answered. He forwarded the dispatch to Attorney General Caleb Cushing, who ignored it.

When Hawthorne arrived back in the United States, he found his old friends and neighbors more violently inclined than ever. Thoreau, following the trial of Anthony Burns, declared in his journal that rather than "consent to establish hell upon earth—to be a party to this establishment,—I would touch a match to blow up earth and hell together" (VI 315). In a similar mood, Emerson had subscribed "lavishly" to help furnish Sharp's rifles to the "Free State men," according to his son Edward (579), and though not a member of John Brown's "Secret Six," Emerson had befriended Brown and given moral support, after the fact, to his raid on Harpers Ferry that ended with seventeen persons killed. At the beginning of the Civil War, Hawthorne observed that Emerson "is as "merciless as a steel bayonet" (XVIII 544), and this was not an overstatement. "Ah! Sometimes gunpowder smells good," Emerson declared while visiting the Charlestown Navy-Yard, and in an address at Tufts College, he asserted, "The brute noise of cannon has a most poetic echo in these days, as instrument of the primal sentiments of humanity" (qtd. Edward Emerson 579). Lydia Maria Child, another peaceful abolitionist, went through a similar transformation, defending John Brown, and persuading herself that violence on behalf of liberty was right action. To a friend, she confided "I *force* myself to remember that, terrible as an insurrection would be to *white* women and children, the *black* women and children have, for many generations, been living in subjection to things *as* horrid, with no *Union,* no *law*s, no *public sentiment* to help *them*" (qtd. Karcher 1994, 424; emphasis in original).

Hawthorne expressed his opposition to the violence that disturbed him in "Chiefly About War-Matters," signing it "By a Peaceable Man," knowing full well that the Peace abolitionists, whom Garrison once led, had disappeared from the scene. As John Demos has pointed out, at this time, it is "not a little ironic, that the 'ultra' or 'radical' position was the pacific one" (525). In Hawthorne's essay, counterpointed by editorial footnotes he wrote himself, expressing mock dismay at his political views, he describes his excursion to Harpers Ferry and his visit to the old engine house, "John Brown's fortress and prison-house," converted into a prison for Rebel soldiers. Calling Brown a "blood-stained fanatic," Hawthorne challenges Emerson's view that Brown's death had "made the Gallows as venerable as the Cross." "Nobody was ever more justly hanged," Hawthorne declares. "He won his martyrdom fairly, and took it firmly . . . any commonsensible man, looking at the matter unsentimentally, must have felt a certain intellectual satisfaction in seeing him hanged, if it were only in requital of his preposterous miscalculation of possibilities" (XXIII 427–28). Such a harsh view of Brown, along with Hawthorne's expression of sympathy for captured confederate soldiers—vacant-eyed, ragged, lacking "the remotest comprehension of what they had been fighting for, or how they had deserved to be shut up in that dreary hole" (XXIII 429)—contributed to Hawthorne's estrangement from his Concord neighbors and revealed once more the depth of his opposition to political violence.[32] His final thoughts on this matter and his most explicit justification for his political vision appear in "Septimius Felton," where he describes what occurs at moments of "seething opinions and overturned principles":

> In times of Revolution and public disturbance, all absurdities are more unrestrained; the measure of calm sense, the habits, the orderly decency, are in a measure lost. More people become insane, I should suppose; offenses against public morality, female license, are more numerous; suicides, murders, all ungovernable outbreaks of men's thoughts, embodying themselves in wild acts, take place more frequently, and with less horror to the lookers-on. (XIII 67)

This is Hawthorne's nightmare world, one he found himself in the midst of, notable for its absence of calmness and rational thought.

Although the psychohistorical image of revolutionary violence played a major part in the shaping of Hawthorne's political and moral vision, I believe a second image, related to the first, affected him more strongly. I refer to witchcraft, or more specifically, to the Salem witchcraft delusion of 1692. As is well known, Hawthorne's great-great-grandfather John Hathorne, gained infamy as one of the three judges of the Salem witchcraft hearings, and, according to family legend, had a curse placed upon him and all his posterity. Before the delusion ended in 1693, he had presided over the imprisonment of more than 150 persons, the hanging of nineteen innocent persons, and the death by torture of another. In the preface to *The Scarlet Letter,* Hawthorne declares that this ancestor "inherited the persecuting spirit, and made himself so conspicuous in the martyrdom of the witches, that their blood may fairly be said to have left a stain upon him." He adds that he will "hereby take shame upon myself for their sakes, and pray that any curse incurred by them . . . may be now and henceforth removed" (I 10). Though this confession and professed atonement are light and humorous, or at least intentionally melodramatic, it appears that Hawthorne indeed felt guilty about the role his ancestors played in Puritan history, which he studied intently. The historical accounts with which he was familiar, such as Charles Upham's *Lectures on Witchcraft* (1831), Robert Calef's *More Wonders of the Invisible World* (1700), and George Bancroft's *History of the United States* (1840), portray the ministers and magistrates in charge as close-minded and cruel and reveal that the specter evidence used to convict the accused was so obviously fabricated that anyone guided by reason, rather than superstition, would have dismissed it. Yet it prevailed. As Hawthorne writes in "Alice Doane's Appeal" (1835), Gallows Hill became "the spot, where guilt and phrenzy [*sic*] consummated the most execrable scene, that our history blushes to record. For this was the field where superstition won her darkest triumph; the high place where our fathers set up their shame, to the mournful gaze of generations far remote" (XI 267). It was Hawthorne's own mournful gaze, then, that strengthened his resolve to resist the pull of religious fanaticism and righteous causes.

Witch hunting and abolitionism, I would argue, formed a particularly strong bond in Hawthorne's mind due to a number of parallels he would have recognized, including a Puritan religiosity intent on ridding the Devil from the land, the sensationalistic demonization of others (accused witches and slavemasters, respectively), obsession with forbidden sexual relations (such as concubinage and amalgamation), and perhaps most important, a failure of vision caused by fanaticism and madness. Hawthorne may not have discerned these parallels at a conscious level, yet they entered his unconscious mind and shaped his political and moral vision. He sensed, as many of his contemporaries did, that Puritanism and the warrior spirit of Cromwell were alive and well in New England, despite the efforts of the Unitarians and Transcendentalists to proffer a new view of humankind. Moral purity remained the national goal. By the beginning of the Civil War, as Joanne Pope Melish (1998) has observed, "the New England nationalist trope of virtuous, historical whiteness, clothed as it was in a distinctive set of cultural, moral, and political values associated with New England's Puritan mission and Revolutionary struggle, had come to define the Unionist North as a whole" (224).[33] Although Hawthorne himself at times seems a proponent of Puritanism, especially due to his skeptical view of human nature, he was also its harshest critic, dramatizing its narrowness and blindness. Intellectual historians have credited the "erosion of Calvinist orthodoxy and the emergence of a powerful alternative often labeled liberal Protestantism" with becoming the "primary source for abolitionist arguments about the inherent brutality of slavery" (Clark 471), yet a Puritan sensibility inspired much of the righteous indignation of antislavery thought.[34]

As a consequence, Hawthorne's critique of his reform-minded contemporaries often coincided with his critique of his ancestors. At their worst, both could become iron men whose repressed fears and desires became externalized in demonic shadow figures resembling themselves. In "Alice Doane's Appeal," for example, Cotton Mather appears riding at the rear of a procession of witches, "a figure on horseback, so darkly conspicuous, so sternly triumphant," says the narrator, "that my hearers mistook him for the visible presence of the fiend himself." Proud and hateful, Mather is described as "the one blood-thirsty man, in whom were concentrated those vices of spirit and errors of opinion, that sufficed to madden the whole surrounding multitude" (XI 279). In "Main-Street," Hawthorne likewise depicts Mather on horseback overseeing a pitiful group of witches being taken to the gallows, and there he asks,

> May not the Arch Fiend have been too subtle for the court and jury, and betrayed them—laughing in his sleeve the while—into the awful errors of pouring out sanctified blood as an acceptable sacrifice upon God's altar? Ah! No; for listen to wise Cotton Mather, who . . . tells them that all has been religiously and justly done, and that Satan's power shall this day receive its death-blow in New England. (XI 77)

Hawthorne's heavy irony here suggests that Mather has unwittingly placed himself in league with the devil, under the delusion that he has successfully resisted him. In a similar psychological process, the protagonist of "Young Goodman Brown" encounters in the forest a devil who bears "a considerable resemblance to him, though perhaps more in expression than features. Still, they might have been taken for father and son" (X 75). As Brown rushes deeper into the forest, "brandishing his staff with frenzied gestures, now giving vent to an inspiration of horrid blasphemy, and now shouting forth such laughter, as set all the echoes of the forest laughing like demons around him," he himself becomes a demon and generates a nightmare world of his own creation. And in "The Hall of Fantasy" (1843), delusion and doubling receive additional, yet less serious, treatment as Hawthorne satirizes a "herd of real or self-styled reformers," many of whom "had got possession of some crystal fragrance of truth, the brightness of which so dazzled them that they could see nothing else in the wide universe." Among them stands the abolitionist, "brandishing his one idea like an iron flail" (X 180), and the resemblance of this figure to a demonic slave master, whip in hand, is surely intentional.

As he read accounts of the Salem witchcraft delusion, Hawthorne would have encountered imagery linking witch hunters, devils, and slave-masters, as well as witches and slaves. He would also have noticed the ways in which the evil perceived by the most prominent witch hunters revealed more about themselves than about the devil. The most striking example appears in the case of the Reverend Samuel Parris, whose slave Tituba first confessed to being a witch, accused others, and told a wild tale of how the Devil became her master—"he Tell me he god, & I must believe him and Serve him" (Breslaw 1996, 195). After the executions stopped, she retracted her confession and declared "that her Master [Parris] did beat her and oth-erways abuse her, to make her confess and accuse (such as he call'd) her Sis-ter-Witches" (Calef 1914, 343). Thus the Reverend Parris, leading witch hunter and enemy of Satan, becomes, as Bancroft puts it, "the beginner and procurer of the sore afflictions to Salem village and the country" (86). (In her confessions, Tituba, significantly, described the devil not as the Black Man, as others did, but as a tall man from Boston with white hair who wore a black coat, which was sometimes serge.)[35] In 1862, Hawthorne reminded himself, as he planned "Septimius Felton," "The clergyman is the more ter-ribly earnest in his religion, because he is conscious of the devil in his blood" (XIII 515).

Other ministers in Salem village during the witchcraft trials used imagery linking the devil to slavemasters, and, indirectly, to themselves. In a sermon the Reverend Deodat Lawson, Samuel Parris's predecessor, deliv-ered in Salem during the trials, he declared,

It is a matter of terror, amazement, and astonishment, to all such wretched souls . . . as have given up their names and souls to the Devil; who by covenant, explicit or implicit, have bound themselves to be his slaves and drudges, consenting to be instruments in whose shapes he may torment and afflict their fellow-creatures (even of their own kind) to the amazing and astonishing of the standers-by. (Upham [1867] 1971, 2: 82)

Mercy Short, an unstable young woman in Cotton Mather's congregation whom he claimed to save through his fasts and counsel in the fall of 1693, apparently fought off the Devil's attempt to make her his slave. According to Mather, his efforts prevented Short's evil angels from tormenting her, and she "could see their 'Black Master' strike and kick them, 'like an Overseer of so many Negro's' until tiring of their useless attempts they said furiously, 'Well you shant be the last,' and flew from the room" (Silverman 1984, 127). As Mercy's minister, Mather was her overseer—from his pulpit, he literally oversaw all in his congregation. And if religious oppression was a cause of the demonic possession Mercy and the hysterical girls of Salem Village performed, then what spills forth from their frenzy may be forms of religious rebellion. (Mercy's invisible tormentors, Mather reported, frequently indulged in "Railing and Slander against a certain Person in the Town"—Mather himself.)[36] In "The Old Manse" preface Hawthorne alludes to the doubling he sees afflicting Puritans like Mather, when he observes that his own dark study was

made still blacker by the grim prints of Puritan ministers that hung around. These worthies looked strangely like bad angels, or, at least, like men who had wrestled so continually and so sternly with the devil, that somewhat of his sooty fierceness had been imparted to their own visages. (X 5)

For Hawthorne the witchcraft hysteria had been sustained by the "wicked arts of a few children," but "the ministers and wise men were more deluded than the illiterate people" (VI 77–78)

It is important to notice the priority Hawthorne gives to faulty perception in his treatment of witch hunters, abolitionists, and self-righteous reformers, for in his view the violence they cause represents not malice but a failure of vision. In his discussion of John Brown in "Chiefly About War-Matters," Hawthorne writes, "He himself, I am persuaded, (such was his natural integrity) would have acknowledged that Virginia had a right to take the life which he had staked and lost; although it would have been better for her, in the hour that is fast coming, if she could generously have forgotten the criminality of his attempt in its enormous folly" (XXIII 428). Folly, delusion, madness—these were the visual and mental defects Hawthorne saw animating those intent on ridding the land of evil. In his biography of Pierce, in a passage that has become notorious, Hawthorne calls abolitionism "the mistiness of a philanthropic theory," and it is important to recognize the delusion inscribed in this characterization. The relevant passage reads:

> [Pierce] fully recognized, by his votes and by his voice, the rights pledged to the South by the Constitution. This, at the period when he so declared himself, was comparatively an easy thing to do. But when it became more difficult, when the first imperceptible movement of agitation had grown to be almost a convulsion, his course was still the same. Nor did he ever shun the obloquy that sometimes threatened to pursue the northern man who dared to love that great and sacred reality—his whole, united, native country— better than the mistiness of a philanthropic theory. (XXIII 292)

What is unusual about the dichotomy Hawthorne sets up, between the "reality" of the United States and the "mistiness" of abolitionism, is that it is an effect, not a cause, he questions. Beyond its reference to climatic conditions, mistiness, as the *OED* points out, can also refer to the obscuring of mental vision or outlook, when the real character of a thing is veiled from one's eyes and mind. For Hawthorne, mist also suggested ocular and mental deception, such as that surrounding specters and ghosts.

Hawthorne's contemporaries shared his familiarity with this usage, as their writings show. Margaret Fuller, in a well-known dispatch she wrote from Scotland in September 1846, tells about the mist that arose on Ben Lomond, before she could descend, and the night spent on the mountain during which she saw "visionary shapes, floating slowly and gracefully, their white robes would unfurl from the great body of mist in which they had been engaged, and come upon me with a kiss pervasively cold as that of Death" (76). In *Walden*, Thoreau also suggests the supernatural and bewitching effects of the mist as he describes how the rising sun revealed the "soft ripples" and "smooth reflecting surface" of the pond, "while the mists, like ghosts, were stealthily withdrawing in every direction into the woods, as at the breaking up of some nocturnal conventicler" (58). In Hawthorne's writings, mists and mistiness are used to suggest not only ghosts and witchcraft, but also mental failure. Clifford goes into a mist in *The House of the Seven Gables* when his mental torpor settles upon him; Priscilla appears as behind a mist in *The Blithedale Romance* after she enters her trance as the veiled lady.

When individuals most often suffer from the inability to see beyond their narrow obsessions in Hawthorne's works, often it is an "ism," such as Puritanism, transcendentalism, or abolitionism that has blinded them.

These are the "theories" or enthusiasms he thought preyed upon the weak-minded and harmed actual persons. He once commented in his notebook, "I find myself rather more of an abolitionist in feeling than in principle" (VIII 112), thus expressing his privileging of persons over abstractions. The way Sophia put it in their journal was to say her husband was "without theories of any kind,"[37] which distinguished him from their Concord neighbors. In "The Celestial Railroad" (1843), Hawthorne describes the Giant Transcendentalist who occupies a cave deserted by those "vile old troglodytes" Pope and Pagan. German by birth, the Giant looks "like a heap of fog and duskiness" and fattens unsuspecting travelers for his table by feeding them "plentiful meals of smoke, mist, moonshine, raw potatoes, and saw-dust" (X 197). Less comically, Hawthorne in "Septimius" places his protagonist within the heart of Transcendentalism, the town of Concord, and shows him struggling unsuccessfully to make his way out of this bewitched land: "with every step that he took, it seemed as if he were coming out of a mist, out of an enchanted land, where things had seemed to him not as they really were" (XIII 129). Linking the mist to witchcraft, Hawthorne claims that Septimius had wandered unawares into a mental landscape inconsistent "with all that really is, with men's purposes, fates, business; into such a misty region had he been, and strayed many days, deeming himself at home; but now the mists were thinning away, he was passing the witch-like boundaries, and might never find his way over them again" (XIII 129).

If Hawthorne recognized, if only subconsciously and imaginatively, the psychohistorical parallels between the Salem witchcraft delusion he felt guilty about and the Concord abolitionism that came to possess his friends and family, then his resistance to and comments upon the latter become more understandable if not less morally irresponsible. When Curtis in his condemnation of Hawthorne in 1864 claimed that Hawthorne failed to appreciate "the fine moral heroism" and "the spiritual grandeur" of the Puritans, he anticipated the link I have been trying to forge between witch hunting and abolitionism. In the process, he also unwittingly supported Hawthorne's case against the abolitionists. Referring to "Young Goodman Brown," Curtis assails Hawthorne's quietism about slavery by asserting

> that the Devil, in the form of an elderly man clad in grave and decent attire, should lead astray the saints of Salem village, two centuries ago, and confuse right and wrong in the mind of Goodman Brown, was something that excited [Hawthorne's] imagination, and produced one of his weirdest stories. But that the same Devil, clad in a somber sophism, was confusing the sentiment of right and wrong in the mind of his own countrymen he did not even guess. (418–19)

Curtis would have it that Hawthorne himself was in league with the devil, saying, "the mind of Justice Hathorn's descendant was bewitched by the fascination of a certain devilish subtlety working under the comeliest aspects in human affairs. It overcame him with strange sympathy. It colored and controlled his intellectual life" (544). Curtis not only misreads Hawthorne's short story, and its critique of specter evidence, but also unwittingly puts himself in the false position of the Puritan witch hunter. He indicts Hawthorne for failing to see the Devil at work in the Slavocracy, thus making himself an advocate for those willing to kill the innocent in order to drive the Devil from the land.[38] Such ahistorical moral absolutism is precisely what motivated that mad Puritan John Brown at Pottawotamie Creek and Harpers Ferry.

The demonization of one's enemy is clearly a transhistorical, cross-cultural phenomenon, yet in American history, there has been an unusually full and dynamic set of persons who have been demonized. As Michael Rogin points out, "the Indian cannibal, the black rapist, the papal whore of Babylon, the monster-hydra United States Bank, the demon rum, the bomb-throwing anarchist, the many-tentacled Communist conspiracy, the agents of international terrorism" (Rogin 1987, xiii) are a consistent, repressed feature of American sociopolitical history. Rogin does not mention the Salem witches, but of course they too form part of this series, as does the Southern slave owner in abolitionist iconography and rhetoric. I would assume that the latter fact has not been a topic of interest in recent American studies because it serves no obvious purpose in advancing a politics of liberation, or "transformative social action" (Cheyvitz 1994, 545); however, it would not have escaped Hawthorne's notice, not only because of its link to the Puritan past, but also because Southerners made a point of objecting to it. Stowe's Simon Legree was the most obvious example of this demonization, but others appeared throughout anti-slavery periodicals, literature, and speeches. Moncure Conway, the Virginian turned New England abolitionist, after participating in the famous July 4, 1854 meeting in Framingham Grove, Massachusetts, which featured speeches by Thoreau, Sojourner Truth, and Garrison, decided,

> I could not join the Antislavery Society. There was a Calvinistic accent in that creed about the "covenant with death and agreement with hell" [Garrison's description of the Constitution, which he burned on stage]. Slavery was not death, nor the South hell ... my peace principles inclined me to a separation between sections that hated each other. Yet I knew good people on both sides. (*Autobiography* 2: 185)

Just as John Hathorne and Cotton Mather sought to drive Satan from New England, Garrison and his followers sought to drive him from the Union. In Mather's eyes, the devil had "decoy'd a fearful knot of proud, froward, ignorant, envious and malicious creatures, to lift themselves in his horrid Service . . . each of them have their *Spectres,* or Devils, commission'd by them, & representing of them, to be the Engines of their Malice. By these wicked *Spectres,* they seize poor people about the Country, with various & bloudy *Torments*" (Mather 1950, 67–68). For Garrison, whose rhetoric, like Mather's, drew upon the Bible, Southern slave owners were the devil's agents, "an adulterous and perverse generation, a brood of vipers, hypocrites, children of the devil, who could not escape the damnation of hell" (180). Such demonization appeared in iconography as well as rhetoric, outraging those accused of depravity. In the summer of 1835 Senator John Tyler of Virginia held up a copy of the *Anti-Slavery Record* and showed his fellow Southerners "a picture upon the external covering, designed to represent each of you gentlemen. A scourge is in your hand, and three victims bound and kneeling at your feet. You are represented as demons in the shape of men" (qtd. Richards 1970, 56–57). As Bertram Wyatt-Brown has pointed out, the abolitionists looked to the past for their imagery, and primitive woodcuts of lustful masters and abject slaves became the gargoyles and relics of a gothic revival" (23).

Northern fascination with the sexual relations between Southern masters and their female slaves (coded as "concubinage," not rape, by male abolitionists) in many ways mirrored seventeenth-century Puritan fascination with the sexual relations between the devil and his concubines. Licentiousness took on political significance, and the black female body, like those of accused witches, could be identified as a threatening site of sin and vice. Few noticed the injustice of blaming the victim such identification involved. Drawing upon first-hand knowledge, one assumes, Thomas Jefferson addressed this aspect of the slavemaster relationship in his *Notes on the State of Virginia,* warning that slavery allowed "a perpetual exercise of the most boisterous passions, the most unremitting despotism" (289). Just as the religious persecution of witches, especially on the Continent, involved avid exploration of the "filthy rites" practiced by the devil and his female worshippers, so, too, the abolitionists focused upon the appetites and lusts of the slavemasters, indulged through the bodies of their female slaves. Wendell Phillips, for one, called the South "one great Brothel, where half a million of women are flogged to prostitution, or worse still, are degraded to believe it honorable" (11). Similarly, Hawthorne's brother-in-law Horace Mann, in his "Speech on the Institution of Slavery" (1852), identified slave owners as those wanting to "introduce a foul concubinage

THE

ANTI-SLAVERY RECORD.

VOL. I.   MAY, 1835.   NO. 5.

CRUELTIES OF SLAVERY.

When we narrate the cruelties of individual masters upon their slaves, it is not for the purpose of exciting public indignation against those masters, nor of drawing the inference, that all masters are equally cruel; but to show that cruelty is the fruit of the system. Every tree must be known by its fruits. Cruelty may occur under good and impartial laws, but then it is in spite of the laws, not in consequence of them. On the other hand, where the laws themselves violate rights, make one class the property of another, and withhold redress of wrongs, cruelty, in ten thousand forms, is the necessary result. If the amount of cruelty perpetrated upon the slaves of this republic could be known to the world,

Figure 2. Cover of the May 1835 *Anti-Slavery Record.* Courtesy of the Boston Public Library.

in place of the institution of marriage, and who would remorselessly trample upon all the tenderest and holiest affections which the human soul is capable of feeling" (267).

A certain sexual anxiety as well as prurience at times seems to surface in Puritan attacks on the "luxurious" South, and such anxiety is an issue Hawthorne explored in "Young Goodman Brown," where he dramatizes the competing desires of the "holiest affections" of marriage and the unholy sexual attractions offered by the Devil and his sex slaves. Brown's departure from his wife, Faith, to pursue forbidden sexual knowledge deep in the forest demonstrates his moral weakness, as does his susceptibility to spectral evidence, which he accepts as real. Witchcraft in Salem is the focus of the tale, however, not slavery; but when the "dark figure" of the devil reappears as the "Black Man" in *The Scarlet Letter,* the issues of witchcraft and slavery merge, as does the imagery of revolutionary violence and witchcraft. Hester tells Pearl she met the Black Man only once, and we know she means not the devil but the Reverend Dimmesdale, and that forbidden desire impelled their union. It is not the Black Man as devil or minister, however, that poses the greatest threat to the peace of the community. Rather, it is the violence-prone mob of "gossips" who surround the scaffold and reveal a frightening bloodlust, wanting Hester to be branded or executed. (The actual Mistress Hibbins, whom Hawthorne fictionalizes in his novel, died at the hands of Godfearing Puritans in1646, hanged as a witch.) For Hawthorne, specter evidence, lies, and mental weakness go hand in hand, and the multitude, when aroused by false stimuli, especially if it is salacious, can be positively fatal.

Hawthorne's politics, growing out of an aversion to violence, social unrest, moral absolutism, and faulty perception, expressed itself in *The Scarlet Letter* and throughout his works in allegories of self-delusion and faulty vision, where lies and myths of salvific action, rather than devils, take possession of people and lead them toward a hell they do not see ahead. Hawthorne's writings of the 1850s and 1860s, especially, show us that the historical novelist, like the historian, can acquire as a blessing and a curse the ability to come at political issues with imagination and understanding, to approach emotive discourse with skepticism and insight, seeking truth through structural links to the past, both fabulous and real. As a romance writer familiar with Gothic conventions, Hawthorne understood how language and imagery can serve to manipulate a reader's emotions, and he was a resistant reader as a result, especially of sensational or partisan rhetoric aimed at exciting his passions. (He surely noticed and perhaps resented the incredible success of *Uncle Tom's Cabin.*) Though charged with a "politics of 'indeterminacy'" by one recent critic, and "ideological fixation by another,"[39] which supposedly prevented him from commitment to political action, Hawthorne can more fairly be credited with a "politics of imagination," which allowed him to resist the kind of groupthink leading to violence and death. His habitual assumption of the perspectives of different persons (essential to the craft of fiction) and his exposure to the viewpoints of those in foreign cultures, in England and Italy, enabled him to appreciate multiple points of view in the midst of partisan propaganda and radical violence. The one key point of view he failed to assume, however, was that of the slave.

Perhaps the most morally responsible aspect of his incomplete vision was its revelation of the ways in which righteousness can become totalitarian as it tries to impose one narrow view of the world upon others. In a letter to Francis Bennoch, ca. July 1861, Hawthorne tells him we

> have gone to war, and we seem to have little, or, at least, a *very misty* idea of what we are fighting for. It depends upon the speaker, and that, again, depends upon the section of the country in which his sympathies are enlisted. The Southern man will say, We fight for state rights, liberty, and independence. The middle and Western states-man will avow that he fights for the Union; whilst our Northern and Eastern man will swear that, from the beginning, his only idea was liberty to the Blacks, and the annihilation of slavery. All are thoroughly in earnest, and all pray for the blessing of Heaven to rest upon the enterprise. (XVIII 387, emphasis added)

Although his fellow New Englanders did not appreciate this cast of mind, Hawthorne's wife, Sophia, apparently did. In the spring of 1862, while he was in Washington D.C., she wrote him:

> I could wish thou mightest be President through this crisis, and show the world what can be done by using two eyes, and turning each thing upside down and inside out, before judging and acting. I should not wonder if thy great presence in Washington might affect the moral air and work good. (qtd. Lathrop [1897] 1969, 437).[40]

This high praise was echoed by Henry James, who in his biography of Hawthorne, defended "Chiefly About War-Matters," calling it "interesting as an example of the way an imaginative man judges current events—trying to see the other side as well as his own, to feel what his adversary feels, and present his view of the case" (James [1879] 1966, 151). If Hawthorne had extended his imagination to take in the plight of the slaves, which even Lincoln found it impossible to do, it would be difficult to find a more thoughtful "peaceable man" of the times.

NOTES

1. Richard Hold Hutton, *Essays Theological and Literary,* 2 vols. (London: Strahan, 1871), 2: 416.

2. In "Chiefly About War-Matters," Hawthorne spoke of the Civil War in the same terms: "No human effort, on a grand scale, has ever yet resulted according to the purpose of its projectors. The advantages are always incidental. Man's accidents

are God's purposes. We miss the good we sought, and do the good we little cared for" (XXIII 431).

3. *The Journals and Miscellaneous Notebooks of Ralph Waldo Emerson.* 16 vols. Ed William H. Gilman et al. Cited hereinafter as *JMN.*

4. Some twenty years after Hawthorne's death, Philip R. Ammidon recalled, "with what concern I once heard a resident of Concord, a man not unknown in the world of letters [Emerson?], speak of certain evils like to result from 'Hawthorne's fall.'" The speaker was referring to Hawthorne's "effort in behalf of his college comrade and life-long friend [Franklin Pierce], that was supposed to imply a state of moral declension fitly indicated by the sinister word" (516). Emerson's friend the abolitionist Moncure Conway even held Hawthorne responsible for the Civil War. He reasoned that Pierce was a political unknown until Hawthorne's campaign biography elevated him to national attention and "extolled" him "into the presidency whose oppression in Kanzas [*sic*] . . . made the war inevitable" (203).

5. Curtis's brother Lieutenant J. B. Curtis lost most of his regiment at Antietam, and Curtis's brother-in-law Colonel Robert Gould Shaw was killed along with hundreds of his all-black regiment during their celebrated assault on Fort Wagner.

6. See, for examples, Hall 1966, 147; Miller 1991, 474; and Bercovitch 1993, 236.

7. For the most severe judgments, see Cheyvitz and Yellin.

8. See Arac 1986; Bercovitch 1991, 1993; Goddu, Grossman, Madsen, Person, and Yellin.

9. See Hansen 1974 on Tituba's metamorphosis.

10. In a speech delivered before the Nashville Convention in 1851, General Felix Huston of Mississippi declared that the San Domingo insurrection "having occurred so near to us, and being within the recollection of many persons living, who heard the exaggerated accounts of the day, has fastened itself on the public imagination, until it has become a subject of frequent reference" (qtd. John Weiss, "The Horrors of San Domingo," *Atlantic Monthly* 11 [June 1863]: 773).

11. See Elkins 1976, 175–93, for a narrative of how this occurred.

12. See Pease and Pease 1965.

13. Thus, in *Uncle Tom's Cabin,* Stowe has Augustine St. Clair declare, "If ever the San Domingo hour comes, Anglo Saxon blood will lead on the day. Sons of white fathers, with all our haughty feelings burning in their veins, will not always be bought and sold and traded. They will rise, and raise with them their mother's race" (392).

14. See Brancaccio, who points out that the American Colonization Society listed the *Journal* in its annual report for 1846 as "one of the most prominent events in the history of colonization for the past year" (1980, 39).

15. See Brickhouse 1996, 1998; Goddu 2001; Grossman 1993; Yellin 2001; Person 2001; Anthony 1999; and Bentley 1990.

16. See Mayer 1980, 120–21.

17. See Kearns 1964, Teichgraeber 1995, von Frank 1999, and Rosenwald 2000. In an 1844 journal entry, Emerson described the abolitionists as an "odious set of people, whom one would be sure to shun as the worst of bores & canters" (*JMN* 9: 120), and in his "Ode, to William H. Channing" (1846), he questioned abolitionist methods by asking,

> What boots thy zeal, O glowing friend,,
> That would indignant rend
> the northland from the south?
> Wherefore? To what good end?
> Boston Bay and Bunker Hill
> Would serve things still;
> Things are of the snake.

Emerson's social conservatism matched Hawthorne's at this time, and his racial fatalism went even farther, for he includes in the poem the following lines:

> The over-god
> Who marries Right to Might,
> Who peoples, unpeoples,—
> He who exterminates
> Races by stronger races,
> Black by white faces,—
> Knows to bring honey
> Out of the lion. (*Collected Poems* 61–64).

18. See Arac 1986 and Bercovitch 1991.

19. Emerson's idealism impels his writings of the 1830s, of course, such as *Nature* (1836), but even in his 1844 Anti-slavery address, he saw "blessed necessity" at work in the emancipation of slaves in the British West Indies, thus anticipating Hawthorne's own gradualist sentiments that so outraged abolitionists (see von Frank 1999, 402). Thoreau, too, sought to elevate himself above the "tintinnabulation," as he called it, of reform movements of the day. In his poem "The Spirit of Lodin" (1851), he fantasized, "I look down from my height on nations,/ And they become ashes before me;/ Calm is my dwelling in the clouds;/ Pleasant are the great fields of my rest" (*Journal* 3: 213–14).

20. As Michael Colacurcio has pointed out, this account of early colonial history calls into question "the flagrant idolatries of America's pseudo-Puritan civil religion." In its place, Hawthorne offers "a Tory view" emphasizing "provincial unruliness, a mob scene" (*Province* 136–38). See also McWilliams 1976.

21. In an illuminating statement, Hawthorne's daughter Rose recalled of her father, "He hated failure, dependence, and disorder, broken rules and weariness of discipline, as he hated cowardice. I cannot express how brave he seemed to me" (Lathrop [1897] 1969, 478).

22. On the internal contradictions of Hawthorne's Jacksoniansm, see Herbert 1993, 88–112.

23. Bell makes the excellent point that, though hostile toward "the radical ideal of revolution," Hawthorne "saw the essential connection between the unleashing of fantasy and the unleashing of revolutionary violence" (Bell 1980, 170–71).

24. See chapter 5 of Reynolds 1988.

25. For an account of Thoreau's knowledge of Brown's past, see Meyer 1980.

26. *"These Sad but Glorious Days": Dispatches from Europe, 1846–1850,* ed. Larry J. Reynolds and Susan Belasco Smith. Cited parenthetically as *SGD*.

27. For a full account of the Hawthorne-Fuller relationship, see Mitchell 1998.

28. Richard Brodhead has done so most cogently, declaring "typically, the quickening of Hawthorne's sense of involvement in the larger struggles of a society in conflict ends up producing not deepened commitment but deepened irony toward such commitment. The main source of this irony is Hawthorne's unregenerate fantasy" (1984, 98).

29. In a June 14, 1854 letter to George Sanders, Hawthorne reacted to a letter Kossuth had written about his decision to remain neutral with regard to the slavery controversy in the United States. "Does he not trim and truckle a little?" Hawthorne asked. "Doubtless, he says nothing but what is perfectly true; but yet it has not the effect of frank and outspoken truth. I wish he had commenced his reply with a sturdier condemnation of slavery . . ." (XVII 230).

30. Horace Greeley later recalled,

> The passage of the Nebraska Bill was a death-blow to Northern quietism and complacency, mistakingly deeming themselves conservatism. To all who fondly dreamed or blindly hoped that the Slavery question would somehow settle itself, it cried, 'Sleep no more!' in thunder-tones that would not die unheeded. . . . Systematic, determined resistance was now recognized as imperative duty. (294)

Thus was born the Republican Party.

31. The debate over the Nebraska Bill became heatedly moralistic thanks to the publicity efforts of a small group of free-soil Democrats in Congress. As David Potter points out, "increasingly after 1854, they had a strength which derived not only from the righteousness of their cause but also from the technical skill of a dis-

tinctive style of publicity, which discredited their opponents as not only wrong on principle but also morally depraved and personally odious" (Potter 1976,164–65).

32. For a full account of Hawthorne's stance with regard to John Brown and his supporters, see Moore 2000.

33. See also Michael Colacurcio, who points out that Hawthorne "had the critical intelligence to discern how much of the familiar politics of mission and destiny was but the public face of a piety that flourished in America distinctively. And eventually, especially in the 1840s, he acquired the perspective to notice how much of the morale of his own generation of intellectuals was suitably understood as neo-Puritan, despite their vigorous rejection of the theological idioms of the older orthodoxy" (1987, viii).

34. The Virginian Moncure Conway, who became an abolitionist and friend of Emerson, observed John Brown's Puritan appeal: "[I]t appears to me now that there had remained in nearly every Northern breast, however liberal, some unconscious chord which Brown had touched, inherited from the old Puritan spirit and faith in the God of War. I had been brought up in no such faith, but in the belief that evil could be conquered only by regeneration of the evil-doer" (*Emerson* 303).

35. See Breslaw's Appendix C, "Transcripts of Tituba's Confessions."

36. See Burr 1914, 267, and Mather's whole account of "A Brand Pluck'd Out of the Burning" (1693) (Burr 203–88).

37. "Sophia Peabody Hawthorne's *American Notebooks,*" ed. Patricia Dunlavy Valenti, in *Studies in the American Renaissance, 1996,* ed. Myerson, 146

38. As Emily Budick has pointed out, "Young Goodman Brown" not only explores the power and nature of spectral evidence, it also reveals Hawthorne's appreciation of moral relativity by dramatizing "Brown's failure to question the sweeping and unsubstantiated claim that his ancestors willingly accepted the devil's help, that they performed deeds that they (and not a subsequent generation) considered evil" (Budick 1986, 221).

39. See Arac 1986 and Bercovitch 1991.

40. See also, *Our Old Home* (1863), where he describes the effect of studying the Cathedral of Lichfield, which becomes "a kind of kaleidoscopic mystery, so rich a variety of aspects did it assume from each altered point of view" (V 124–25).

4

Hawthorne and the Problem of "American" Fiction: The Example of *The Scarlet Letter*

LAWRENCE BUELL[1]

This essay is intended as a kind of contemporary equivalent to Lionel Trilling's (1964) landmark centennial assessment of changing conceptions of the tenor of Hawthorne's work. Trilling's "Our Hawthorne" concentrated on a particular shift in critical perception from the delicate ironist imaged by Henry James to the troubled Kafka-esque Hawthorne descried by Herman Melville but not prevalent until the twentieth century. Hawthorne emerges from this analysis both as a moving target fascinating in and of itself and as a barometer of changing dispensations of critical inquiry (Trilling). Since Trilling wrote, the variability and contestedness of the "essential" Hawthorne and his legacy, or legacies, have been further underscored by such excellent influence/reception studies as Richard Brodhead's *The School of Hawthorne* (1986) and by a plethora of fictive reworkings of his plots, particularly *The Scarlet Letter*. Not only is the issue of what ought to count as "our" Hawthorne far more problematic now than it seemed in 1964. To reflect seriously about the issue through a turn-of-the-twenty-first-century lens also requires engaging the much vaster question of what ought to count as "American" literary history. The case of Hawthorne's masterpiece demonstrates this especially.

1

The Scarlet Letter holds a unique place in Anglo-American literary history. It was the book that made Hawthorne famous, his most incontestably "perfect" book, the book most crucial in establishing him as the most consummate artist in American fiction before James. James was not alone in looking back upon it as a landmark event in U.S. literary emergence: "Something might at last be sent to Europe as exquisite in quality as anything that had been received" (James [1878] 1984, 403).

The Scarlet Letter's exquisite self-circumscription has been held against it as well. James thought it lacked passion. New historicists have seen it as evading the slavery issue, or giving aid and comfort to a conservative consensualism through some of the very strategies of ambiguation that make it so aesthetically resplendent (Arac 1986). Fault has been found with the practice of making this text and/or "Hawthorne" generally so central to the narrative U.S. literary history, as in Jane Tompkins's argument that Hawthorne's high critical reputation relative to the "scribbling woman" he denigrated is an artifact of a "dynastic cultural elite" (Tompkins 1985, 30).[2] Yet *The Scarlet Letter* will surely continue to be a key reference point for U.S. literary history. It remains the single most taught long work of premodern American literature. Although far from being the earliest U.S. novel of consequence, it is widely looked upon as "the inaugural text of the indigenous canon" (Gilmore 2003, 84). Were a vote taken among Americanist critics as to the first indisputable Anglo-American classic in the genre, *The Scarlet Letter* would almost surely win.

This status derives not just from its qualities as a freestanding text but from its historical representation and historical impact. Among major premodern U.S. fictions, *The Scarlet Letter* comes closest to rendering a myth of national origins. It has also become a masterplot for American writers, from Harold Frederic (*The Damnation of Theron Ware*) and Henry James to Toni Morrison (*Beloved*) and Bharati Mukherjee (*The Holder of the World*). In this sense James was prophetic in his explanation of why, in addition to its craftsmanship, *The Scarlet Letter* seemed "in the United States a literary event of the first importance." For "the best of it was that the thing was absolutely American; it belonged to the soil, to the air; it came out of the very heart of New England" (James [1878] 1984, 402, 403).

Some have not found the connection between Americanness and Hawthornian romance so self-evident. In a contentious essay as significant in its own way as James's assessment a decade later, novelist J. W. DeForest looked in vain for "The Great American Novel" he wished to call into

being. Hawthorne, "the greatest of American imaginations," was part of the
problem. His "personages" seemed to "belong to the wide realm of art
rather than to our nationality," to be "as probably natives of the furthest
mountains of Cathay or of the moon as of the United States of America"
(DeForest 1868, 28). This was actually quite close to the view Hawthorne
himself expressed in his Preface to *The House of the Seven Gables* (3):

> The personages of the tale—though they give themselves out to be of
> ancient stability and considerable prominence—are really of the author's
> own making, or, at all events, of his own mixing. . . . He would be glad,
> therefore, if . . . the book may be read strictly as a Romance, having a great
> deal more to do with the clouds overhead than with any portion of the
> actual soil of the County of Essex.

Of course, in *this* instance Hawthorne had a special interest in distancing
himself from actual personages and locale (to ward off charges of libel),
whereas "The Custom-House" makes the opposite appeal—to lococentric-
ity and provincial antiquarianism—under the guise of observing the law of
literary "propriety" that justifies an account of how the "authentic" manuscript came into the author's possession (4). Hawthorne scholarship has
demonstrated the accuracy of *The Scarlet Letter*'s historical geography
(Ryskamp 1959), and the uncanny correspondence of its plot and two
main protagonists with those of the Antinomian Controversy (Colacurcio
1972). But these meticulous historical readings also presuppose a detached
cosmopolitan intelligence. It wasn't *just* a dodge for Hawthorne to claim
that *Seven Gables* came from cloudland, nor was he concealing his dependence on documentary sources in affirming of *The Scarlet Letter* that, save
for "the authenticity of the outline," he had allowed himself "nearly or altogether as much license as if the facts had been entirely of my own invention" (33).

Americanists, who constitute the overwhelming majority of Hawthorne
scholars, have generally read such disclaimers in the spirit of James rather
than of DeForest: as attempts to claim elbow room for romantic stylization
without taking his protestations of detachment from native place and history too seriously. Even if Hawthorne invokes New England and/or national
ideology only to dismantle it, surely the cultural reference point remains
U.S.-ness, New England-ness, post–Puritanness, antebellum ideological ferment.

Lately, however, a more quizzical conception of *The Scarlet Letter*'s
investment in the national has begun to emerge. "Underlying the primary
attention given to New England history in the novel," has been described "a

subsurface of English history that Hawthorne has carefully structured in order to examine American Puritans within a framework larger than the provincial boundaries of New England" (Newberry 1987, 168). Again and again "residual attachments to Old World culture and theology" seem to "permeate the consciousness of these emigrant characters" (Giles 1962, 178), making *The Scarlet Letter* as much a text about cultural migration and diaspora as a text about settlement, founding, and the Puritan origins of national culture. Hester and Pearl seem more like creatures of the author's fascination with the "Orient" than figures who belong in a Puritan colonial setting (Luedtke 1989, 181–87). And what are we to make of the oddity that a text so influential for national letters as *The Scarlet Letter* should be so tenuously affiliated, so tenuously committed in its own cultural allegiances? We need to rethink once more that penultimate flourish in "The Custom-House," "I am a citizen of somewhere else" (44).

The old, now widely discredited way of thinking about such a remark only takes us back to Americanness again: Hawthorne was declaring allegiance to the romance mode because the cultural "thinness" of the comparatively young, open country made impossible the thick social representations of the novel. From such fictions as his (and Cooper's and Melville's and others), the distinctive shape of the "American novel" took form.[3] So it was once thought. We can do better than that, better too than anti-romance revisionist theory has done. To do so, at the risk of seeming perverse I should like to start at the very end of *The Scarlet Letter* and work back from there.

The Scarlet Letter confirms its residual skepticism about the possibility of radical breaks and new departures by ending with a glimpse of the spot where Hester Prynne is buried, next to the "old and sunken grave" of Arthur Dimmesdale, with a space between but a single tombstone marking both, those markings worn by the weathering of two hundred years. "On this simple slab of slate,

> —as the curious investigator may still discern, and perplex himself with the purport—there appeared the semblance of an engraved escutcheon. It bore a device, a herald's wording of which might serve for a motto and brief description of our now concluded legend; so sombre is it, and relieved only by one ever-glowing point of light gloomier than the shadow:—
> "ON A FIELD SABLE, THE LETTER A, GULES"

Well indeed might "the curious investigator" be perplexed, so encrypted is this passage. To be sure, there is an obvious return-to-starting-point fitness to the book's ending: Chapter 1 mentions the cemetery, in the same breath as the prison, as being among a colonial government's first allotments of space for public use; and "The Custom-House" is suffused with elegiac images of burial, exhumation, and mystified musing *à propos* the musty packet containing the "original narrative" of Surveyor Pue. But so strange a return! What seems as if it ought to be a distinct visual image cannot be visualized. The basic *idea* is plain enough: a red letter against a black background. But the rhetoric is teasingly oblique. The carving on the gravestone is rendered neither quite as language nor quite as picture, but *via* the arcane semiotics of heraldry.

To be sure, it is typical of Hawthorne's colonial tales to proliferate emblematic schemata and instill a sense of remoteness of past from present. They squint back at quaint old tombstones, houses, furniture, and other colonial artifacts from an immense aesthetic distance, like Henry Thoreau prompted by an old painting of seventeenth-century Concord to wonder whether real people could truly have existed then. In this Hawthorne and Thoreau were both engaging in a familiar ritual of romanticized gothicization of the Puritan primordium and revealing themselves—more than they let on—as children of the early industrial age, the first generation to undergo what we now call future shock. Yet *The Scarlet Letter*'s closing scene feels alien even by that standard. Though identified as a particular burying-ground, the colony's first, it feels more like an English graveyard than a New England one, whose old slabs generally sported no such adornments.[4] Is the reader to assume the design is the work of the grown-up Pearl, the new world's richest heiress long since resocialized into old-world elegance? Might it also, or alternatively, be a potshot at the rising interest in pedigree among northeastern elite families as the nineteenth century unfolded? (The New England Historic Genealogical Society, the nation's first such organization, had been founded just five years before the novel's publication.) In any case, the inscription is atypical of standard colonial and antebellum funerary design.

But I want to concentrate especially on a still more occluded element: the intertextual palimpsest the heraldic reference creates. The text here recalls two passages by classic English writers that turn on the symbolic contrast of sable and gules. One is the concluding stanza of the English Puritan poet Andrew Marvell's "The Unfortunate Lover," a weirdly contorted metaphysical lyric that dates from the approximate time of Hawthorne's plot. The other is a passage from Walter Scott's "Introduction" to *Waverley,* the first in the series of fictionalized renderings of Scottish history from the mid-seventeenth to the mid-eighteenth century that secured his reputation as the father of the historical romance, Hawthorne's own genre. Neither of these texts is unknown to Hawthorne criticism, but neither have they been much discussed (cf. Gale 315, Stubbs 175–76).

This is the only *Banneret*
That ever Love created yet:
Who though, by the Malignant Starrs,
Forced to live in Storms and Warrs;
Yet dying leave a Perfume here,
And Musick within every Ear:
And he in Story only rules
In a Field *Sable* a Lover *Gules.* (Marvell 1: 29)

[My story will emphasize] those passions common to men in all stages of
society, and which have alike agitated the human heart, whether it throbbed
under the steel corslet of the fifteenth century, the brocaded coat of the eighteenth, or the blue rock and white dimity waistcoat of the present day. Upon
these passions it is no doubt true that the state of manners and laws casts a
necessary colouring; but the bearings, to use the language of heraldry,
remain the same. . . . The wrath of our ancestors, for example, was colored
gules; it broke forth in acts of open and sanguinary violence against the
objects of its fury. Our malignant feelings, which must seek gratification
through more indirect channels, and undermine the obstacles which they
cannot openly bear down, may be rather said to be tinctured *sable.* But the
deep-ruling impulse is the same in both cases; and the proud peer who can
now only ruin his neighbor according to law, by protracted suits, is the genuine descendant of the baron, who wrapped the castle of his competitor in
flames, and knocked him on the head as he endeavoured to escape from the
conflagration. It is from the great book of Nature, the same through a thousand editions, whether of black-letter, or wire-wove and hot-pressed, that I
have venturously essayed to read a chapter to the public. (Scott 1901,
1:13–14)

We cannot be sure if Hawthorne had either passage consciously in mind,
though almost certainly he knew them both. He was an attentive reader of
Renaissance allegorical poetry, and he read and reread Scott, "his boyhood
favorite among novelists" (Dekker 1987, 131), from youth until near his
death.[5] In any case, the passages underscore fundamental implications of the
main plot: that love-longing is fulfilled in fantasy, not in real life, and that
ancient and modern forms of deviance and oppression are nonidentical but
akin. Hawthorne's romance fuses the discrepant sable-gules polarities from
the two pre-texts. Marvell and Scott use heraldry to achieve a stylized diag-
nostic control over very different passions. For Marvell, the passion of love;

for Scott, aggression. Marvell's sable/gules antithesis refers to violently con-flicted emotions within the lover, which can be resolved only in a certain kind of idealizing story. Scott's antithesis is between different kinds of revenge. *The Scarlet Letter* subsumes both antitheses within *its* dominant polarity between the one passion and the other: love versus patriarchal repression, whether exerted from without or from within.

Would the author of *The Scarlet Letter*—supposing him to have had these pre-texts in mind—have expected readers to catch the allusions? I suspect not, seeing that a basic *gestalt* of some sort can be grasped without perceiving the esoterica, although it piquantly enhances the effect when you do. You're bound to feel a sense of the story of Hester and Dimmesdale being converted into "legend" even if you remain oblivious to the antecedent realms of legend—all the more so given that the scene of grave-yard pondering was a stock memorial and literary device in the eighteenth and nineteenth centuries, Thomas Gray's "Elegy Written in a Country Churchyard" and the frame narrative of Scott's *Old Mortality* being famil-iar to most middle-class readers of Hawthorne's day.

To catch the two more deeply buried allusions helps make better sense of the ending's strangeness, however. The injection of heraldry seems less freakish, seems indeed a sophisticated preemption of tradition by a mind steeped in the Anglo-European inheritance. For Marvell, the device urbanely evokes such courtly love topoi as the typical lover's proverbial throes. Only in never-never land can he attain the apotheosis of the ban-neret (knighthood on the spot for valor in the field of battle). Abstraction underscores the remoteness of the prospect. Scott's invocation of the topos is more complex, simultaneously bringing the past nearer and exoticizing the bourgeois present by the parallel to bygone feudalism. But here, too, the formal sable versus gules contrast urbanely rises above and displaces the phenomenon of aggression by rendering it as design. In *The Scarlet Letter,* the two levels of signification merge (the contortions of love and the aggressions of patriarchy), and on Scott's complex terms, dramatizing a counterpoint of opposition versus affinity between the then and the now.

In so doing, Hawthorne and his precursors also emphasize something timeless, perennial, about their stories. Costumes differ, emotions remain the same. Marvell's hapless wight is a perennial lover-loser. *The Scarlet Let-ter's* quiet affiliation with these texts helps establish *its* story not just as a Puritan tale but also as part and parcel of Euro-diasporic collective mem-ory stretching back to the Middle Ages. Hawthorne's redeployment of the sable-gules schema is no more hermetically American than filmmaker Akira Kurosawa's retelling of Shakespeare's *King Lear* in *Ran* is hermetically Japanese.

The more we start to think of Hawthorne in relation to figures like Scott and Marvell, the less *The Scarlet Letter* looks like a text firmly and unshakeably embedded within a line of American descent from Puritan history or as a critique of American Transcendentalism or nineteenth-century American Victorian moralism. The more it makes sense that the precursor to which Henry James thought to liken it was Scottish writer John Gibson Lockhart's *Adam Blair* (1822), a novel of ministerial adultery in an old-world puritanical culture. The more it begins to make sense that the first rewriting of *The Scarlet Letter* was not an American novel but George Eliot's *Adam Bede*. It, too, is a historical fiction that features a pair of illicit lovers named Hester and Arthur, with an illegitimate child—also in a provincial social context that intensifies the mixture of guilt, suffering, and repression. Why should not an English country town of the turn of the nineteenth century be every bit as promising a venue for a Hester-Arthur story as seventeenth-century New England?

That is not the way the majority of Hawthorne scholars, who are mostly Americanists, have been conditioned to think about Hawthorne's legacy. We are much more inclined to think of Hawthorne in relation to William Faulkner or John Updike or Toni Morrison than to compare him to George Eliot, even though Eliot is on record as declaring Hawthorne "a grand favorite of mine" (Eliot 1954–78, 2: 52). The underlying assumption is that Hawthorne was a classic American writer chiefly of importance to "our" literary history as an agent of U.S. literary emergence and the propagation of distinctive strains in national fiction thereafter.

With one side of his mind this was also how Hawthorne himself thought. He was attracted to the idea of writing "tales of my native land" (the working title of an early, uncompleted project). He was one of the several dozen antebellum New England authors who answered lawyer-orator Rufus Choate's call for a series of New England-based fictions—in a lecture given in Hawthorne's native Salem, Massachusetts—that would rival Scott's Waverley novels (Choate 1852, 1: 319–46). Hawthorne was by far the most talented of the lot (Bell). Historically ordered, his colonial tales together with his first three book-length romances constitute an episodic epic of New England history from the first generation of settlement through Transcendentalist communitarianism.

Yet with another side of his mind, Hawthorne doubted whether a distinctively national fiction or narrative was possible or even desirable. Much of his late writing was devoted to the Anglo-American connection and unfinished romances of ancestral linkage and/or inheritance. His American masterpiece indicates a hesitancy about the viability of the story of an autonomous American history repeated soon afterward in seriocomic form

in his last published historical tale, "Main-Street," in which an earnest, voluble, but self-undermining showman attempts to stage a series of tableaux
of colonial history to a marginally invested audience of townsmen, only to
break down during the Great Snow of 1717 when his crude mechanical con-
trivance fails. So much for the patriotic boosterism of Rufus Choate.

In *The Scarlet Letter*, likewise, the story of Hester and Arthur is not
shown as having any lasting American issue. The mother country is pic-
tured wistfully as a place of healthy vitality and merriment, the new world
of Puritan Boston seen as a diminished shadowland by contrast. "We have
yet to learn again the forgotten art of gaiety," the narrator sighs (232) as he
describes the book's one festive scene. "The Custom-House" portrays a
nineteenth-century America already moribund. That this was an age of
unparalleled national expansion and economic growth one could never tell
from Hawthorne's essay. The author's home town is in decay. The country
doesn't seem to be going anywhere. That is perhaps the most strikingly
idiosyncratic aspect of this novel's vision of history: not its representation
of Puritan nostalgia for the mother country (for many Puritans *did* return
home, as Hawthorne would have known); not the comparison between
Puritan austerity and latter-day lightening-up (already a cliché in
Hawthorne's day), but rather the sense that the whole new world experiment may be fizzling out. Two centuries of New England history end in the
anticlimax of the aptly named Custom-House.

This was not, of course, the biographical Hawthorne's full view of the
matter. In other moods, George Dekker usefully reminds us, "Hawthorne
could argue earnestly that the sadly imperfect liberal democracy nurtured
in the United States, and especially in New England, was the best hope of
mankind" (Dekker 1987, 170). This may even have been his prevailing view
as a citizen. But it was not a view that Hawthorne could make prevail in
either his fictive renditions of New England or in his history for children,
Grandfather's Chair, neither of which manages to draw the line between
colonial New England and the present-day national efflorescence that was
axiomatic to the likes of Choate and Daniel Webster, not to mention the
New England-dominated schoolbook industry of Hawthorne's day. In *The
Scarlet Letter*, the one moment during either the introduction or the
romance proper that the grand narrative is told with any enthusiasm, it
remains inaudible and suspect. That is the point before the denouement
when Dimmesdale sermonizes on the glorious destiny of New England—
a standard topic for ministers on certain ceremonial occasions, then and
(even more) in Hawthorne's day. *The Scarlet Letter* makes sure to put the
reader at a great distance from this performance—outside the church
alongside Hester, who doesn't catch a word of it. All we know for sure is

that Dimmesdale is in an abnormal and agitated state. His rapturous prophecy is not to be believed.

The skepticism Hawthorne generally evinces toward historical pieties in both "The Custom-House" and *The Scarlet Letter* has generally been explained in Americanist terms. Lauren Berlant brilliantly reads Hawthorne as offering "a counter-National Symbolic marked by a hermeneutic of negativity and defamiliarization" (Berlant 1991, 34). Catherine Jones, in a thoughtful comparative discussion of the uses of history and tradition in Hawthorne and Scott, sees in Hawthorne a distinctly American tendency to disown the past. ("The self-definition of America precludes direct access to a continuous folk memory" [Jones 2000, 136].) There is much to be said for these views of the case: the image of Hawthornian narrative practice as a process of wily skeptical negotiation within certain forms of ideological blockage attendant upon his inevitable embeddedness within his national and/or regional culture at a particular point in time. But we also need to question the prior assumption that the most fruitful way to situate Hawthorne should be in terms of his or his text's standing as an "American" discourse, whether acquiescent or dissenting. The cosmopolitanism of perspective that his historical fictions imply in the course of engaging in their provincial struggles—as with *The Scarlet Letter*'s glimpses backward to the motherland, or the intertextual knot at the close—may indeed be so construed, but it is hardly imperative so to construe them. Hester's return to Boston to her old role as letter-wearer, which Sacvan Bercovitch reads— thoughtfully, subtly, learnedly—as an enactment of the national covenant of consent (Bercovitch 1991),[6] might also be conceived as confirmation of the impoverished options to which the decision to emigrate condemns one. The old world past cannot be disowned in this romance because the new world avatar is only a diminished version of the old. The reduction of the protagonists to ghosts of their former selves shows this plainly enough. Dimmesdale "had come from one of the great English universities, bringing all the learning of the new age into our wild forest-land" (66). It's all downhill from there. Internalization of the provincial thought police socializes him into such timidity that Hester's challenge in the forest ("[B]e a scholar and a sage among the wisest and the most renowned of the cultivated world. Preach! Write! Act!") sickens rather than invigorates him (198). Hester's mind, by contrast, expands to the point that she assumes "a freedom of speculation, then common enough on the other side of the Atlantic." But by colonial Puritan standards this is "a deadlier crime than that stigmatized by the scarlet letter" (164). In this brave new world, what Hester has become cannot socially exist. Despite the fact that *The Scarlet Letter* takes place entirely on American soil, despite its attention to colonial culture and institutions, despite its having been written in the heyday of national expansion, it remains at heart a diasporic rather than a nativized imagination of place, in the sense that the standard of cultural vitality remains transatlantic and colonial life and culture by contrast diminished, underactualized, and without issue—with characters, narrator, author all self-consciously detached from the new world place that is supposed to be their habitat.

As such, *The Scarlet Letter* seems less a reflection on issues of national consensus and less a template for narratives of American nationalization than a story of transnational dislocation whose investment in issues of nationhood is peripheral at best. To the extent that we take it as a barometric indicator or reference point for new world imagination, its closest affiliations are narratives of rebuffed or imperfect assimilation of a place conceived through unassimilated eyes as alien ground, from the narratives of Mary Rowlandson and Olaudah Equiano to James's *The Europeans* to Cather's *O Pioneers!* and Flannery O'Connor's "The Displaced Person" to Chang Rae Lee's *Native Speaker* and *A Gesture Life.* Like all these texts and others like them, *The Scarlet Letter* does not so much insinuate "Here is national fiction" as pose the question: "Can there be such a thing?" or "Why should there be?"

2

Here, then, is the "problem of 'American' fiction" *The Scarlet Letter* exemplifies and to which the title of this essay alludes. The cultural work that *The Scarlet Letter* has been made to perform is not quite the work it undertakes to perform. The book is arguably not an "American" performance so much as one that critical and creative repossessions have by and large tended to Americanize in ways that play down its cosmopolitan and deracinated aspects. In this respect, it is hardly unique among the canonical writings of our literary history. On the contrary, the larger significance of belaboring the point at hand is precisely that it is exemplary of a much larger-scale foreshortening of vista. The foreshortening I have described is akin to the centripetalism that leads Americanists to claim Equiano as an "American" writer or to block out the transnationalism of (say) Melville's account of business culture in "Bartleby the Scrivener" (Why not Dickens? Why not Gogol? Why not Joyce's "Counterparts"?). The examples are endless, especially for immigrant and expatriate writing. But *The Scarlet Letter* is an especially imposing case, insofar as more than any other premodern American novel it has come to stand as a point of origin in the history of American literary-cultural emergence and as a point of textual origin for later artists. Few other novels have seemed for so many critics so pivotal for the solidification of national historical imagination.

Indeed, the sequence of American reinventions of *The Scarlet Letter* plot from Frederic and James to Updike and Mukherjee—the legacy of Hawthorne's masterpiece as a master-plot for national writers—has unquestionably helped to create a solider sense of national literary tradition than Hawthorne could ever have felt. The ironic effect of this remarkable success story is its tendency to distract one from how desolidifying a text *The Scarlet Letter* is—although the plethora of rewritings testifies to that, too. "Most persons of ability," Emerson remarks, "meet in society with a kind of tacit appeal," as if to imply "I am not all there" (Emerson 1971–, 3: 127). *The Scarlet Letter* imparts just such an impression through its structural tightness, its laconic restraint of emotional tone, and its oscillation of narrative judgment—suggesting tortuous, self-conflicted operation within the reluctant confines of the mind's own making. Among the various explanations for the amount of exegesis and reenactment that *The Scarlet Letter* has provoked, *one* is that its uneasy, self-conscious narratorial reticence invites second-guessing reappraisal and active rewriting of the author's version of his own tale. That is why it is not *utterly* outrageous for the 1990s Hollywood adaptation of *The Scarlet Letter* to end with the Indians rescuing Hester, Dimmesdale, and Pearl and burning down Boston. For the narrator repeatedly emits signals to the effect that he might wish that things could work out differently, even though he fears they can't and (in some moods, particularly near the end) agrees they shouldn't.

One of the book's early reviewers praised *The Scarlet Letter* on just such grounds: for the author's ethical restraint, allowing "his guilty parties to end, not as his own fancy or his own benevolent sympathies might dictate, but as the spiritual laws, lying back of all persons dictated to him" (Whipple 346). Modern readers have tended by contrast to long for a breakaway from the book's self-imposed emotional/ ethical/ ideological confines—most especially as they constrain its heroine. So Frederic I. Carpenter, in the classic essay in this vein, assigns Hawthorne a grade of A-minus for inability to get past "emotional" to full "intellectual" realization of Hester's potential for "embodying the authentic American dream of freedom and independence in the new world" (Carpenter 1944, 180). Since the advent of critical feminist studies, debate around the general issue of whether the narrative undercuts Hester has continued—at a far higher level of sophistication—as in Nina Baym's defenses of *The Scarlet Letter*'s feminism ("Hester has certainly changed the Puritans more than they have changed her") and David Leverenz's critique of its misogyny (Baym 1986, 29; cf.

Baym 1976, 142–51; Leverenz 1983). Even more variable have been the fictive rewritings of Hester, such as Frederic's flirtatiously sophisticated Celia Madden; Faulkner's matriarch-victim Addie Bundren; Updike's wily, self-indulgent, misnamed Sarah Worth; and Mukherjee's picaresque world-traveling Hannah Easton. Read them in a series, throw in for good measure the filmic Hesters from Lilian Gish to Demi Moore, and well might the curious interpreter perplex him or herself with the question: "Whose Hawthorne?"

Even if one agrees that *The Scarlet Letter* is the kind of text that provokes revision, it does not follow that the revisions thereby provoked will question the legitimacy of reading Hawthorne in Americanist terms. Indeed, few of the just-mentioned texts do so. One that does, however, and with a metahistorical self-consciousness whose perspicacity compensates for its intervals of zany froth, is Mukherjee's *The Holder of the World* (1993). This novel is equally instructive for its resistance to *The Scarlet Letter*'s status as a founding document in the history of imagined nationness and for the form in which it eventually succumbs to a version of the temptation that it critiques in Hawthorne.

The Holder of the World features a female latter-day narrator, Beigh Masters, who, like Hawthorne, is a skilled historian conscious of her family's New England antecedence, nominally engaged in money-making ("asset management") but overtaken—more wholeheartedly than Surveyor Hawthorne—by an identification with the novel's primary Hester-figure, Hannah. (*Holder* also features two other characters provocatively named Hester.) This Hannah is not an immigrant but a Massachusetts frontier child whose widowed still-youthful mother deserts her during King Philip's War for the sake of her Indian lover. Thus begins a picaresque plot that takes Hannah through a Puritan girlhood in Salem, brief residence in London, then to the original India—the obverse transit from that of the Indo-American author. There she becomes the mistress of the ruler of a Hindu state, fleeing it after his death (which she unintentionally helps bring about) at the hands of the Moghul emperor in order to return to New England with her unborn child, predictably named Pearl. The shady merchant-pirate who whisks her from Salem to England to India is a blow-up of the swashbuckling sea captain who makes a cameo appearance near the end of *The Scarlet Letter*, contracting to take Hester, Dimmesdale, and Pearl back to England. Hannah's marriage to Gabriel Legge, in order to escape stultifying Salem, is one of several exploitations of *The Scarlet Letter*'s fleeting glimpses of the wider, livelier world beyond—and behind—the infant colony.[7]

Hannah's extrication from her stiff, monitorial Puritan foster-parents does not save her from a series of irksome domestic enclosures thereafter.

But it makes for a vertiginous and mind-expanding *peripeteia* starkly different from *The Scarlet Letter*'s intense confinement. Hawthorne multiculturalized, Hawthorne transnationalized, Hawthorne in technicolor. *Holder* wants to put the New England experiment in the global Anglophone context just barely visible in Hawthorne's text: to connect the remotest ends of Empire, and dramatize in the process the hyperactive, raffish fortuity of colonial enterprise, as against the tightly regimented affair *The Scarlet Letter* foregrounds. Significantly, two of the clues by means of which the narrator reconstructs Hannah's lifeline are a youthful fantasy-sampler of "the uttermost shore"—yes, like Hester Prynne, Hannah is deft with the needle—and an Indian artist's renditions of "the Salem Bibi": two happenstance mirror images of the termini of the Anglophone world.

In all this one sees a more lighthearted version of Carpenter's judgmentalism: *The Scarlet Letter* lacked the courage of its best convictions. Hawthorne "sh[ied] away from the real story of the brave Salem mother and her illegitimate daughter," even though it was Hannah's "stories of the China and India trade" that induced Hawthorne's great-grandfather to become the first of the clan to go to sea (Mukherjee 1993, 283–85). In applying her corrective, Mukherjee's narrator far outdoes "The Custom-House"'s ponderously whimsical anecdote of imagined reconnection with the past, when the surveyor puts the moth-eaten letter to his chest and feels that strange, unexpected pulsation of heat. With the aid of virtual reality simulation software designed by her Indian boyfriend, an MIT researcher, Beigh is transported back to the moment Hannah and her servant-companion Bhagmati (whom she has renamed Hester after a childhood friend) are fleeing the emperor with "the world's most perfect diamond." One-upping Hawthorne, Beigh feels the diamond as it is handed off by faltering Hannah to the fleeing Bhagmati/Hester, feels herself mowed down by the sharpshooter's bullets that mortally wound Bhagmati, then feels herself wield Bhagmati's knife and "plunge the diamond into the deepest part of me" (283). The boyfriend's program doesn't get Beigh precisely where she'd expected—into *Hannah's* mind/body—but at least she meets Hannah (virtually) face to face.

Given *Holder*'s insistence on deterritorializing Hawthorne, one of its most arresting moves is its Americanization of the denouement. Mukherjee's Hester *and* Pearl come back to New England to stay. What's more, they come back as proto-republican libertarians. "'We are Americans to freedom born!' White Pearl and Black Pearl [their local nicknames] were heard to mutter, the latter even in school." *Holder* here sets itself against Hawthorne's "morbid introspection into guilt and repression that many call our greatest work. . . . He wrote," she adds, "against the fading of the light, the dying of the old program, the distant memory of a shameful, heroic time," whereas *this* novel seeks to "bring alive the first letter of an alphabet of hope and of horror stretching out, and back to the uttermost shores" (285, 286). This is intriguingly congruent with Colacurco's and Bercovitch's diagnoses of a Hawthorne fascinated by America's Puritan origins—although *Holder* posits a(n even) more culturally embedded Hawthorne and arrives at the diagnosis through a very different route: locating national beginnings in the experience of global roaming rather than in the localized Puritan experiment per se.

Holder might have given *The Scarlet Letter* more credit for anticipatory resistance to Americanist-centripetal historical criticism. For *The Scarlet Letter* anticipates something of Mukherjee's geocultural plenitude at those moments when it pauses to wonder whether "we perhaps exaggerate the gray or sable tinge" of early Puritan manners, when, after all, these "were native Englishmen, whose fathers had lived in the sunny richness of the Elizabethan epoch; a time when the life of England, viewed as one great mass, would appear to have been as stately, magnificent, and joyous, as the world has ever witnessed" (230). Asides like this one show that the author was aware—as was his heroine—that *The Scarlet Letter*'s here and now was not the whole seventeenth-century world, certainly not the whole Anglophone world and indeed not even the whole world of early Massachusetts settlement culture. Such passages are calculated fissures in the seeming monolith, standing invitations to tell this provincial tale differently if one feels so moved. But nothing more than hints. *The Scarlet Letter* finally leaves it to the curious inquirer to decide whether to read the book more as an open secret (deliberately a fragment of all that it knows might be said) or as a closed book (a resolutely self-contained local tale "of human frailty and sorrow" [48] notwithstanding whatever cracks and fissures). *The Holder of the World* seems—too hastily—to have presumed the latter intent, at least for the purpose of establishing by contrast its own wider geocultural horizon.

Mukherjee is not alone in this sort of rewriting. English novelist Christopher Bigsby's concurrent *Hester* (1994) is in some ways an even more de-centered retelling than *The Holder of the World*. Its best energies are devoted to the in-England, voyage-over, and pre-*Scarlet Letter* backstory of Hester's involvements with Chillingworth and Dimmesdale. Bigsby's elaboration of Hawthorne's Hester's memory-snatches, on the scaffold, of her former family and married life are comparable to Mukherjee's exfoliation of Hawthorne's skipper into Gabriel Legge; and the result is almost as much of a re-Englishing of *The Scarlet Letter* as *Adam Bede*. The New England phase of the novel, particularly the recapitulation of *The*

Scarlet Letter plotline, is perfunctory by comparison to the earlier life and adventures of the three principals. *Holder of the World* expends an even smaller percentage of text than *Hester* on American shores; but it is careful to begin in New England initially so as to make its protagonist an American original whose idiosyncracies are brought out, broadened, then returned home through globalization. The contrast makes sense in light of Mukherjee's insistence that "I am an American writer, in the American mainstream, trying to extend it ... I am not an Indian writer, not an exile, not an expatriate. I am an immigrant" (Alam 1996, 11). So *Holder of the World,* relative to *Hester,* participates in the "Americanization" of *The Scarlet Letter,* even as it critiques Hawthorne for Yankee parochialism. Participates not only in the sense that *Holder* finally becomes still another self-identified American writer's rewriting of an American classic, but also in that it strives to make its version of *The Scarlet Letter* into an image of /reflection on Americanness no less strenuously than do (say) Updike or Berlant or Bercovitch in their own quite different ways. So too with Toni Morrison's *Beloved,* whose reweaving of the tropes of the pariah-mother, the elf-child, and remembered diaspora turned potential cul de sac constitute in its own way perhaps the single most brilliant contemporary heterodox re-Americanization of *The Scarlet Letter* plot, though less to my purpose here since for Morrison *The Scarlet Letter* is a secondary and more occluded pre-text.[8]

Altogether, the 500-year palimpsest from Marvell to Mukherjee reviewed here shows, I hope, that the absorption of *The Scarlet Letter* as American discourse makes cultural-historical sense, but that it is not the only plausible outcome. The romance offers itself as a portable archetype. "The Puritan community in *The Scarlet Letter,*" as Baym declares, can be thought of as "a symbol of society in general" (Baym 1976, 141). Solemn visitants to Hester's grave who "on a certain day still lay blood-red roses in the tangled grass," opines Bigsby's narrator in similarly generalizing fashion, "tell the story of a woman's love and of man's capacity for good and ill" (Bigsby 1994, 186). England, New England, India, the essential story is the same, one might argue. This is not to deny the presence of cultural particularities. Bercovitch writes no less cogently that "Hawthorne rendered Puritan intolerance more vividly than any other historical novelist," because "better than any other" he understood the complexities of Puritanism *"as an interpretive community"* (emphasis in original)—as well as both the dead and living dimensions of that legacy for the nineteenth century (Bercovitch 1991, 48). But then again, insofar as Puritanism itself is diasporic, one might reply that Hawthorne's chief glory is of a transcultural kind: to have represented Puritan doctrines "as an expression of an enduring states of the human soul," or to have rendered Puritanism "lyrically, with a purity of intensity of focus which makes it, for the time, inescapable" (Manning 1990, 181). And beyond that, insofar as the Puritan experiment in Massachusetts was but a variant manifestation of the Anglophone diaspora generally, an experiment itself fissiparous and pluriform, should not a more sprawling and unglued diasporic rendition like Mukherjee's be prized, however fanciful at certain points?

There is no end to such rumination. No end to the reinterpretations and the retellings. After 150 years, it is clear that the percolation effect of *The Scarlet Letter* won't diminish anytime soon, and with it the multiplication of possible Hawthornes. Lionel Trilling anticipated this, though somewhat grudgingly. For Trilling, some versions (the modernist) were undeniably closer to the true Hawthorne than others (James's), and there seemed something wrong with Hawthorne's artistry "in the degree that he does not dominate us" but leaves us with unresolved questions. In closing, Trilling went so far as to blame Hawthorne for instilling in readers the "sensation of having been set at liberty. . . . We find ourselves at a loss and uncertain in the charge of an artist so little concerned to impose upon us the structure of his imagination." Yet in final qualification Trilling speculates that even though "our judgment of Hawthorne may have to be that he is not for today, or perhaps not even tomorrow," he may nonetheless, as Nietzsche remarks in another context, be "one of the spirits of yesterday—and the day after tomorrow" (Trilling 1964, 457). Early-twenty-first-century postmodern transnationalism bears this speculation out. Today Hawthornian indeterminacy (at the heart of James's admiration for Hawthorne's delicacy, I think) is more in phase. No longer does it seem necessary to posit, much less to defend, *an* essential Hawthorne. We can feel more at home with the kind of interpretative liberty *The Scarlet Letter* invites, even while holding its narration under restraint.

The particular form of liberty for which this essay has argued, is willingness to suspend, even if not to scrap, the assumption that *The Scarlet Letter* must be read as a symptomatically "American" tale, as a cornerstone of "American literature." It can, of course, be so read. It will continue to be so read. But it is neither necessary nor desirable that it should inevitably be so read. And if it is to be so read, it should be in consciousness of the extraterritorial circles of discourse, history, and migration lurking—often unseen by Americanist eyes—in such underexplored portions of the text as the encrypted closing allusions, and elaborated in transnational readings and repossessions of Hawthorne of the past dozen years or so. Reimagining in such terms a text like *The Scarlet Letter*—so salient and durable a cornerstone in the organization of Americanist thinking about national narrative imagination—might go a long way toward a more expansive understanding of how "American" narratives actually do take form and work.

NOTES

1. For preparation of this essay I am grateful to Jared Hickman.

2. It is important to stress that Tompkins does not deny the excellence of Hawthorne or *The Scarlet Letter;* her concern is rather to demonstrate the contingency as against the inevitability of what counts as literary merit. As such she provides a more self-consciously theoretical account than Trilling does—though by no means the only possibly account—of the instability of what counts as "our Hawthorne."

3. The first comprehensive critical formulation of the romance-as-American-fictional-difference hypothesis was Chase. The most influential attack has been Baym (1976, 1981). The two most significant recent attempts at reviving a more critically scrupulous version of the romance hypothesis, in both of which Hawthorne figures significantly, are Budick and Thompson/Link.

4. An earlier scene, however, offers a glimpse of Pearl skipping among the tombstones of the same burying ground, stopping to dance upon "the broad, flat, armorial tombstone of a departed worthy,—perhaps of Isaac Johnson himself," the lot's first owner.

5. Hawthorne wrote his sister Elizabeth in 1820 that he had read all of Scott's books except for *Lord of the Isles* (*Letters, 1813–1843,* 132). His son Julian Hawthorne remembered his father reading aloud to the family "the whole of Walter Scott's novels" a few years before his death (J. Hawthorne 2: 9).

6. Like Berlant's serendipitously concurrent study, Bercovitch argues that "Hawthorne sought to rise above [party] politics not by escaping history, but by representing it ironically" (Bercovitch 1991, 107).

7. Of the several critical discussions of Mukherjee as a reviser of Hawthorne, the most helpfully informative and satisfyingly complex to my mind is Newman, although I disagree with its argument that the novel attempts a "deconstruction" of new historicism.

8. For published discussions of Hawthorne-Morrison, see especially Stryz. I am especially indebted, however, to a comparative study still in ms. by C. Namwali Serpell, "Ghostly Secrecy and Palimpsest Secrecy."

5

Nathaniel Hawthorne and Transnationality

John Carlos Rowe

> Thus, between two countries, we have none at all, or only that little space of either, in which we finally lay down our discontented bones. It is wise, therefore, to come back betimes—or never.
>
> Nathaniel Hawthorne, *The Marble Faun* (1860)

> Hawthorne's career . . . had few perceptible points of contact with what is called the world, with public events, with the manners of his time, even with the life of his neighbours.
>
> Henry James, *Nathaniel Hawthorne* (1879)

Henry James's judgment of Hawthorne's provincialism is taken too often for the truth. Although Hawthorne cultivated his isolation, even helped mythologize his dreamy detachment from the world, he was both a man of the world and the author of fiction that focuses with special intensity on the conflict among peoples from different worlds. Today we are interested in the history of our current global situation and the transnational forces that challenge the nation state and other traditional sociopolitical organizations. In order to understand these phenomena, we would do well to study Hawthorne's fiction, which represents an older world transformed by the new forces of modernization, first announced by the industrial revolution in England and made more urgent and dangerous in the expansionist frenzy of Jacksonian America. What makes Hawthorne especially worthy of reconsideration in today's debates over globalization is his conflation of the new U.S. nation with its transnational others and of the allegorical transposition of the misty European past into the democratic (and usually U.S.) present. Hawthorne usually does this work in a politically conservative manner, and it is just his ability to "Americanize" international and transnational issues in this manner that makes him relevant to our present situation.

Hawthorne appears to prefer the premodern era and its relative stability, and his characteristic narrative strategy of retreating to some moonlit, fantastic region also involves his return to a forgotten or misremembered past. His historical romances quite precisely manipulate our tendency to forget the past by rendering it remote and fantastic, thus irrelevant to our contemporary concerns, an effect heightened by a modernization process focused quite narrowly on present accomplishments and future possibilities. But Hawthorne wrote his historical romances often to dramatize just this modern inclination to romanticize the past for the sake of ignoring its continuing effects in the present. Even before Richard Chase famously identified the curious combination of romance and realism in Hawthorne's fiction as a distinctive formal characteristic of American literature, Hawthorne was interpreted as a writer whose historical consciousness depends upon the tension and conflict between realistic and romantic uses of the past (Chase 1957, 67–79). Understanding as he does how powerfully human beings are inclined to delude themselves, especially where the past is concerned, Hawthorne finds literature an especially powerful, perhaps unique, means of working through our fantasies of the past toward more precise and useful interpretations of history.

Hawthorne thus renders illusory the debate between the Ancients and the Moderns, insofar as the concerns of the present are usually traceable to a forgotten historical past still operating secretly within our everyday lives. This is "The Skeleton in the Closet" Harry Levin chooses as his title for the chapter on Hawthorne in *The Power of Blackness: Hawthorne, Poe, Melville* (1958), and that skeleton is the *memento mori* buried in our unconscious that Hawthorne seeks to revive, if only to help us understand the consequences of repressing and forgetting it. Levin considers this journey into the unconscious to be a "cosmic adventure in introspection, as much as in exploration," and thus one means by which Hawthorne can be redeemed from Henry James's judgment of his "provincialism" (Levin 1958, 100). To be sure, this interior voyage tends to substitute personal for political history, psychobiography for ideology, often in ways meant to be read allegorically from one domain to the other, but often for that very reason ambiguous in its broader national and transnational significance.

Yet if we remain attentive to the allegorical character of the psychological journey in Hawthorne's fiction, then we can understand this adventure as a series of related border crossings between the conscious and the unconscious, the present and the past, the individual and the citizen, the nation and the alien. Difficult as Hawthorne sometimes makes it for the reader to follow these allegorical links, he also teaches us an important lesson often lost in more recent discussions of transnationality: to go beyond the "nation" is not merely to connect with other nations, but to consider the great variety of different social formations and personal identities *excluded* by a particular nation and nationalism in general. In the case of the United States in the nineteenth century, these exclusions are quite various, often interrelated, and surprisingly well represented in Hawthorne's fiction. Taken together, the *extranational* social and personal alternatives in Hawthorne often serve a utopian function, what Sacvan Bercovitch has termed "the ideological marks of the unthinkable (un-American, anti- or nonliberal)" and thus pose "the ideological prospects for dissent, the grounds for a resistant subjectivity that is potentially . . . the source of radical insight and social change" (Bercovitch 1991, 153).

Pearl's mysterious marriage into a European aristocratic class "unknown to English heraldry," yet made possible in large part by Roger Chillingworth's bequest to her of "a very considerable amount of property, both here and in England," exemplifies this sort of transnational utopianism in ways that are both radically ambiguous and in certain respects allegorically clear and distinct (I 262, 261). Some new "aristocracy" may possibly grow out of the tragic narrative of original sin told emblematically in *The Scarlet Letter* and realize thereby the millennial promise of "New England" in America. In Hawthorne's Calvinist version of American romanticism, the lesson to be learned is not too difficult to understand: the United States must realize the liberal individualism seventeenth-century New England Puritanism failed to produce, even though its theology promised such moral self-reliance. For whatever reasons, historical or theological, Puritanism did not liberate its followers from the feudal hierarchies and spiritual dependencies of Europe. Hester's insistent display of her original sin in the figure of the scarlet letter, even when the elders no longer require it, reminds us that she is a prophetess of democratic individualism, including full responsibility for her human weaknesses as the sign of a new beginning and humanity.

Bercovitch complicates this liberal individualism, which is certainly compatible with American transcendentalism and the general ethos of Jacksonian America, by insisting upon its utopian dimensions: "That liberal both/and includes an alternative either/or: the concept of an un-American place of freedom, Europe; the possibility of an American nonliberal future, some still undetermined 'surer ground of mutual happiness' whose structures will contravene those of actual individualism" (Bercovitch 1991, 152). But the abstraction of liberal individualism from its historical and geopolitical possibility in nineteenth-century America is Hawthorne's way of contributing to what today we recognize as cultural colonialism, whereby the promise of the American self-reliant individual would become the model for the rest of the world and "America" would transcend its *national* destiny by achieving the *spiritual* or *religious* empire that is implicit in Hawthorne's imaginative transumption of Hester's otherwise restricted destiny at the edge of the North American wilderness. Not surprisingly, literature is the utopian space in which such imaginative projection best occurs, so that Hawthorne's romantic regionalism is a trick that serves expansionist political and cultural purposes.

The Custom-House's upper floor in Hawthorne's famous preface to *The Scarlet Letter* is the *locus classicus* of this aesthetic, transnational space. More explicitly liminal than either the study where Hawthorne wrote *Mosses from an Old Manse* or the other marginal spaces he claimed for himself as author, the Custom-House marks precisely the national border as the model for other boundaries, such as those dividing past from present, civilization from wilderness, divine from human, spiritual from material. Yet such precise distinctions belong to the official and commercial work on the ground floor of the Custom-House, where the identification of products according to their national origins is crucial for the imposition of duties and tariffs and the general regulation of what is permissible and forbidden within the republic. It is not surprising that Hawthorne represents the lives of the workers on this level as full of ennui and lacking in real sociability and conversation, epitomized by the octogenarian Inspector, General Miller, "the patriarch" (16), whose preternatural youth and health grotesquely represent "the rare perfection of his animal nature" at complete odds with humanity: "He possessed no power of thought, no depth of feeling, no troublesome sensibilities; nothing, in short, but a few commonplace instincts, which . . . did duty . . . in lieu of a heart" (I 17). In typical romantic fashion, Hawthorne quickly transforms this figure of sheer animality, "so earthly and sensuous," into a mere illusion: "so shallow, so delusive, so impalpable, such an absolute nonentity" in all human respects that matter (18). Hawthorne's great fear is that his work in the Custom-House will transform his more serious vocation as an imaginative writer into some version of the labor of commodification and classification that has rendered the Inspector so inhuman.

In contrast, the upper floor is structured like an unconscious of both the nation and the author who will attempt to represent it, a ratio established by parallelism with the Inspector's patriarchal representation of the U.S. government on the lower floor: "The patriarch, not only of this little squad of officials, but, I am bold to say, of the respectable body of tide-waiters all over the United States—was a certain permanent Inspector" (I 16). Hawthorne names this Inspector General Miller, whose official relationship to these "tide-waiters," servants of the state, parallels the author's relationship with his audience, on the understanding that the writer and his readers will transcend the dehumanized conditions of all those toiling on the ground floor. Lauren Berlant has written that "The Custom-House" "can be read as a study in the genealogy of national identity, as it discloses the variety of historical forms that descend on America, in 1850," including the baser impulses of Jacksonian America on the ground floor and the more utopian desires discoverable on the upper floor (Berlant 1991,165). This "neutral territory, somewhere between the real world and fairy-land, where the Actual and Imaginary may meet" is obviously intended to represent the more flexible meanings of literature in place of the fixed duties and values imposed on the commercial objects passing through the ground floor of the Custom-House (I 36).

Both Bercovitch and Berlant argue that Hawthorne's "neutral territory" is the aesthetic space where he attempts to reinvent the U.S. national symbology (Bercovitch 1991, 115–16; Berlant 1991, 182), but it is also an explicitly, albeit very *abstract*, transnational space. Whereas the patriarchal Inspector, General Miller, combines military, economic, and legal authorities to "police" the border of the United States, Nathaniel Hawthorne creates what Berlant terms a deliberately "unstable" territory, wherein strictly national concerns are reconnected with colonial history. As he bids farewell to his public service in the Custom-House and commits himself anew to literary work, Hawthorne states directly: "I am a citizen of somewhere else" (I 44). His use of "citizen" in this particular context may not attract much attention beyond the rhetoric of the two competing nationalisms Hawthorne has included in his preface: Jacksonian America's commercialism and the utopian democracy Hawthorne's romance promises to revive. But Hawthorne's definition of the "citizen" is complicated when we recall his extended metaphor of political execution by "the guillotine" to represent both his predecessor, Survey Pue's, and his own removals from their political offices (41). In one sense, Hawthorne is a "citizen of somewhere else" when he leaves the material world of the Custom-House to enter the realm of his imagination, but it is also a consequence of just such an imaginative act that he links his own citizenship with that of the *citoyen* declared by the French Revolution.

Hawthorne's identification with the French Revolution is clearly ironic, insofar as he links citizenship with the Terror and thus follows the conservative interpretation of how the French revolt against monarchy was a democratic failure. This sober warning about the dangers of populist revolutions, provoked by widespread anxieties in the U.S. regarding the socialist uprisings of 1848 in Europe, takes another transnational turn as Hawthorne compares himself with "Irving's Headless Horseman," a version of "my figurative self" (I 43). Hawthorne's allusion is complex, because by means of it he identifies with American literature's first internationally recognized author, Washington Irving, with the spectral figure of the Headless Horseman, and with the hapless figure Ichabod Crane, to whom this ghost appears in Irving's famous "The Legend of Sleepy Hollow." Drawing on old Dutch and German folklore, Irving renders fantastic the rush of modern democracy in Brom Bones's "Headless Horseman," even as he represents the schoolteacher Ichabod Crane, "whose mind is haunted by ghost tales reaching back to Puritan times," as defeated both in his suit for Katrina Van Tassel and his effort to preserve the quiet pastoral world of the Hudson River valley from modernization (David Reynolds 1988, 447).

Insofar as he feels alienated from his literary and imaginative powers in the Custom-House, Hawthorne identifies with Irving's defeated Ichabod Crane; both undergo symbolic castration, embodied in Hawthorne's extended metaphor of decapitation and in that "pumpkin" head left behind by Bram Bones to remind Ichabod who has won the game in Irving's story. By association, then, the U.S. "Terror" may result in part from the trivialization of those imaginative powers Hawthorne claims by association with his greatest American precursor, Washington Irving, and their mutual recovery of the historical past, including Puritan America and its European heritage. Perry Miller has argued that "none of Irving's admirers" in the 1820s recognized his reliance, verging on plagiarism, on such old German tales as "Peter Klaus" and "Bürger's *Der wilde Jäger*" in "The Legend of Sleepy Hollow," but the great popularity of Irving's style in *The Sketch Book* was based in large part on Irving's success in invoking venerable European legends and folkore in U.S. settings (Miller 1961, 377).

The charm of Irving's ghosts and goblins assumes a terrifying moral seriousness in Hawthorne's interpretation. The U.S. nation risks repeating the sins of its European and colonial past, unless it discovers some means of confronting and overcoming these repressed moral problems. At the conclusion of "The Custom-House," Hawthorne embodies in his "autobiographical . . . person" these ghostly warnings and poses as "a gentleman who writes from beyond the grave," right down to his parody of supernatural communications from beyond the mortal realm: "Peace be with all the world! My blessing on my friends! My forgiveness to my enemies! For I am in the realm of quiet!" (I 44). Hawthorne uses spirit-rapping, mysterious veiled ladies, and other gothic effects in his fiction as metaphors for the aesthetic imagination, unless they are not exposed as frauds. Literature, especially the romance, allows the dead to live again in ways that reverse quite precisely the living death Hawthorne describes as the condition of General Miller and his "tide-waiters" on the ground floor. Like Dickinson's poetic speaker able to claim "I Heard a Fly Buzz when I Died," Hawthorne's author is capable of crossing boundaries conventionally imagined to be absolute: between life and death, present and past, democratic citizenship and aristocratic title (Dickinson 1960, 223–24).

Berlant equates the authorial body with "Hawthorne's representation of this new 'state,'" both a metaphor for his ontological condition and for the democratic nation, but this body can claim to be "a citizen of somewhere else" precisely because it offers a model of transnational, cosmopolitan identity (Berlant 1991, 185). Far from being the provincial figure doomed to a life of drudgery maintaining proper national and regional borders in the Salem Custom-House, Hawthorne's "decapitated Surveyor" functions as any good ghost to connect the past with the present and the unconscious with consciousness, which in this specific case links Pue's service in "his Majesty's Customs . . . in the Province of Massachusetts Bay" with Hawthorne's service to the U.S. federal government and the state of Massachusetts (I 30). Both Pue's and Hawthorne's missing "heads" turn out to be the texts for which they are responsible. Recalling a story "in a newspaper of recent times . . . of the digging up of [Pue's] remains in the little grave-yard of St. Peter's Church," Hawthorne notes that "nothing . . . was left of my respected predecessor, save an imperfect skeleton, and some fragments of apparel, and a wig of majestic frizzle; which, unlike the head that it once adorned, was in very satisfactory preservation." It is in the papers Pue leaves behind, including the icon of Hester's embroidered letter, where Hawthorne "found more traces of Mr. Pue's mental part, and the internal operations of his head, than the frizzled wig had contained of the venerable skull itself" (I 30). Indeed, the famous scene of authorial investiture wherein Hawthorne places Hester's letter on his own breast and experiences "a sensation not altogether physical, yet almost so, as of burning heat" seems to confirm that the physical and mental "realities" for which Hawthorne appeals belong to the language of the historical romance, rather than to any natural, biochemical body (I 32).

"The Custom-House" reincarnates the national as an authorial body in the rhetorical language of literature, which Hawthorne claims has the special qualities of transgressing otherwise inviolable boundaries and thus enabling both author and reader to become "citizens of somewhere else." In this sense, literature becomes the proper "custom-house" through which cultural and psychological goods circulate far more ambiguously and complexly than ordinary imports and exports do, and for this very reason literature (and the other fine arts, including painting and sculpture) enables readers to identify themselves with a nation (or other bounded community) by establishing relations with other histories and places. For Hawthorne, "American literature" will have to be simultaneously national and transnational, regional only to the extent it is cosmopolitan, historical only insofar as it is romantic. Literature's transnational purpose in connecting contemporary readers with different "nations," such as England, Germany, and Italy, is complemented by its *transmigratory* function, which enables the reader to experience spirits of history and ghosts of the past to be imaginatively reincarnated in the characters of a literary fiction, whose temporality is the present.

The cultural anthropologist Akhil Gupta, who has studied cases of Hindu reincarnation, has argued that "taking the ideas and beliefs of reincarnation seriously may raise fundamental questions about *western* cultural, social, and political theory . . . by forcing to the surface the hidden folk of religious underpinnings of secular social theory" (Gupta 2002, 4; original emphasis). Although western enlightenment reason treats the transmigration of souls as religious superstition, many western literary texts allow us to *reinhabit* past places and bodies either for the mere pleasure of nostalgia or to cope with unresolved historical traumas. This literary contribution to social practice tends to be conservative, insofar as it attempts to regulate a trauma that threatens social order, has for that reason been collectively repressed, and yet by virtue of such forgetting returns to "haunt" us. It is in this theoretical context, then, that I refer to Hawthorne's use of the literary imagination to transmigrate across the borders of historical time as well as national space, and I propose that other considerations of how the transnational imaginary functions spatially include some treatment of how this transmigratory imaginary works temporally. Because the time-space continuum of the transmigratory and transnational work together, we should pay special attention in literary narratives to the primary sites of such interaction: "characters," including that of the author.

At one level, we might understand such "transmigration" merely as a complex system of cultural allusion, whereby the English heritage of Hester's and Dimmesdale's Puritan Bay Colony continues to operate in the mid-nineteenth-century United States. Traditional interpretations of Hawthorne as a romantic intent on secularizing Puritan theology generally follow this pattern, so that his allusions in *The Scarlet Letter* to Peter Ramus, Milton, and the traditions of European biblical exegesis should be considered important features of his transnational consciousness. Recognizing such worldly reading as typical of many transcendentalists' claims to cosmopolitanism, I also want to suggest that Hawthorne's aesthetic of transmigration has a more complex significance for his work of constructing himself as an American author with transnational ambitions (Rowe 2003, 80–81). Hawthorne often invokes earlier historical periods and their communities to remind us that some of their social and psychological problems still haunt us. Recalling in "The Custom-House" his own ancestors' responsibility for the trial and execution of witches in colonial Salem, Hawthorne offers the reader a compensatory narrative in *The Scarlet Letter* that both attempts to explain the Puritans' intolerance and to overcome such prejudices with his own aesthetic claims to moral honesty and self-reliance. Even as he acknowledges his descent from the first Hathorne in America, that "soldier, legislator, judge," who was remembered by the Quakers as a "bitter persecutor," and his son, who "inherited the persecuting spirit, and made himself so conspicuous in the martyrdom of the witches, that their blood may fairly be said to have left a stain upon him," Hawthorne identifies with Hester, whose crime is not witchcraft or even adultery, but finally her stubborn refusal to violate the sanctity of a human heart (I 9).

Literary transmigration thus enables Hawthorne to claim a different ancestry by means of his historical imagination: one that aligns him with the persecuted and thus frees him from his genealogical ties with his "blood-stained" family history. Indeed, Hawthorne enacts a strategic transvestism when he dons Hester's scarlet letter in the upper chamber of the Custom-House, anticipating the radical gesture Judith Butler has identified in more recent and explicit acts of gender transgression: "[As] figurative productions, these [gender] identifications constitute impossible desires that figure the body, active principles of incorporation, modes of structuring and signifying the enactment of the lived body in social spaces" (Butler 1990a, 334). In the space and time of Hawthorne's romance, identifications of all sorts are seen as consequences of individual choices made in response to social laws and conventions. By becoming Hester and feeling in his own body the "burning heat" of both her sin and her sex—his act is ineluctably erotic, especially because he uses the fetish "A" instead of Hester's visual or textual image—Hawthorne dons her radical, creative power as a "prophetess," in the same way as he has imbued her with his imaginative power as an author. Indeed, transmigration always works dialectically between past and present, thereby positing an imaginable or utopian future. Just as Hester will transform her potential for overt social revolution into the subtler, psychological transformation she helps Dimmesdale achieve on his own and in the "family" tableau they constitute with Pearl, however tenuously and briefly, so Hawthorne will change his appeal in "The Custom-House" for a political revolution in Jacksonian America into his narrative version of what I term "aesthetic dissent": "the romantic idealist assumption that rigorous reflection on the processes of thought and representation constitutes in itself a critique of social reality and effects a transformation of the naive realism that confuses truth with social convention" (Rowe 1997, 1).

The rhetorical process through which Hawthorne disengages himself from the commercial values of Jacksonian America and his family ancestry to which he traces such social degradation is necessarily complicated, because it involves an aesthetic sleight-of-hand by which the literary author (Hawthorne), the marginalized and abused woman (Hester), and the bastard child (Pearl) are transformed into leaders of a spiritual and moral revival of an otherwise corrupt U.S. democracy. The redemptive narrative of *The Scarlet Letter* opens the two prisons from which both Hawthorne and Hester emerge at the introduction of their stories—"The Custom-House" and "The Prison-Door"—to the wide, wide world in which Pearl is both citizen and titled lady in the open-ended "Conclusion." The apparently solid, brick edifice of the federal Custom-House is displaced by the narrative organization of Hawthorne's romance, which may claim the attention and interest of both readers in the U.S. and elsewhere, especially in the English-speaking world, as it has certainly done in the century and a half since its publication.

Yet Hawthorne's transmigrational narrative in *The Scarlet Letter* remains obliquely and abstractly cosmopolitan, so it is difficult to assess the extent to which his transnational ambitions in the romance contribute to or challenge the work of U.S. cultural colonialism. Berlant refers to Hawthorne's "critical National Symbolic of 'The Custom-House'" as an alternative to the burgeoning capitalism of Jacksonian America, but Sacvan Bercovitch concludes that the radical ambiguity of *The Scarlet Letter* represents an American ideology in which consensus is "founded upon the potential for dissent" and cultural forms are "designed to consecrate the uncontained self" (Berlant 1991, 188; Bercovitch 1991, 159). If we follow Berlant's more optimistic interpretation, then we should interpret Pearl's curious international destiny at the end to be an allegory of Hawthorne's own special aristocracy as a successful romancer, whose own "letters" arrive "with armorial seals upon them," as literary symbols do, but with "bearings unknown to English heraldry," precisely because they are truly American letters (262). In Bercovitch's terms, Hawthorne's aspiration to ruling-class authority through the profession of letters is based upon his imaginative play with political dissent within the perfectly recognizable conventions of American self-reliant individualism, which relies on myths of progressive development and the secular adaptation of Puritan Election and *felix culpa*.

The Scarlet Letter leaves the international and imperial consequences of these interpretive choices in suspension, but Hawthorne appears to work out their logic in the more explicit transnational circumstances of *The Marble Faun* (1860). Published in England as *Transformation*, Hawthorne's Italian romance is another transmigrational narrative, in which the American author proposes to channel spirits of the past but now from explicitly foreign lands. In his preface to the romance, Hawthorne claims "Italy, as the site of his Romance," primarily as "a sort of poetic or fairy precinct, where actualities would not be so terribly insisted upon, as they are, and must needs be, in America" (IV 3). This claim apparently absolves the author from "attempting a portraiture of Italian manners and character" or the folly as a "foreigner" of "endeavouring to idealize its traits"; it permits him to treat Italy as a metaphor for his own aesthetic playground, the flexible domain of the upper floor of the Custom-House where the author can pose as a "citizen of somewhere else" (3). *The Marble Faun*'s Italian setting is sufficiently concrete and historically specific, especially between 1858 and 1859 when Hawthorne was composing the romance, to suggest that his imaginative transumption of Italy is a form of cultural colonialism that is also perfectly compatible with the aesthetic position he develops in "The Custom-House" preface (IV xxi–xxii). Hawthorne's composition of *The Marble Faun* in Florence and Rome takes place in the midst of the formation of the modern Italian nation, its struggle against the French military occupation of Rome (1849–1870) and Austrian colonization, especially in Piedmont and Lombardy, and its internal fight with the secular empire of the Catholic Church in the Papal States (including its governance of Rome until 1870).

In his *Italian Notebooks*, Hawthorne makes consistently superficial observations about the great political events taking place around him. The Italian nationalists Cavour, Garibaldi, and Mazzini are not even mentioned, whereas Hawthorne makes only brief references to Napoleon III and to the papacy. He takes comfort and even finds a certain charm in the French troops occupying Rome (XIV 63–64), whom he sometimes criticizes for excessive military exercises "to keep the imperial city in awe" (XIV 144), but generally praises as "young, fresh, good-looking men, in excellent trim as to uniform and equipments" and concludes "I was not sorry to see the Gauls still pouring into Rome" (XIV 232). Hawthorne makes most of these favorable observations about the French military in 1858, when Italian republicans still considered the French their bitter enemies and colonial occupiers of their homeland. However oblivious Hawthorne appears to be about these admittedly confusing political events in 1858–1860, he was certainly aware of the deep enmity of Italian nationalists toward the French between 1848 and 1859. Hawthorne and his family had been touring Marseilles in January 1858 when the news arrived from Paris that "Felice Orsini and three other Italian revolutionary conspirators had hurled powerful bombs at the imperial carriage as Napoleon [III] and the empress arrived at the Opéra" (XIV 729).

What seems remarkable in Hawthorne's otherwise touristic impressions is the pleasure he takes in the cosmopolitan atmosphere in Rome and Italy, even when it is an effect of the political violence reshaping modern Europe. As the family prepares to depart Italy aboard a steamer in the harbor of Leghorn in 1859, only to be "detained by order of the French government, to take on board dispatches," Hawthorne observes first "a disembarkation of French soldiers in a train of boats" and then on his own ship "a number of Sardinian officers, in green uniform, came on board, and a pale and picturesque-looking Italian, and other worthies of less note,— English, American, and of all races,—among them a Turk with a little boy in Christian dress; also a Greek gentleman with his young bride" (XIV 527–28). Such political events as French military reinforcements arriving at Leghorn in May 1859—part of 100,000 sent to Italy in 1859—and Sardinian officers boarding a steamer bound for France five months after Cavour, prime minister of the Kingdom of Sardinia (1852–1859), ratified a formal treaty of alliance with Napoleon III in France's war against Austria (January 1859), are rendered strangely picturesque by Hawthorne.

Although Hawthorne claims in his preface to *The Marble Faun* to choose Italy as his setting for the "shadow," "antiquity," "mystery," and "Ruin" necessary for "Romance and poetry . . . to . . . grow," he admires the cosmopolitan atmosphere of *modern* Rome, in which French troops mingle with Papal Guards, Italian Carabiniere, English and American expatriates, and middle-eastern travelers. Yet Hawthorne also recoils from the political disorder, the economic confusion, and the cultural upheaval in Italy. Complaining about the minor chicanery of Roman vendors, poor public hygiene, and other tourists' woes, he generalizes about the moral decadence of Italy as part of both its historical ruin and present political crisis. Although Pope Pius IX (r. 1846–1878) is the secular and religious ruler of Rome at the time, Hawthorne complains he is old, stout, "waddles," and is "not particularly impressive" (XIV 150). Hawthorne prefers the surviving artistic glory of imperial Rome and the Italian Renaissance, concentrating most of his observations in *The Italian Notebooks* on sculptures, paintings, and jewelry from these past eras. Such attitudes are quite typical of American travelers in Italy in the nineteenth century. From Hawthorne and William Wetmore Story to Henry James and Henry Adams, Rome's ruin promised American glory as the neoclassical revival in American arts made graphically clear in so many American public buildings and monuments (Rowe 2002, 94–102). Hawthorne Americanizes nineteenth-century Italy by projecting onto it his own fantasy of the transnational ideal for the American citizen, drawing both on the aura of ancient imperial Rome in its global reach and at the same time emphasizing the American transumption of this "ruined" heritage. Hawthorne gives historical concreteness to this idea in *The Marble Faun* by modeling Kenyon, Hilda, and Miriam on various members of the expatriate community of American artists in Rome in the 1840s and 1850s, such as Hiram Powers (Kenyon), Harriet Hosmer (Hilda), and Maria Louisa Lander (Miriam) (Rowe 2002, 83–94). His allegorical narrative allows him to work through cathartically those aspects of modern cosmopolitanism that frighten him, purging them by way of the Italian character Donatello and the Anglo-Italian-Jewish character Miriam, and embody safely those qualities he finds acceptable in Kenyon and Hilda, who return at the end to America to be married. *The Marble Faun* is in certain respects Hawthorne's most *American* romance, because it offers clear, albeit troubling answers to the questions regarding U.S. cultural colonialism raised by "The Custom-House" preface and "Conclusion" to *The Scarlet Letter*.

Miriam Schaefer condenses Hawthorne's fears of cosmopolitan modernity, even as she represents his fascination with the sexual, psychological, political, and aesthetic powers with which she is variously associated. Like Hester in *The Scarlet Letter* and Zenobia in *The Blithedale Romance*, she embodies the threat of liberated femininity in the arts and politics, so that her associations with such historical figures as Margaret Fuller and the expatriate American sculptors Harriet Hosmer and Maria Louisa Lander allow Hawthorne to suggest her "unpardonable sin," thus combining nineteenth-century women's rights and the artistic freedom many women considered essential for such political emancipation. Hawthorne not only renders Miriam the dark other to the fair Hilda, but he also estranges and racializes Miriam, whose "English parentage, on the mother's side" has "a vein, likewise, of Jewish blood, yet connected through her father, with one of those few princely families of southern Italy, which still retain a great wealth and influence" (IV 429–30). Jews were associated explicitly with a threatening cosmopolitanism in the nineteenth century, an antisemitic convention reinforced by such popular works as Eugène Sue's *Le Juif Errant* (*The Wandering Jew,* 1844–1845) and in much Victorian and nineteenth-century American literature (Rowe 1998, 79–83; Ben-Joseph 1996, 49, 85–86).

Miriam is also vaguely associated with political intrigues in occupied Rome, such that when Hilda attempts to deliver the packet Miriam has addressed to "Signor Luca Barboni, at the Palazzo Cenci, third piano" (IV 68), she is imprisoned for two days in "the Convent of the Sacré Cœur, in the Trinità de' Monti . . . in such kindly custody . . . I could willingly have dwelt there forever" (IV 466). Miriam's confinement in a French Catholic convent in Rome reminds the reader that the French military defended the papal government of Rome against Italian nationalists until 1870, even though Napoleon III and Cavour joined forces to drive Austria out of northern Italy. Miriam's unnamed "crime" is indeed associated frequently in the narrative with some offense against papal secular rule in Rome as well as its moral law, so that the reader gathers the general impression that Miriam is at least allegorically identifiable with the republican revolutions in Europe of 1848 and, more specifically, with the Italian Risorgimento.

Such associations are only reinforced by Miriam's identification with Beatrice Cenci, especially in Guido Reni's famous painting of her displayed at the time in the Palazzo Barberini in Rome, because this tragic figure from the Italian Renaissance was much celebrated in the nineteenth century as an icon of misguided feminine and proto-republican rebellion (Rowe 2002, 86; 1998, 43). Indeed, the address to which Miriam's packet is to be delivered seems to condense "Barberini" into "Barbaro," with the added connotation of "barbarian," and then combine both with the fabled history of Francesco Cenci's sexual violation of his daughter and her vengeful parricide. Nathalia Wright's speculation that Hawthorne based Miriam on Henriette Deluzy-Desportes, the French governess implicated in 1847 in an affair with her employer, the Duc de Choiseul-Praslin, who "murdered his wife and a week later died of arsenic poisoning," only adds to Hawthorne's process of aesthetic mystification whereby "Miriam" condenses his fears of uncontrolled feminine sexuality, Jewish "contamination" of Euroamerican racial "purity," and republican rebellions against established religious and aristocratic rule (IV xlii; Wright 1942, 5–14). By linking these modern threats with the ruthless rule of the aristocracy in the Italian Renaissance, Hawthorne not only enhances the aura of Italian "ruin" but warns his readers of the dangers of this historical repetition-compulsion, whereby both women's rights and republican revolution will follow a venerable will-to-power and cycle of revenge. Recalling conservative responses to the French Revolution like Edmund Burke's and his own in "The Custom-House," Hawthorne warns the reader of *The Marble Faun* about certain universal human inclinations to dominate others through force and the consequences of social anarchy. As Larry Reynolds has pointed out, Hawthorne shared the anxieties of many of his compatriots regarding the anti-monarchical, republican, sometimes socialist-inspired revolutions transforming Europe after 1848, and such concerns were frequently entangled with irrational fears of the international calls for women's rights, such as those expressed at the Women's Rights Convention held at Seneca Falls, New York in 1848 (Larry Reynolds 1988, 55).

What, then, are we to conclude is the allegorical significance of Kenyon's and Hilda's engagement and return to America at the end of the romance? At the most literal level, Hawthorne's happy ending cathartically purges his fears of modern cosmopolitanism and yet sublimates what he finds so charming in Italy in two American artists, who are also models for good citizenship, not unlike the figure of the author who emerges from "The Custom-House." Miriam paints only herself and her sexual violence in the different Scriptural women she chooses for her subjects: Judith, Salomé, and Sisera. Even when she invites Donatello to pose for her, she paints herself, transmitting her threatening sexuality to him and rendering both monstrously transgendered (Rowe 2002, 98). Miriam relies on an aesthetic of unsublimated expression, a naive "realism" that takes for its subject the darkest impulses of the unconscious and thus of the anarchic drives of sex and murder. In these respects, she typifies the limitations Hawthorne found in women artists. As Lora Romero writes: "Even when Hawthorne spoke well of his female competitors, he referred to their work as though it were an unmediated transcription of their private lives" (Romero 1997, 103).

In contrast, Kenyon and Hilda develop an aesthetic of sublimation that locates and controls such dangerous powers of the unconscious in mediated works of art. Hilda's decision to become a copyist of the old masters, rather than an original painter, prepares the reader for her eventual marriage to Kenyon. Hilda's "copies were indeed marvellous," because they express "that evanescent and ethereal life—that flitting fragrance, as it were, of the originals—which it is as difficult to catch and retain as it would be for a sculptor to get the very movement and varying colour of a living man into his marble bust" (IV 58). This passage clearly links Hilda's "genius" for copying *male* artists' paintings—"Guido, Domenichino, Raphael" are Hawthorne's examples (58)—with Kenyon's sculptural vocation long before they have developed a romantic relationship. Hawthorne's sexual politics in regard to Hilda are typical of other conservative, male transcendentalists, such as Emerson in "Woman" (1855): "When women engage in any art or trade, it is usually as a resource, not as a primary object" (Rowe 2003, 246). Becoming in effect Kenyon's aesthetic "resource," then, she will help him as once she played "the handmaid of Raphael, whom she loved with a virgin's love"; both roles Hawthorne judges far worthier than her own art, "the counterpart, in picture, of so many feminine achievements in literature!" (IV 61).

Responding more diplomatically to American women sculptors in Rome than he did in 1855 in his unguarded complaint against the "d[amne]d mob of scribbling women," who had "occupied" the "public taste . . . with their trash," Hawthorne nonetheless judges both groups of women artists to pose a serious threat to his own artistic authority (Ticknor 1913, 141). Racializing Miriam—insofar as Hawthorne, like other nineteenth-century writers, treats Judaism as a "race" rather than a religion, he also renders her decidedly transnational and cosmopolitan, just as he returns Kenyon and Hilda to their native America. What they import through the literary custom-house of *The Marble Faun* is not only what Romero terms the patriarchal "protocols of gender and sexuality" Hawthorne considers crucial to a well-organized nation, but they bring along Kenyon's aesthetic genius, ready to be adapted to the expansionist agenda of the young republic (Romero 1997, 105).

In chapter 13, "A Sculptor's Studio," Hawthorne dismisses as bad art the adaptation of the neoclassical style for the purpose of ennobling American politicians, as Horatio Greenough famously sculpted George Washington in classical pose and garb (IV 118). For Hawthorne, great sculpture expresses the "genius" of its subject, as he claims Kenyon's bust of Milton spiritualizes the marble by virtue of Kenyon's study of "all known representations of the poet," including his "long perusal and deep love" of Milton's writings (118). Kenyon's own genius and study culminate in his *Cleopatra,* which Hawthorne modeled after William Wetmore Story's *Cleopatra* (1858), and which Miriam declares "'a great work,'" in which Kenyon has succeeded in combining "all those seemingly discordant elements" to represent "the womanhood" of his subject (IV 127). Capitalizing on Story's emphasis on the African features of his *Cleopatra,* Hawthorne stresses the foreignness of the sculpture in Kenyon's studio:

> The face was a miraculous success. The sculptor had not shunned to give the full Nubian lips, and other characteristics of the Egyptian physiognomy. His courage and integrity had been abundantly rewarded; for Cleopatra's beauty shone out richer, warmer, more triumphantly, beyond comparison, than if, shrinking timidly from the truth, he had chosen the tame Grecian type. The expression was of profound, gloomy, heavily revolving thought; a glance into

her past life and present emergencies, while her spirit gathered itself up for some new struggle, or was getting sternly reconciled to impending doom. (IV 126–27)

In Hawthorne's description, Cleopatra resembles Hester in *The Scarlet Letter*, both in Hester's "impressiveness belonging to a marked brow and deep black eyes" (I 53) and the speculative and meditative qualities Hawthorne claims might have made her "the foundress of a religious sect" or "a prophetess" (I 165).

Whatever "Oriental" qualities Hawthorne attributes to Hester, however, she is never African. Hester displaces and condenses religious radicalism from Anne Hutchinson to Jonathan Edwards in the manner of what Bercovitch terms "an intermediary prophetess . . . a *figura medietatis*," who will redeem the flawed Puritan legacy in a renewed democratic nationalism (Bercovitch 1975, 177). Kenyon's *Cleopatra* incorporates feminist and abolitionist political activism in a similarly liberal and aesthetic gesture, mediating thereby U.S. nationalism on the eve of the Civil War with the transnational legacies of the European revolutions of 1848 and of the fight against slavery. In *The Marble Faun*, *Cleopatra* expresses Kenyon's genius; in William Wetmore Story's studio in Rome, *Cleopatra* represents to Hawthorne "a terribly dangerous woman, quiet enough for the moment, but very likely to spring upon you like a tigress" (XIV 177). What better media to keep women "quiet" than marble and romance?

Just as Hawthorne imaginatively embodies his own authorial powers in Hester Prynne, so Kenyon embodies his imagination in his *Cleopatra*. Miriam recognizes the genius of Kenyon's work, but she mistakes it as an expression of womanhood: "'What a woman is this!'" Kenyon corrects her: "'I kindled a great fire within my mind, and threw in the material—as Aaron threw the gold of the Israelites into the furnace—and, in the midmost heat, up rose Cleopatra, as you see her'" (IV 127). In the witty dialogue of this chapter, Kenyon mocks himself by comparing himself with Moses' brother, Aaron, who forged the gold of the Israelites into the false image of the Golden Calf they worshiped until Moses returned with the true scripture of the Ten Commandments (Exodus 32), but Kenyon also suggests that what the great artist produces is an icon of the divine—not of earthly feminine or masculine celebrity. Kenyon also uses an Old Testament story to remind Miriam he is conversant with her Jewish origins. *Cleopatra* thus refers neither to the historical Cleopatra nor to the contemporary struggles of nineteenth-century women for equality nor to the fight for the abolition of slavery—all interpretations Story's *Cleopatra* would attract at the time of its first exhibition in London in 1862—but to the creative genius of the artist, that "liberating god" Emerson celebrated in "The Poet" (1844) (Rowe 2003, 201). Henry James could only admire Kenyon's "admirable answer" to Miriam as "the artist's only possible account of the origin of any work" (James 1903, 2: 86).

Sacvan Bercovitch interprets Hester Prynne as one of several characters in Hawthorne's fiction who offers revolution only to "overcome such 'vain imaginings'" by incorporating them into a "vision of continuity" (Bercovitch 1991, 80). Bercovitch compares Hester's contribution to U.S. ideology with those allegorical feminine figures of national identity—Freedom, Liberty, Columbia, America—who increasingly organized the public space of nineteenth-century America. Bercovitch refers specifically to "the statue of 'Liberty' sculpted by Hiram Powers" begun "in Florence in 1848" and entitled on its completion *America,* which Hawthorne admired in Powers's studio and "urged Franklin Pierce to purchase . . . for the U.S. Capitol" (80). Hawthorne's admiration for this statue of "a female figure, youthful, vigorous, beautiful, planting its foot lightly on a broken chain, and pointing upward," wavers between his admiration for Powers's departure from the sculptural conventions of "the cold allegoric sisterhood" and Hawthorne's concern about making "a genuine woman out of an allegory" (XIV 436). If the feminine form in sculpture is not allegorical and especially when there is some nudity (*America* is "nude to the middle"), then Hawthorne complains, "Who is to wed this lovely virgin? who is to clasp and enjoy that beautiful form?—and are not satisfied to banish her into the realm of chilly thought" (436). Often dressed, decorated, or surrounded with signs of North American Indian, African, and European cultures together with the instruments of scientific progress, such allegorical women herald U.S. imperial expansion and global domination (Fryd 1992, 10–23). Hawthorne reminds us that our very ability to interpret these feminine allegories as representing neither womanhood nor the colonized cultures whose signs they bear but as "America" depended on the complex ideological work of our literary authors. If the sculpted versions are either too "cold" or too sexually graphic, then the literary allegories might succeed better in giving life to national ideals and controlling political and sexual threats from domestic and foreign sources. However distant the historical continuity between Hester's seventeenth-century Bay Colony and Hawthorne's nineteenth-century Massachusetts, they share common soil; revising the pre-national, colonial, Puritan past to suit the national, capitalist present was a difficult but by no means unreasonable literary task. Taming the threats of Europe's mid-century, nationalist revolutions and the international claims of women's rights and turning their related social problems into the aesthetic concerns and allegorical figures of an American romance was indeed a miraculous transformation. As obscure, fantastic, and mysterious as *The Marble Faun* remains, this American romance makes its own contribution to the transnational ambitions of U.S. ideology at the beginning of the Civil War and prophetically anticipates how U.S. cultural work today incorporates the histories and cultures of other peoples for its own glory and their control.

6

Revisiting Hawthorne's Feminism

Nina Baym

I n this essay I swim against the tide to argue—again—for Hawthorne as a feminist writer from *The Scarlet Letter* onward. I argued this in essays published throughout the 1970s and 1980s, as well as in *The Shape of Hawthorne's Career* (1976). My readings have been contested, debated, revised, extended; the idea of Hawthorne as a feminist has been overwhelmingly rejected. In what follows I'll describe my original positions, summarize the important critical challenges to them, and finally—in view of these challenges—propose the idea of a feminist Hawthorne anew.

The Shape of Hawthorne's Career pointed to a significant change in Hawthorne's thematic emphasis around the time of *Mosses from an Old Manse* (1846). He began publishing as a neoclassicist strongly critical of non-conforming individualism, became increasingly Romantic during the 1840s, and emerged with *The Scarlet Letter* into full daylight as a partisan of his outcast heroine, Hester Prynne. The character type faulted by the neoclassicist, however, did not now earn the approval of the Romanticist. That Hester was a woman made all the difference. With one exception (Catherine in "The Gentle Boy,") the denigrated Romantic characters had been men. The later, admired Romantic characters were women.

Guided by my perception of this important distinction, I made several claims about Hawthorne and women characters, about Hawthorne and the feminine (defining the feminine as an assemblage of traits associated with persons socially identified as women), and about Hawthorne and feminism.

I proposed that as the fiction increasingly centered on sympathetic women characters struggling against a murderous male authority, Hawthorne frequently contrasted such characters to an alternative female type. This structure deployed the traditional literary contrast between "dark" and "fair" ladies. I called the dark lady a "real" woman and the fair lady a "social myth" invented by patriarchal culture to discipline "real" women; I proposed that real women embodied creative force while fair women, if favored by men, destroyed not only the women they had bested but also the men who chose them. I also suggested that Hawthorne linked artistic creativity, including his own, with traits that might be fairly called "feminine" because they were represented by these sympathetic, embattled "real" women as natural expressions of their womanhood. I further proposed in two essays—"Hawthorne's Women" (1971) and "Thwarted Nature" (1982)—that, because Hawthorne represented women simultaneously as embodiments of misogynistic male fantasies about women and as "real" women struggling against these fantasies, it was appropriate to call him a feminist.

I excepted Hawthorne from feminist arguments that the canonized authors were patriarchal sexists, even though it was he who infamously referred to literary women as a "d——d mob of scribbling women." No true patriarch, I thought, could have invented Hester. In proposing Hester as the novel's protagonist—initially in "Passion and Authority" (1970)—I was not offering a new reading but reviving an approach that had languished under Perry Miller's powerful influence. The "Miller" line understood Hawthorne to be writing about Puritan theology from a perspective close to the Puritans themselves, and criticizing his own culture for foolish optimism about human nature. This approach assumed that Arthur Dimmesdale was *The Scarlet Letter*'s protagonist. If *The Scarlet Letter* retold Genesis, Hester was the temptress Eve; if it retold Puritan history, she was Anne Hutchinson. Yes, Hawthorne began *The Scarlet Letter* with reference to "the sainted Anne Hutchinson"; but that was irony, as recourse to his early, uncollected "Mrs. Hutchinson" (1830) made clear. No matter that twenty years had elapsed between the works; Hester was no more than a sexual and doctrinal temptress whose scheming led poor Arthur Dimmesdale, the novel's beset hero, astray.

Having interpreted the novel as a story about Hester (an interpretation which, no matter how my feminist angle has been rejected, is now standard in discussions of the novel), I then reread "The Custom-House" as an autobiographical allegory about a blocked artist breaking out by identifying himself with an imaginary, stigmatized woman ("The Romantic Malgré Lui," 1973). When "Hawthorne" wanders into the upper floor of the Custom-House, finds the letter, puts it on his chest, and feels it burn, he is saying in several senses, "this is my character." He associates the creative flood that sweeps him out of the Custom-House backwater with the life force inhering in this admirable woman. For, as the novel unfolds, the letter, intended by the Authorities to signify harsh but just condemnation, is made by Hester to signify something entirely different—able, admirable. From this perspective, I thought at the time, the novel's feminism was self-evident.

I interpreted Dimmesdale as Hester's foil—weak, orthodox, conventional—and as her temptation rather than she his. As an actor in his own story, Dimmesdale, like so many other Hawthorne male characters, rejects the woman at his own cost as well as hers. In *The Scarlet Letter,* oppression or rejection of women, rather than surrender to them, led to male downfall. This motif, incipient in earlier stories like "Young Goodman Brown" (1835) and "The Minister's Black Veil" (1836), became dominant in the 1840s; this change gave Hawthorne's career its "shape."

How to explain this development? Between 1841 and 1846 Hawthorne encountered the Transcendentalists via his eight-month sojourn at Brook Farm and several years in Concord. He came into close contact with Romantic ideas as they were vividly articulated by living people. The iconoclastic idealists who became his friends—Thoreau, Fuller, Emerson—had an intellectual vigor and courage he could not help but admire. These provocations coincided with his marriage. They also coincided with his recognition that New England literary culture was itself moving in a more liberal direction.

Then, in 1849, having returned to Salem three years earlier to work in a dull job secured through political patronage, he suffered two bereavements. He lost this boring yet remunerative occupation when his party lost the elections, and his mother died. According to Sophia, Hawthorne's wife, and also according to Hawthorne's courtship letters, his mother was reclusive and remote. Julian Hawthorne's biography of his parents affirmed the characterization; but Hawthorne's journals, along with his letters to his mother and sisters, testify to her strong and much-loved presence. Her loss was shattering. In "Hawthorne and his Mother" (1982), I proposed that this death, in complex ways, might have motivated *The Scarlet Letter.* I imagined Hester as a version of the mother, and the novel as allying with her—she who had always supported his literary ambitions—rather than with the stultifying, untrustworthy authority of Uncle Sam's Custom-House.

Challenges to these readings have countered that Hawthorne's use of the feminine was always in the service of masculinity issues, that he viewed assertive or aggressive or rebellious women as threats to masculinity; that his inevitable punishing or containing of truant women demonstrated deep hostility to them and a profoundly conservative view of their proper place; that this penalizing reflected discomfort over the ongoing feminization of the literary profession; that women characters are tools of the state, upholding or instilling conservative, bourgeois values, "naturalizing" the capitalist agenda by a politics of domesticity. These points recur and overlap throughout six critical approaches, of which I now offer representative examples: Puritan/traditionalist, masculinity, gay/queer, feminist, political, and biographical studies.

Puritan/traditionalist criticism, masculinity studies, and gay/queer studies converge in Hawthorne studies by agreeing that men are central and women ancillary in his writings. Traditionalist studies of Hawthorne took the male center for granted; Baym (as I will now call myself) questioned this. Traditional critics now started insisting that, yes, Hawthorne's main characters were, indeed, male. Michael Colacurcio's "Woman's Own Choice" reads *The Scarlet Letter* as Dimmesdale's overcoming Hester's literalist temptation. Saying that "the fiercely logical structure of *The Scarlet Letter* points to Dimmesdale as the indubitable center of literary organization" (Calacurcio 1985, 119), that "structural analysis . . . must always privilege Dimmesdale" (133), Colacurcio thinks Hester's choice of "a human lover" rather than "the figure of salvation in covenant" (Dimmesdale's choice) demonstrates her female incapacity for abstract thought. When her moment to choose comes, "she passionately chooses the literal. To which she almost converts even Dimmesdale" (124). Dimmesdale, however, demonstrates his manhood and admirable orthodoxy by rejecting her temptation.

Masculinity studies and gay/queer studies also focus on men. Masculinity critics identify "feminine" tendencies in the self or the culture, and consider how masculinity is defined as their opposite. Some critics in this mode—e.g., Leland F. Person, who writes that Coverdale, Kenyon, and Dimmesdale briefly "enjoy creative relationships with women before repressing the self-creative impulse within themselves which the woman evokes" (1988, 115)—take the Baym-like position that men need the feminine; others, like T. Walter Herbert (*Dearest Beloved*) and David Leverenz, argue that rejecting women is (unfortunately) necessary for men dedicated to Jacksonian masculinity. Leverenz writes: "story after story presents conventional manliness as aggressive, insensitive, and murderously dominant" (Leverenz 1989, 231); "as male rivalry takes center stage, the narrators disengage from their heroines. . . . They put up a fog of ambiguities, ironies, self-consciousness, and multiple points of view to screen their covert participation in the men's struggle for narcissistic self-empowering" (246–47).

Some critics propose that the biographical Hawthorne is uncomfortable about operating in an increasingly feminine profession (the opposite of Baym's point that a good male artist has to accept the inner feminine). Millicent Bell observes that "his authorial mode was that of the feminized male author who knows he has entered a female world in becoming a writer rather than a businessman or politician" (Bell 1993, 15). Kenneth Egan proposes that Hawthorne made Hester an adulteress specifically to express the author's sense that to be a male writer in his culture "was necessarily to be an adulteress or feminized adulterer of the truth" (Egan 1995, 41). James D. Wallace (1990) says that Hawthorne's hostile reaction to women writers originates in his uneasy identification with them. Herbert brings the lessons of *The Scarlet Letter* home to men: "Men whose manhood compels them to hate what they conceive as the womanhood in them lead psychic lives that are characterized by a continuous internal assault that is gendered male-on-female. . . . [Men] may find inspiration in Hester, as we seek to rework the manhood that dooms us to pornographic enchantments and cripples our capacity for intimacy with real women" (Herbert 2001, 116, 119).

Gay/queer criticism is male-centered by definition. Homosocial and homoerotic moments are excavated and attributed either to Hawthorne's own suppressed sexual inclinations or to the sublimated, affect-laden idealizations of male-male relationships in antebellum culture. Robert K. Martin points to "the dynamics of male relationship" in *The Scarlet Letter* and *The Blithedale Romance*—noting, for example, the "extraordinarily erotic moment" when Chillingworth half-undresses the sleeping Dimmesdale, and claiming that Coverdale's disquisitions on polymorphous sexuality at Blithedale register his attraction to Hollingsworth (Martin 1990, 132). Lauren Berlant also finds Coverdale's attraction to Hollingsworth central in *The Blithedale Romance* (Berlant 1989). Scott S. Derrick (1995) identifies the erotic connection between Dimmesdale and Chillingworth as the affective center of *The Scarlet Letter;* Leverenz writes, "the cuckold and the lover rise together to an all-male paradise, while Hester mutely returns to Boston" (Leverenz 1989, 275). Karen L. Kilcup (1996) argues that the relationship of author to reader in Hawthorne's work is erotically charged and—supposing that Hawthorne imagines his reader as male—specifically homoerotic.

Although academic feminism is rife with internal dissention, most self-identified feminists writing about Hawthorne agree in rejecting Baym's readings. Stressing the way Hawthorne inevitably punishes and/or silences unconventional women, they find his plots antifeminist, reinforcing a culturally conservative agenda, and a testimony to authorial misogyny. A preponderance of feminist criticism thinks Hawthorne felt threatened by emergent feminism, female activism, female sexuality, and women writers—in fact, by any sign of women's desire to improve their lot or determine their own lives. For this group, Hawthorne's narratorial hand-wringing over the intractability of social institutions and the misery of women is a sentimental sham.

The first scholar to make this argument was probably Judith Fetterley, who sees "The Birth-mark" as illustration of "the great American dream of eliminating women" (Fetterley 1978, 24). Louise Desalvo concedes that Hawthorne "portrayed, with superb accuracy, the condition of women in the nineteenth century and the psychological processes of men who could not tolerate the notion of female equality," but decides that because "he shared the misogynistic view of his age, he could not condemn what he saw and drew back from defining the implications, for society, of what he so astutely observed about the reality of women's lives" (Desalvo 1987, 121–22). Barbara Bardes and Suzanne Gossett use *The Blithedale Romance* and *The Scarlet Letter* to observe that while Hawthorne's novels reveal "distrust of almost anyone with the power of speech," he was especially wary of "women with 'tongues'" because he connected women's public speech with sexual exposure and expression" (Bardes and Gossett 1990, 59). Joyce W. Warren finds him especially severe on strong women, who "are never allowed to pursue what might seem to be the implications of their characters; they do not become heroic leaders or independent public figures. . . . This hesitation is owing in part to Hawthorne's belief in a conventional image of feminine behavior" (Warren 1984, 189). Jean Yellin thinks *The Scarlet Letter* "seriously considers the new feminist definitions of womanhood and, rejecting them, replicates traditional imagery and endorses patriarchal notions" (Yellin 1989, 126). Amy Schrager Lang complains about Hester's unfeminist subsidence into a "vague politics of patience and inaction" (Lang 1987, 191).

More recently, Jamie Barlowe's "Rereading Women" (1997) and follow-up *Scarlet Mob* (2000) coins the term "Hester Prynnism" to denote anti-feminist silencing and ignoring of women's voices, of which the first and most egregious practitioner was Hawthorne himself. Barlowe idealizes the Hester of Roland Joffé's 1995 film; she sees Joffé's plot—in which Hester spends a lot of time naked, Dimmesdale professes undying love, and the couple (with Pearl recently born rather than seven years old) successfully run off together—as a feminist way to tell Hester's story. Although the idea of an entirely different Hester in an entirely different narrative (along with an entirely different Dimmesdale) may seem bizarre, and although not every feminist will share Barlowe's idea of feminism, most feminist criticism does fantasize a different ending to Hester's story. Sandra Tomc, invoking Hawthorne's "notoriously conservative ideas about women [and] feminism," agrees that Hawthorne "repudiates both his heroine and the genre [of seduction novel] that inspired her" (Tomc 2002, 469, 472). Todd Onderdonk imputes an obsession with sexual purity to Hawthorne deriving from the author's conviction that women have only one "necessary function—motherhood" (Onderdonk 2003, 97).

Political, new-historical, and ideological critics perceive Hawthorne's women as servants of bourgeois capitalism. Gendered spheres, here, are key to the consolidation of middle-class, capitalist culture in Hawthorne's era; women were pressed into bourgeois service by persuading them that their natural abilities suit them for the domestic sphere, where they are cherished and protected. And Hawthorne went along with this project, which relies heavily on what such critics consider sentimental hocus-pocus. Michael Davitt Bell calls sentimentalism "a medium of psychological repression and social control" that, in his view, the conservative Hawthorne deployed against women's rights and other movements for social change (Bell 1980, 191). Gillian Brown argues that a female domestic subculture "based on self-denial and collectivity—the ethos of sympathy customarily and disparagingly called sentimentalism" (Brown 1990, 6)—has not produced "an antithetical model of selfhood" but only further domesticated "an already domesticated selfhood. . . . Far from an account of the female subject, domesticity signifies a feminization of selfhood in service to an individualism most available to (white) men" (7). The novel most suited to this approach is *The House of the Seven Gables;* but other novels also figure. Lori Merish, for example, reads *The Blithedale Romance* as an exposure of "the extent to which the bourgeois ideology of romantic love and consensual familial ties produces new species of patriarchal power, reconfiguring, rather than undermining, women's construction as property" (Merish 2000, 172). Ellen Weinauer says that, "Despite his effort to situate himself in an alternative and indeed antipatriarchal history, *The Scarlet Letter* taken as a whole suggests that . . . Hawthorne needs the possessed female body" (Weinauer 2001, 107).

Psychologizing this political class-and-gender analysis, Joel Pfister thinks Hawthorne's plots about "the feminization of women" (Pfister 1991, 8) reflect and contribute to a middle-class discourse of sexuality. Still, Pfister says that Hawthorne recognizes the artificiality of this discourse: he is "product, agent, and critic of an emerging middle-class interiority, and is aware that his participation in reproducing the forms of subjectivity of his class is political" (183). Herbert (*Dearest Beloved*) interweaves Hawthorne's fiction with family letters to show how internalized social ideas of true woman and manly man are experienced as authentic. He develops a poignant portrait of a Sophia who has violently disciplined herself to become the woman Nathaniel required as the condition of his adoration. And he shows a Nathaniel imprisoned in turn by the surveillance of the monstrous woman he created. According to Herbert, this paradigm implicates the entire culture; the Hawthornes "vividly exemplified the domestic ideal of family relations that became dominant in the early nineteenth century" (Herbert 1993, xvi). For Herbert, Hawthorne is both participant in and critic of the represented scene, seeking to "contain his material within the rhetoric of the domestic ideal, even as he lays open the dilemmas intrinsic to that ideal" (199).

Three important ideological readings make Hester into a problem or opportunity for the state. Sacvan Bercovitch reads Hester's return to Boston and resumption of the letter as the novel's most important event. In a "woman's own choice" quite unlike Colacurcio's, Hester elects "to become the agent of her own domestication" (Bercovitch 1991, 11); "in the most carefully prepared-for reversal in classic American literature, Hester herself imposes the symbol" (92). Her choice, Bercovitch says, illustrates the workings of liberal capitalism, a political form "designed to make subjectivity the primary agency of change while keeping the subject under control," a double function accomplished "by representing interpretation as multiplicity flowing naturally into consensus" (23–24). Where Bercovitch finds Hester a type of the citizen in her free acceptance of social control, Berlant describes her citizen type less forgivingly as a "mutual articulation of woman, privacy, and political submission" (Berlant 1991, 106) and proposes that 'woman' is a "manifest public problem of law and order" that is solved by containment (ibid., 108). Brook Thomas (2001) likens Hester's final community of women to Habermas's public sphere, a zone of independent activity that guarantees the state's democratic functioning. Curiously, of these three readings only Berlant makes a point of Hester's gender, and even she perceives "the male body" (Dimmesdale's male body) as "the major stress point in the social order" (Berlant 1991, 115).

All lines of criticism fret over Hawthorne's self-awareness. Even Bercovitch, in a troubled and troubling footnote, remarks that Hawthorne, not liberal culture, ultimately "compels Hester to resume the A"; this "sense of compulsion . . . adds a discordant note to Hawthorne's orchestration of pluralist points of view" (Bercovitch 1991, 157). For if Hawthorne knew about the woman-centered reform initiatives in antebellum culture, if he knew well some of the women actively involved in such efforts, if he knew that the literary market he sought to enter and dominate was filled with women authors, then it becomes likely that his strategies of plot containment represent his own intentions rather unthinkingly reproducing social platitudes. Hawthorne was well acquainted with, even close to, many women who lived undomestic lives but who neither killed themselves nor kept silent. He knew women scholars, writers, artists, and activists: among others, Elizabeth Peabody; Mary Peabody Mann; Sarah Josepha Hale; Grace Greenwood; and, perhaps above all, Margaret Fuller. Thomas R. Mitchell (1998) has written compellingly about traces of Fuller in Hawthorne's writing; he sees her in Hester, Zenobia, and Miriam. He finds sentences in *The Scarlet Letter* appropriating "The Great Lawsuit" almost verbatim. It would seem to follow that if he created powerful women only to silence them, Hawthorne did so as a way of rejecting the signs of the times that he saw all around him.

To suggest a feminist Hawthorne in the face of all this criticism is foolhardy. Nevertheless, I will give it a try. I grant at the outset—a point that criticism usually ignores, perhaps because it's so obvious—that while Hawthorne featured an occasional woman character who was not a New Englander (Miriam in *The Marble Faun*, Beatrice in "Rappaccini's Daughter"), his work rarely ventured beyond white American women of New England background, presumably heterosexual, and of English descent. Hawthorne knew his own limits in this regard very well; when he wrote "women this" and "men that," he asked to be understood as an interpreter of mainstream New England life and character, not the universe. I grant, too, that if a feminist position must be manifested by plots wherein women live happily ever after on their own terms, Hawthorne fails. Happy endings on such terms are impossible in his novels—men are not what women imagine. One might argue that, given the kind of man Dimmesdale is, *The Scarlet Letter* is far more feminist for refusing the bogus finale of a happy escape than had it allowed the two (three, actually) to make their getaway. The mismatch between women's illusions and the realities of male character is a leading motif in the later romances.

Hawthorne's observation that smart women often make foolish choices is not erroneous; the problem is still with us. There are, of course, other imaginable endings than a happy marriage; much feminist writing today exists to show how women might get along without men (or, more strategically, to show what social reforms are necessary so that women can actually get along without men). In which case, since Hawthorne's work exactly fits this description, his feminism should be obvious. Smart, independent women like Hester, Zenobia, and Miriam are his heroines in *The Scarlet Letter, The Blithedale Romance,* and *The Marble Faun.* But even the more conventional women—Phoebe, Priscilla, and Hilda, not to mention the amazing Hepzibah, who deserves much more careful appraisal than I have space for here—are women used to living alone and fending for themselves.

They can and do get along without men, but they would prefer not to. No question but that this author is preoccupied with the heterosexual couple and the obstacles that make of a supposedly fulfilling social form something so fraught with misery. Why this is so, and what to do about it, are questions his plots repeatedly ask. But if his plots do not—cannot—lead to happy outcomes in a conventional romantic sense, neither do they end in utter social futility. They offer limited, incremental change, although often at a great cost to the agent of such change.

By the time he wrote *The Scarlet Letter,* Hawthorne had become aware of and deeply involved in ideas about women's grievances as they were expressed by articulate women he knew, especially Margaret Fuller. He understood that, since he had chosen to write fiction, many if not most of his readers would be women; he anticipated their thoughtful familiarity with these ideas. Virtually alone among male authors of his generation, he made space for feminist analysis in his fiction. Hester is made to introduce feminist ideas at least twice in *The Scarlet Letter:* once in chapter 13, where, brooding over the situation of woman, she wonders whether existence was "worth accepting, even to the happiest among them" (I 165), and again in chapter 24, where she tells sorrowful women about her hope for a new truth that would "establish the whole relation between man and woman on a surer ground of mutual happiness" (I 263).

The subject runs constantly through *The Blithedale Romance,* especially in chapter 14, where Zenobia insists that "when my sex shall achieve its rights, there will be ten eloquent women, where there is now one eloquent man" and goes on to say that "thus far, no woman in the world has ever once spoken out her whole heart and her whole mind! The mistrust and disapproval of the vast bulk of society throttles us, as with two gigantic hands at our throats!" (III 120). True, Coverdale attributes "the animosity with which she now took up the general quarrel of women against men" to "Zenobia's inward trouble"—but this is at least to concede that such a quarrel exists. When Coverdale adds that he personally would be happy to give woman "all she asks, and add a great deal more, which she will not be the party to demand, but men, if they were generous and wise, would grant of their own free motion" (III 121), he is saying men are neither generous nor wise. Hollingsworth's behavior (and his own) bear this out.

Feminist ideas typical of Hawthorne's era also circulate through *The Marble Faun*, as in chapter 13, when Miriam tells Kenyon that men wrongly believe

> Nature has made women especially prone to throw their whole being into what is technically called Love. We have, to say the least, no more necessity for it than yourselves—only, we have nothing else to do with our hearts. . . . I can think of many women, distinguished in art, literature, and science—and multitudes whose hearts and minds find good employment in less ostentatious ways—who lead high, lonely lives, and are conscious of no sacrifice, so far as your sex is concerned. (IV 121)

Miriam's reference to distinguished professional women, which Kenyon does not contest, alludes to a situation that few male authors of Hawthorne's day recognized in print.

Certainly, Hawthorne's novels point to errors that reform-minded women typically make—mainly through lack of self-understanding and unwitting complicity in the conditions they deplore. But unless a feminist perspective requires asserting that women are perfect, his observations might be seen as attempts to intervene on the feminist side. That feminist ideas are uttered by flawed women, that activist women generalize from their own situations, does not invalidate the ideas. The imperfect women who utter feminist sentiments are treated sympathetically and admiringly. They have enormous courage and considerable intellect. Even when defeated, they make things happen. Bercovitch presumes that the liberal polity absorbs Hester's dissent; but I think her resumption of the letter permanently changes her public world. Hawthorne writes: "The scarlet letter ceased to be a stigma which attracted the world's scorn and bitterness, and became a type of something to be sorrowed over, and looked upon with awe, yet with reverence too" (I 263).

Had Hester never returned, she would have been forgotten. Had she returned and not worn the letter, she would have escaped the letter's meaning without changing it. Returning and wearing the letter when "not the sternest magistrate of that iron period would have imposed it" alters the way the letter is perceived, changes its definition. People look on the letter "with reverence." Hester preaches a model of change involving sudden revelation from a sinless apostle of joy, but she practices a model of slow change brought about by persons visibly scarred by battles fought and ignominy endured. This is not entirely a sentimental outcome, resulting from pity ("sorrowed over"); it is also the outcome of reverence, of awe. Re-entering civil life adorned with the letter by her own choice, Hester moves Puritan Boston from the Dark Ages toward enlightened modernity. Now, a century and a half after *The Scarlet Letter,* popular references to a scarlet letter invariably imply unjust stigmatization. In the wider world, this novel has performed that cultural work.

One concedes that Hester and Hawthorne understand women's plight in reference to intimacy with men. This was the overwhelming focus of feminist reformers of his day, the overwhelming subject of the novel (his chosen genre), and is (after all) the overwhelming concern of feminist reformers now. The underlying sources of the difficulty in thinking of a feminist Hawthorne, as I see it now, are his beliefs in such a thing as human nature and, worse still, in essential differences between human nature in the two sexes. The key point is that, for Hawthorne, the age-old, relentless history of male exploitation of women could only be explained as the outgrowth of essential characteristics of human selves.

If the two sexes are essentially different, as I now think Hawthorne thinks they are, then the social change sought by feminism would seem impossible to achieve. But, oddly, Hawthorne's work does not offer these essentialist beliefs as conservative excuses to keep women down. On the contrary, it struggles to plot a way in which, given these "facts" about the human, women may be raised up. His novels are replete with objections against social arrangements that tell so heavily and unjustly against women. I used to think that Hawthorne presented romantic love as a social myth invented to ensnare women, because woman after woman in his texts suffers from what might be called "a broken heart." Passages in the novels seem to support this idea of love as a social myth; for example, Coverdale, at the end of *The Blithedale Romance,* laments that,

> It is nonsense, and a miserable wrong—the result, like so many others, of masculine egotism—that the success or failure of woman's existence should be made to depend wholly on the affections, and on one species of affection; while man has such a multitude of other chances, that this seems but an incident. For its own sake, if it will do no more, the world should throw open all its avenues to the passport of a woman's bleeding heart. (III 241).

But now I notice that this social asymmetry stems from "masculine egotism," not a constructed condition but a fact about men, and see that these sentences argue explicitly for social change.

Hawthorne's point, one might say, is not that essentialism makes social change impossible, but that it makes social change impossible unless differences between women and men are taken into account. The slow, uneven pace of social change occupies Hawthorne much in these later works wherein—unlike so much anti-feminist rhetoric of his day, of which

Hollingsworth's tirade in chapter 14 of *The Blithedale Romance* is a splendid example—inequality of physical strength is unimportant. What matters is the internal difference to which Hollingsworth refers when, after threatening violence against female reformers ("petticoated monstrosities," as he calls them), he says that force is unnecessary because "the heart of true woman-hood knows where its own sphere is, and never seeks to stray beyond it" (III 123). That the heart of womanhood knows its sphere, as Hollingsworth would define it, is repeatedly given the lie in Hawthorne's writings; but that women have more heart than men is something he counts on. In women's excess of heart, compared to men—or in men's deficiency of heart, com-pared to women—lies the explanation for an asymmetrical culture.

Male egotism and its associated cold-heartedness had been a Hawthorne obsession from far back in his career: "Wakefield" (1835); implicitly in "Young Goodman Brown" (1835) and "The Minister's Black Veil" (1837), "The Man of Adamant" (1837), and "The Shaker Bridal" (1838); on through the 1840s: "Egotism; or, the Bosom Serpent" (1843), "The Birth-mark" (1843), and "Rappaccini's Daughter" (1844). Still prominent in three of the four later romances (the contrast between Hep-zibah and Clifford introduces it into *Seven Gables* as well)—these traits are now considered entirely in terms of their meaning for women's lives. In *The Blithedale Romance,* Coverdale's speculations about Hollingsworth in chapter 7—"Sad, indeed, but by no means unusual" that he has mistaken his "terrible egotism" for "an angel of God" (III 55)—and in chapter 9: "Men who have surrendered themselves to an over-ruling purpose" are almost never able to "recognize the process, by which godlike benevolence has been debased into all-devouring egotism" (III 70–71)—acquire their significance because of the way this man behaves toward women. In chap-ter 28, as noted above, Hawthorne deplores the masculine egotism that makes women's success wholly dependent on love (III 241). Most memo-rably, in chapter 14, he interprets Hollingsworth's anti-feminist tirade as an

> outrageous affirmation of what struck me as the intensity of masculine ego-tism. It centred everything in itself, and deprived woman of her very soul, her inexpressible and unfathomable all, to make it a mere incident in the great sum of man. Hollingsworth had boldly uttered what he, and millions of despots like him, really felt. Without intending it, he had disclosed the well-spring of all these troubled waters. (III 123)

Masculine self-absorption is the source, but it prevails because women lack a corresponding self-absorption. When, rather than rising to Hollingsworth's challenge, Zenobia mildly counters that, if man were "but manly and godlike," woman would be "only too ready to become to him what you say" (III 124), she demonstrates the other side of the intractable equation. Coverdale, appalled, wonders whether her words express women's "nature" or "the result of ages of compelled degradation" and whether, in either case, it could "be possible ever to redeem them." He does not, however, notice that this meditation has been sparked by his peevish awareness that the women are more attracted to Hollingsworth than to him: "how little did these two women care for me, who had freely conceded all their claims, and a great deal more, out of the fullness of my heart" (III 124). Hawthorne lets readers see that Coverdale's self-labeled feminism is also exploitative of women; he is not exempt from the situation that he analyzes so cannily.

Nor is Zenobia exempt; her capitulation here puts a feminist conundrum squarely before us. If millions of men behave like Hollingsworth and millions of women behave like Zenobia (and their gendered behavior is reproduced more palely in Coverdale and Priscilla), what can be hoped for? The intransigency of the problem, rather than their weakness of intellect, baffles Hawthorne's women characters. The more acute their minds, the more they recognize the conundrum. When the narrator comments on Hester's meditations, he says: "A woman never overcomes these problems by any exercise of thought. They are not to be solved, or only in one way. If her heart chance to come uppermost, they vanish" (I 166). This passage has been read as a misogynistic dismissal of female intellectuality. But it can be read to mean, not that women lack intellect, but that nobody can solve these problems by sheer intellectual force, and that a woman happily in love will likely stop worrying about them. Yes, but how many women are happily in love in Hawthorne's world? Too, if unhappiness makes women into reformers, it does the same with men. As Holgrave says, "The world owes all its onward impulse to men ill at ease. The happy man inevitably confines himself within ancient limits" (III 306–7).

Thus, to say that Hawthorne's women have more heart than his men does not imply that they have less brain. Mind does not unsex a woman; Zenobia is smarter than Hollingsworth, Miriam than Kenyon. Hester leaves Dimmesdale in the dust. True, all that thinking in Hester's case is associated with an apparent loss of beauty, insofar as female beauty means sexual attractiveness to heterosexual men. That Hawthorne might have reconsidered this facile association is inferable from the fact that neither Zenobia nor Miriam are less sexually appealing because of their intellects. With these two later heroines Hawthorne seems to propose that beauty and braininess are different expressions of the same force, a force lacking in the counter-heroines Priscilla and Hilda whose appeal lies in both their physical plainness and intellectual timidity.

But if Hester's thinking makes her less conventionally sexy, it does not make her less loving, and if motherhood is Hawthorne's test for true womanhood, then Hester is a paragon. I read *The Scarlet Letter* as an "anti-seduction" novel. The protagonist does not die; she succeeds as a single mother supporting herself and her child (see Elbert 1990, 199) and, when her child is grown, becomes a valued and valuable member of the community.

In the plot's unfolding, the significant result of Hester's independent thinking is a profoundly womanly decision (in Hawthorne's terms) to "rescue" Dimmesdale by telling him who Chillingworth is. Thus the forest meeting where Dimmesdale's cold heart triumphs over her warm one, his appeal to the great heart of womanhood effectively seducing Hester for a second time.

Herbert, like other critics, says, "Hester has already contrived the plan that she now persuades Arthur to adopt. She wants them to leave the colony" (Herbert 1993, 201). No; she wants *him* to leave the colony. Horrified by Dimmesdale's condition as she sees it in the second scaffold scene, inferring that Chillingworth is somehow to blame, Hester determines first to "meet her former husband"—not her former lover—and "do what might be in her power for the rescue of the victim on whom he had so evidently set his gripe" (I 167). "I must reveal the secret," she tells Chillingworth; "what may be the result, I know not" (I 173). Chillingworth releases her from her oath of secrecy, freeing her to follow her conscience: "Go thy ways, and deal as thou wilt with yonder man" (I 174).

As chapter 16 tells us, Hester's one intention is "to make known to Mr. Dimmesdale, at whatever risk of present pain or ulterior consequences, the true character of the man who had crept into his intimacy" (I 182). Beyond this she has no plan. Their forest meeting makes her, at last, "fully sensible of the deep injury for which she was responsible to this unhappy man" (192). No plan already decided on, even if she had one, could possibly be useful in view of what she sees Dimmesdale to be: "She now read his heart more accurately" (I 193).

Dimmesdale then commandeers the conversation in typical passive-aggressive fashion by pleading for her help: "Be thou strong for me! . . . Advise me what to do" (I 196). Hester answers by counseling him to leave Boston—whether heading west into the forest or east over the ocean—in ringing rhetoric that implies no intention to go with him: "Leave this wreck and ruin here where it hath happened! Meddle no more with it! Begin all anew. . . . The future is yet full of trial and success. There is happiness to be enjoyed! There is good to be done! . . . Up, and away!" (I 198). But then Dimmesdale replies, "There is not the strength or courage left me to venture into the wide, strange, difficult world, alone!" and, as the narrator stresses, repeats the word *alone.* Hester hears his unvoiced plea and responds to it: "Thou shalt not go alone!" (I 198). In this exchange Dimmesdale manipulates Hester—no doubt sincerely—through a senti-mental appeal to (as he put it earlier) the "wondrous strength and gen-erosity of a woman's heart" (I 68). Only a woman's heart can be so worked upon.

Dimmesdale's thoughts in this scene are all for himself, Hester's all for him. He is, after all, a true man as she is a true woman. One might suppose that it was always thus for these two—the woman in love with the man, the man in love with himself. Few seduced women get the chance to express the point with more intensity than Zenobia in her great attack on Hollingsworth: "It is all self! . . . Nothing else but self, self, self! . . . I see it now! I am awake, disenchanted, disenthralled! Self, self, self!" (III 218). Certainly, Hester never approaches this level of feminist rage, even though Dimmesdale's death amounts to yet another disavowal of human love. What Hester achieves through Dimmesdale's death, however, is unique in that it is a loving—that is, womanly—life without a man. It prefigures and registers the eruption of women into the public sphere through various forms of culturally acceptable womanly activity, what historians have come to call "domestic feminism."

Herbert writes that *The Scarlet Letter* "does not work out a solution to the male-on-female sexual abuse that it so pervasively depicts, but in Hes-ter Prynne [Hawthorne] dramatizes the struggle of women to disentangle themselves from this enslavement, and to find lives of independent self-respect, and to define an autonomous sexual selfhood" (Herbert 2001, 119). What Herbert calls male-on-female sexual abuse, Hawthorne would call the inequality of egotism versus love; I see no male character in the whole Hawthorne repertory who "loves" a woman the way a woman loves him. However, that Hester is struggling to find a life of independent self-respect is not so clear, still less that she is trying to define an "autonomous sexual selfhood"; on the contrary, Hawthorne proposes, it is exactly her disregard for self (including, yes, her celibacy) that changes the public mind. Because Hester "had no selfish ends, nor lived in any measure for her own profit and enjoyment," people look up to her (I 263).

This change is not a reversal, but a continuation of what had been hap-pening over the seven years of her earlier sojourn in Boston:

> She was self-ordained a Sister of Mercy; or, we may rather say, the world's heavy hand had so ordained her, when neither the world nor she looked for-ward to this result. The letter was the symbol of her calling. Such helpfulness was found in her—so much power do do, and power to sympathize—that

many people refused to interpret the scarlet A by its original signification. They said that it meant Able; so strong was Hester Prynne, with a woman's strength. (I 161)

Pearl, too, is crucial to understanding Hester as a loving woman in the less heterosexualized sense that Hawthorne represents in *The Scarlet Letter*. Much has been written about Pearl as her mother's disciplinarian, the externalization of her mother's sin, and so on (e.g., Budick 1994, Nudelman 1997). But Pearl is also a human person, somebody for Hester to love, her child. The quiet and outwardly compliant Hester explodes furiously when the governor threatens to take Pearl from her. "Hester caught hold of Pearl, and drew her forcibly into her arms, confronting the old Puritan magistrate with almost a fierce expression. Alone in the world, cast off by it, and with this sole treasure to keep her heart alive, she felt that she possessed indefeasible rights against the world, and was ready to defend them to the death. . . . 'Ye shall not take her! I will die first!'" To Dimmesdale she cries out, "thou knowest what is in my heart, and what are a mother's rights, and how much the stronger they are, when that mother has but her child and the scarlet letter! Look thou to it! I will not lose the child! Look to it!" (I 113).

Leaving the governor's hall, her mother's rights confirmed, Hester declines Mistress Hibbens's invitation to a witches' gathering: "I must tarry at home, and keep watch over my little Pearl. Had they taken her from me, I would willingly have gone with thee into the forest, and signed my name in the Black Man's book too, and that with mine own blood!" (I 117). Had Pearl been taken from her, Hester would have embraced her social identity as a bad woman; Pearl keeps Hester's loving heart—her identity as a good woman—alive. She thinks, the narrator reports: "How strange, indeed! Man had marked this woman's sin by a scarlet letter. . . . God, as a direct consequence of the sin which man thus punished, had given her a lovely child, whose place was on that same dishonored bosom, to connect her parent for ever with the race and descent of mortals, and to be finally a blessed soul in heaven!" (I 89). Not incidentally, that same dishonored bosom is where people in extreme situations come over time to rest: "Hester's nature showed itself warm and rich; a well-spring of human tenderness, unfailing to every real demand, and inexhaustible by the largest. Her breast, with its badge of shame, was but the softer pillow for the head that needed one" (I 162).

Hester's character cannot be explained through allusions to ideology or social expectations. If anything, the course of her life shows that ideology and social expectations should have made her a very different person from the one she is. As a seduced ingénue, she should have died; as an evil temptress, she should have recanted, gone mad, or been murdered by the mob. Instead, she survives as love's incarnation. Yet, or because of this, she does not find happiness with one man. A new model of love between woman and man is needed, a new kind of couple—"sacred love" Hawthorne calls it at the novel's end (I 263). If only a love of this sort can guarantee mutual happiness between men and women, only a love like this could underpin a society of equals that might supersede present-day exploitation. As long as there are two sexes in the world, a just and humane polity must perceive each as equal to the other. But the very difference between the sexes that demands better forms of human intimacy also impedes their realization.

Awareness of the recalcitrant reality of human nature occupies Hester's meditations on reconstructing the social system, which include the tasks—in order—of tearing down society and rebuilding it, altering what in men is either their "very nature or its long hereditary habit, which has become like nature"; and finally producing, somehow, a "still mightier change" in woman herself—a change "in which, perhaps, the ethereal essence, wherein she has her truest life, will be found to have evaporated" (I 165–66). This "ethereal essence" is her capacity of loving. Should that be destroyed, then the social formation of which Hester dreams is an impossibility, because it is grounded in exactly that love, the only counter to male self-love. The "whole new truth," the "coming revelation" of which Hester later speaks (I 263), would then be beyond human reach.

What, then, is to be done? The only possible changes Hawthorne can imagine—and he does imagine them—are palliative and far from romantic. Society can begin to compensate for the trials and consequences of woman's greater heart. Women's lot can be eased; they can be helped rather than punished; their humanity can be affirmed by recognizing their equality with men, their intellects respected, possibilities opened for them other than the domesticity that has failed them. Above all, perhaps, the institution of marriage needs to be freely elected; neither men nor women should be required to marry. *The Scarlet Letter, The Blithedale Romance,* and *The Marble Faun* all make space for emancipated female rhetoric, place transgressing women at the center, insist on women's equality with men, and deny the universal applicability of domestic ideals. But none imagines different men and different women from the ones Hawthorne believes people foundationally are, or opportunistically describes social outcomes that the author thinks cannot possibly come to pass.

7

Hawthorne's Early Tales: Male Authorship, Domestic Violence, and Female Readers

LELAND S. PERSON

> Perceiving the motion of some object behind a thick veil of under-growth, he fired, with the instinct of a hunter and the aim of a prac-ticed marksman. A low moan, which told his success, and by which even animals can express their dying agony, was unheeded by Reuben Bourne. What were the recollections now breaking upon him?
>
> ("Roger Malvin's Burial," X 356)

This essay originated in my puzzling over the narrative break that occurs in "Roger Malvin's Burial" right after the passage quoted above—a gap between the moment that Reuben Bourne fires his gun and the moment we and Dorcas Bourne discover that he has killed their son Cyrus. Hawthorne postpones discovery of Cyrus's body for two lengthy paragraphs not only to create and maintain readerly suspense. The content of the two paragraphs suggests other motives. In the first, he presents Reuben's recognition that he has found his way—compulsively, in Frederick Crews's well-known view—to the spot where he had left Roger Malvin eigh-teen years before.[1] In the second, longer paragraph, he suddenly switches point of view and breaks chronology to focus on Dorcas as she makes preparations for supper. Little do she and the first-time reader realize that the spectacle they will soon have to consume is the dead body of her son.

Even though the reader witnesses Reuben's gunshot and thus wonders what he has hit, by moving the narrative backward in time coincident with the shift to Dorcas's viewpoint, Hawthorne opens ironic distance between his readers and his female character. This distance widens, of course, upon a second reading because we know that Cyrus is dead by his father's hand all the while Dorcas prepares a supper he will never eat. But even on a first reading we suspect the worst. The shift to Dorcas raises our suspicions, just as such a shift does today in a horror movie. We know something awful is going to happen—in part, because Dorcas, an innocent woman, has been so blissfully preoccupied with domestic business.

In its manipulation of readers' emotions, "Roger Malvin's Burial" offers an appropriate entry point for examining Hawthorne's earliest efforts to define himself as a male writer in relation to an imagined audience. His treatment of Dorcas Bourne shows his willingness to manipulate female characters, as well as readers who identified with them, in order to prove his authorial power over texts and reader responses. The first decade of Hawthorne's career, the period between the publication of *Fanshawe* in 1828 and the publication of *Twice-Told Tales* in 1837, offers fertile ground for such a study, because Hawthorne struggled so remarkably to write a male self into being. His material conditions—his living and working arrangements, as well as the situation of the literary marketplace—did not align themselves with his desire for success.

When Hawthorne wrote to his mother from Bowdoin in 1821, announcing his interest in "becoming an Author, and relying for support upon my pen" (XV 139), he targeted a career path that was just then open-ing. "The profession of authorship in the United States began in the 1820s," William Charvat observes, "when Washington Irving and James Fenimore Cooper discovered that they could turn out regularly books which readers were willing to buy regularly" (Charvat 1968, 29). Lawrence Buell adds that "before 1830 none in New England but the independently rich could pursue belles lettres as a primary vocation," but "by the 1850s Longfellow could earn a living from his poetry" (Buell 1986, 57). Hawthorne enjoyed considerable success in his own right after the publi-cation of *The Scarlet Letter* in 1850, but he began his career on the cusp of the transition Buell remarks. Contributing stories to Samuel Goodrich's gift books, such as *The Token*, he earned very little—and he published anonymously. If not quite the "obscurest man of letters in America," as Hawthorne would later style himself (IX, 3), he enjoyed little public rep-utation before 1837. Publication of *Twice-Told Tales*, therefore, marked a watershed moment in Hawthorne's career. With his name finally on the cover of a book, he had reason to think that his pen might support him and that his writing might be "praised by the reviewers, as equal to the proudest productions of the scribbling sons of John Bull" (XV 139).

Not only did Hawthorne struggle within a literary marketplace to discover any "regularity" of success. During the decade in which he wrote his earliest fiction, he lived with and depended upon his mother and sisters. He would later tell his wife, Sophia, exaggerating for effect, that he had sat in his room "a long, long time, waiting patiently for the world to know me, and sometimes wondering why it did not know me sooner, or whether it would ever know me at all" (XV 494). He "plugged away" for years, in Millicent Bell's words, "at writings which he hoped might make a book of connected tales" (Bell 1993, 1). Hawthorne published *Fanshawe* in 1828 at his own expense, but then quickly suppressed the novel, which did not bear his name. However, he attempted to promote at least three different collections of linked tales: *Seven Tales of My Native Land, Provincial Tales,* and *The Story Teller.* By the time he published *Twice-Told Tales,* Hawthorne had a lot of experience negotiating the vagaries of the literary marketplace. He must have felt frustrated, furthermore, for, as Bell observes, he had "allowed these projects to be cannibalized as he was forced to sell off their intended components one by one to periodicals, in which they were printed anonymously" (2). As his letters make clear, Hawthorne understood how this domestic situation and relative lack of writerly success reflected on his manhood, so it is not surprising that he represents the domestic sphere of marriage and family in a negative light. He was trying to write himself out of house and home both inside and outside of the fictional worlds he created.

Richard Brodhead considers Hawthorne "the most perfectly domestic of all American writers, the one most devoted to the family as the scene of fulfilling relation" (Brodhead 1986, 48). In Douglass Anderson's similar view, Hawthorne's work was "perfectly consistent" with the "sentimental domestic spirit" of his day and "helps to establish its complexity, value, and durability" (Anderson 1990, 5). Situating Hawthorne within a domestic frame of reference proves vexing in light of his early tales, for I think many of those works play off the "perfect" spirit of domesticity that Brodhead and Anderson note. In this respect, David Leverenz's view that "story after story presents conventional manliness as aggressive, insensitive, and murderously dominant" is more consistent with my own. Hawthorne's "fascination with marketplace humiliation," Leverenz concludes, "reflects a profound quarrel with the manhood he feels inside himself, so narcissistically needy for self-empowering through malice and cruelty" (Leverenz 1989, 231). Bringing that profound quarrel into the home, Hawthorne waged a campaign against the domestic sphere of marriage and family and repeatedly represented women's homemaking failures. He also played with female readers by manipulating their emotions, violently disrupting the domestic order with which they identified, and deliberately causing them pain through their identification with the female characters he disappointed or shocked. Whether Hawthorne was rebelling against his own domestic situation or against constraints that an increasingly female audience placed on his writing, his tenuous circumstances in the late 1820s and early 1830s must have influenced his conception of himself as a writer and his conception of his fictional project.

With changes in American publishing came changes in readership. The American audience changed dramatically in the nineteenth century, as women formed an increasingly important part of the reading public. Nina Baym argues that Hawthorne "could not possibly foresee the evolution of both popular and critical taste away from the gothic, romantic, and historical toward the domestic, realistic, and contemporary." "Nor could he realize that the American readership as it grew and acquired character between 1830 and 1850 would come to be composed chiefly of women, and therefore responsive to concerns different from his" (Baym 1976, 17–18). My analysis of Hawthorne's early fiction reveals a clearer sense of audience than Baym's assessment allows. In making this argument, of course, I am speculating that Hawthorne positions female readers in strategically conceived relationship to his fictional materials—that he deliberately creates characters and stages scenes designed to manipulate reader, especially female reader, responses. In positing an audience for Hawthorne's early fiction, furthermore, I am following Stephen Railton's contention that an audience is "'there' in the real world" an author inhabits but, more importantly, is "'there' in the author's mind as his or her sense of the people to whom the text is addressed" (Railton 1991, 8). In other words, I am inferring an internalized sense of audience from Hawthorne's fictional materials, especially from the patterns I see in many of his early tales.

Although Hawthorne had failed in his first efforts to make a book, he had learned valuable lessons about the type of collection he should *not* put together.[2] Donald Crowley suggests that Hawthorne "deliberately included something for everyone—children, delicate ladies, hardheaded businessmen." He carefully edited the tales he included in *Twice-Told Tales* with his audience in mind, deleting passages from "The Vision of the Fountain," for example, "that parodied his readers' favorite gift-book form." Subduing a "strong urge to satirize the sentimental bent of his audience," his "strategy was to minister to rather than exploit the needs of the wide audience he was always hoping to attract" (Crowley 1973, 50). He made "numerous changes which reveal his sensitivity to current, often prudish, standards of taste," Crowley observes (IX 503). Wanting to "avoid any matter his audience might consider prurient," Hawthorne demonstrated that "his acute sense of the limitations of his readers made him unwilling to risk printing in acknowledged tales some words and attitudes he had felt free to publish anonymously" (IX 504). Hawthorne's "acute sense" of his readers and their limitations must also have governed his decisions about the volume as a whole. By the time the first collection was published, after all, he had published about four dozen tales and sketches. *Twice-Told Tales* included eighteen, so Hawthorne excluded more than two dozen tales from the book.[3] Many of those tales, including "Roger Malvin's Burial," feature domestic violence, if not "prurience," and thus reveal a lot about his efforts to negotiate with the literary marketplace and with the potential audience for his writing.

Arguably, the most important single reader response Hawthorne received was not Melville's belated notice of *Mosses from an Old Manse* in 1850, but Henry Wadsworth Longfellow's review of the 1837 *Twice-Told Tales*. In Peter Balakian's words, Longfellow gave to Hawthorne "the same kind of unofficial confirmation that Emerson would later give to Whitman upon the publication of *Leaves of Grass*" (Balakian 1983, 429). When Hawthorne wrote his old classmate that the American Stationers Company would be sending him a copy of *Twice-Told Tales* (XV 249), Longfellow promptly replied, surmising that he had probably already read most of the tales and commenting that "what most delighted me in them is the simple representation of what may be called small-life" (Balakian 1983, 431). Longfellow's review follows in the same vein. These tales and sketches, he assures his readers, "have been gathered fresh from the secret places of a peaceful and gentle heart. . . . The book, though in prose, is written nevertheless by a poet. He looks upon all things in the spirit of love, and with lively sympathies" (Longfellow 1837, 60). Longfellow considers *Twice-Told Tales* a "'sweet, sweet book,'" and he concludes by quoting lengthy passages from "The Vision of the Fountain," "Sunday at Home," and "A Rill from the Town Pump." If his Hawthorne does not much resemble our own, or the "dark" Hawthorne whom Melville would praise a decade and a half later, the reason lies in the choices Hawthorne himself made for *Twice-Told Tales*.[4] As much as anything else, I think, Hawthorne made those choices on the basis of audience—an early version of focus group analysis. I think he recognized that his attack on domesticity in "Roger Malvin's Burial" and other tales would not attract an audience, so he excluded those tales in favor of the gentle-hearted pieces for which Longfellow and others would praise him.

Negative representations of marriage, family, and the whole domestic sphere—what James Mellow calls Hawthorne's "theme of dark nuptials" (Mellow 1980, 68)—haunt so many of these early tales that they constitute a leitmotif of gothic fear and horror. The idea of marrying Ellen Langton causes such inner turmoil in the eponymous hero of *Fanshawe*, for example, that he becomes a study in twisted psychology that anticipates male characters such as Parson Hooper, Richard Digby, and Wakefield, as well as Arthur Dimmesdale and Miles Coverdale. When Ellen "extended her hand to Fanshawe," Hawthorne notes, "to refuse it was like turning from an angel, who would have guided him to Heaven. But, had he been capable of making the woman he loved a sacrifice to her own generosity, that act would have rendered him unworthy of her" (III 458). According to this logic, Fanshawe cannot marry Ellen because he loves her and has (indirectly) saved her from a villain's clutches. He tells her, therefore, that they must "part now and forever," and he immediately resumes his studies with "absorbing ardour" (III 459). Given the other domestic situations that Hawthorne describes in *Fanshawe,* his hero's resistance to marriage seems less idiosyncratic. Doctor Melmoth, for example, has borne the "matrimonial yoke" nearly twenty years (III 336) and has endured the "shrewishness of woman" (III 337) in the person of his wife. The villainy of Hawthorne's antagonist (Butler) has its origins in the home. "A harsh father, and his own untameable disposition, had driven him from home in his boyhood" (III 453), and he has spent his life estranged from the mother who dies at the moment he returns home. Hawthorne's description of Mrs. Butler's body through Fanshawe's point of view, moreover, suggests a pathological view of marriage: "How frightful it seemed!—that fixed countenance of ashy paleness, amid its decorations of muslin and fine linen—as if a bride were decked for the marriage chamber—as if death were a bridegroom, and the coffin a bridal bed" (III 446). In Mellow's terms, Fanshawe's fate reflects the "unwritten prohibition against love and marriage that thwarts many of Hawthorne's heroes" (Mellow 1980, 43). The frightening, necrophiliac vision magnifies the fears that Hawthorne implicitly lodges in other male characters who resist or sabotage marriages.

Published just two years after *Fanshawe,* "The Hollow of the Three Hills" (1830) sketches out a similarly chilling paradigm of domestic trouble in the auditory "visions" an old crone grants an estranged woman. Her mother and father speak of a daughter "bearing dishonor along with her, and leaving shame and affliction to bring their gray heads to the grave" (IX 202). Her husband talks of "woman's perfidy, of a wife who had broken her holiest vows, of a home and heart made desolate" (IX 203). Finally, she witnesses her own funeral procession and hears the "revilings and anathemas, whispered but distinct, from women and from men, breathed against the daughter who had wrung the aged hearts of her parents,—the wife who had betrayed the trusting fondness of her husband,—the mother who had sinned against natural affection, and left her child to die" (IX 204). In varying degrees, Hawthorne's early fiction repeats such visions of estrangement, betrayal, bad parenting, and other domestic evils.

In particular, Hawthorne imagines women's roles far removed from the "cult of true womanhood" then emerging in the nineteenth century and founded on "four cardinal virtues—piety, purity, submissiveness and domesticity" (Welter 1976, 21). In Nancy Cott's words, in the "canon of domesticity, the home contrasted to the restless and competitive world because its 'presiding spirit' was woman, who was 'removed from the area of pecuniary excitement and ambitious competition.' Woman inhabited the 'shady green lanes of domestic life,' where she found 'pure enjoyment and hallowed sympathies' in her 'peaceful offices'" (Cott 1977, 67). Although the notion of separate male and female spheres has been subject to recent revisions (for example, in essay collections edited by Cathy Davidson and Jessamyn Hatcher [2002] and by Monika Elbert [2000]), Hawthorne's early writing seems to reinforce and exploit such differences, even if his own life situation did not. In one of his earliest sketches, "Mrs. Hutchinson" (1830), and twenty-five years before his infamous complaint about "a d—d mob of scribbling women," Hawthorne noted the "changes gradually taking place in the habits and feelings of the gentle sex, which seem to threaten our posterity with many of those public women, whereof one was a burthen too grievous for our fathers" (XXIII 66). If such a statement acknowledges the blurring of gender lines and spheres that the most recent scholarship has noted, Hawthorne's response is to slam the door on such border crossings. "A false liberality which mistakes the strong division lines of Nature for arbitrary distinctions, and a courtesy, which might polish criticism but should never soften it," he concludes, "have done their best to add a girlish feebleness to the tottering infancy of our literature" (XXIII 66–67). Not content simply to remand women to the domestic sphere, Hawthorne took the battle to them in the home. Insofar as he was aiming his tales at women readers, he subverted, often violently so, their power to hold homes and families together. Hawthorne does not simply represent lapsed female characters, however. He uses them to work out a special relationship within his fiction between narrator and character. "The Hollow of the Three Hills" offers this paradigm, too: the artist (in the guise of the old crone) sadistically tormenting a woman with visions of domestic disorder and dishonor—her criminal failure to fulfill her familial duties as daughter, wife, and mother. But there is pleasure represented here as well—even sadomasochistic pleasure, in Richard Thompson's view (Thompson 1993, 62)—for the artist figure who wields the power to represent, judge, and punish a woman. Whether the old crone conjures up "real" events or simply reveals the lady's worst fears, she proves the artist's power over reader response. "Here has been a sweet hour's sport!" she chuckles, in the tale's concluding line (IX 204).

"The Wives of the Dead" (1832) offers another example of Hawthorne's playing with female characters in order to manipulate readers and their feelings. Although Hawthorne purports to describe "simple and domestic incidents," he stages an emotionally wrenching story in which he holds women's feelings in suspense. The tale begins shortly after two "recent brides," habitants of the same household, have received news of their husbands' deaths (XI 192). On the night in question, however, each woman receives news that her husband lives. Although joy "flashed" into Margaret's heart when Goodman Parker, an obvious authorial delegate, informs her that her husband has survived, she hesitates to share the good news with Mary: "'Shall I waken her, to feel her sorrow sharpened by my happiness?'" she asks herself. "'No; I will keep it within my bosom till the morrow'" (XI 196). Even as he highlights the women's feelings, Hawthorne plays with them deliberately, self-consciously, much as he does in "Roger Malvin's Burial"—as if calling attention to his power to kill and then resurrect their loved ones. Ingeniously, he places the women in tortuous positions of abjection—waiting for him to decide their emotional fate in the process of determining the plot. Thus, when Mary learns that her own husband still lives, she faces the same quandary as Margaret. Discovering Margaret sleeping peacefully, she feels reluctant to awaken her. "'My poor sister!'" she says to herself; "'you will waken too soon from that happy dream'" (XI 199). Instead, she arranges the bedclothes, and as "her hand trembled against Margaret's neck, a tear also fell upon her cheek, and she suddenly awoke" (XI 67). Hawthorne creates some confusion in this concluding sentence because the referent of "she" remains unclear—leaving open the possibility that the sisters have only dreamed the news of their husbands' survival—but the falling tear realizes one of the tale's purposes. That is, Hawthorne plays, sadistically, with his characters' emotions by leaving them and the readers who identify with their emotionally wrenching experience in a state of suspense and thus at the mercy of an author who enjoys a "sweet hour's sport" in prolonging it.

Whether the wives of the now-living will live out their days in happy marriages or end up like the estranged woman in "The Hollow of the Three Hills," Hawthorne gives no hint. If they had spent their lonely nights reading such tales as "The Canterbury Pilgrims" and "Young Goodman Brown," the two wives might have developed mixed feelings about their husbands' return from the dead. In "The Canterbury Pilgrims" (1833) Hawthorne tells the story of a young Shaker couple, Josiah and Miriam, who flee the

Shaker Village with the intention of living and marrying in the larger world. Hawthorne confronts the young couple with a group of travelers, the pilgrims of the title, who offer them a cautionary preview of life that includes a forbidding vision of married life. In the wife's obviously self-referential words:

> If you and your sweetheart marry, you'll be kind and pleasant to each other for a year or two, and while that's the case, you never will repent; but by-and-by, he'll grow gloomy, rough, and hard to please; and you'll be peevish, and full of little angry fits, and apt to be complaining by the fireside, when he comes to rest himself from his troubles out of doors; so your love will wear away by little and little, and leave you miserable at last. It has been so with us; and yet my husband and I were true lovers once, if ever two young folks were. (XI 130)

Miriam and Josiah continue on their journey without being dissuaded from their purpose and convinced that the "world never can be dark to us, for we will always love one another" (XI 131). Thus the tale can be read as testimony to the power of romantic optimism in the face of cynical world weariness. The lengthy passage I quoted, however, offers additional evidence that Hawthorne imagined the domestic world of marriage and family in negative terms. However cynical its view of marriage, the prophetic vision Hawthorne attributes to the wife in "The Canterbury Pilgrims" pales in comparison to the apocalyptic account of family values that young Goodman Brown hears from the satanic figure in the forest:

> This night it shall be granted you to know their secret deeds; how hoary-bearded elders of the church have whispered wanton words to the young maids of their households; how many a woman, eager for widow's weeds, has given her husband a drink at bed-time and let him sleep his last sleep in her bosom; how beardless youths have made haste to inherit their fathers' wealth; and how fair damsels—blush not, sweet ones!—have dug little graves in the garden, and bidden me, the sole guest, to an infant's funeral. (X 87)

Brown proves unable to resist the force of the devil's vision, especially when the devil commands him to look at his wife, Faith, in the light of this horrific vision of family life.[5] Whatever else it depicts, "Young Goodman Brown" (1835) is the tale of a man who journeys into the wilderness to learn the worst about his wife. He returns to town and to his marriage, but he returns a cynical and gloomy man whose domestic world feels blighted.

For evidence that Hawthorne was calculating his relationship to his female readers, we have only to look closely at "Alice Doane's Appeal," one of the tales apparently left over from the first collection he destroyed. Hawthorne dramatizes his rhetorical relationship to female readers in the relationship between his narrator and the two women he escorts to Gallows Hill in Salem, and he attends carefully to his narrator's success and failure in controlling the responses of these two female listeners. With its heightened self-consciousness and intrusive narrative frame, the tale offers a metafictional workshop for experimenting with author-audience relations and especially with the male artist's power over female response. As R. McClure Smith suggests, "It appears that the audience that the narrator chooses to detain has been carefully targeted, and his assumptions (or presumptions) about them reveal a particular interest in the perlocutionary effectiveness of his performance" (Smith 1991, 75). After leading his "two young ladies" (XI 266) to the top of Gallows Hill, the narrator hopes to exploit their "feminine susceptibility," the tendency of their emotions to come and go with "quick vicissitude" (XI 268). As Christopher Packard cogently argues, the two young women "represent readers of 'light' sentimental magazines like the *Token*—females susceptible to innocent laughter and sympathetic tears" (Packard 1996, 3). Through the relationship he stages between these two female "readers" and his male narrator, Hawthorne could analyze the writing process dynamically—as if measuring the impact of every word on a focus group of two. "The ladies, in consideration that I had never before intruded my performances on them, by any but the legitimate medium, through the press, consented to hear me read," the narrator modestly says (XI 269); but this is a false modesty, for he masks an aggressive impulse. As Packard observes, the tale begins with the "staples of the sentimental genre, particularly the qualities of purity and its opposite," but within "this familiar territory Hawthorne works with decidedly anti-sentimental themes" (Packard 1996, 5). Indeed, he "subverts the domestic literary conventions by grounding a murder in its sphere" (6).

Theme seems subordinate in this metafictional tale to effect—a means for this male narrator to measure his narratorial power over women. "Their bright eyes were fixed on me; their lips apart," he observes with obvious relish as he nears the end of his narrative. "I took courage, and led the fated pair to a new made grave, where for a few moments, in the bright and silent midnight, they stood alone. But suddenly, there was a multitude of people among the graves" (XI 275). Since Hawthorne actually situates his narrator and readers within the tale's fictional world, he can represent every author's fantasy of controlling his readers' responses so completely that he feels as if he were leading them by the hand. Ironically, however, the male narrator only partially succeeds in capturing and controlling his female listeners' attention. Narrating the tale of Leonard and Alice Doane and Walter Brome does cause the young women to fall into his power—to fix their eyes on him, part their lips, and allow him to lead them to the new-made grave. But when he proceeds, in the company of the dead, to finish the tale of Alice Doane's appeal by revealing that the Wizard who has maliciously orchestrated this tale of murder lies buried "close beside" them, the ladies laugh (XI 277). They have been resisting readers, in some degree, able to thwart the narrator's designs on their feelings. Perhaps, as Michael Colacurcio suggests, the young women simply cannot apply the "moral" of this metaphorical tale to their own situations (Colacurcio 1984, 81). Perhaps they see through the narrative frame the narrator has erected, recognizing that the true wizard is the narrator himself. He is the one who decided to defuse the Doane-Brome story by attributing all responsibility for its outcomes—metafictionally—to the wizard. They laugh, in other words, because they recognize how the narrator has manipulated their responses. In either case, the breakdown of the narrative relationship highlights what Hawthorne has placed at stake.

The tale, of course, does not end with the ladies' laughter—or with them in control of the narrator-auditor relationship. "With such eloquence as my share of feeling and fancy could supply," the male narrator conjures up the moment of the Salem witches' executions. He describes the witches one by one as they walk up Gallows Hill and, presumably at the climax of his narrative, he describes himself plunging "into my imagination for a blacker horror, and a deeper woe" (XI 279). He will describe the scaffold and the executions themselves. "But here my companions seized an arm on each side," he notes triumphantly; "their nerves were trembling; and sweeter victory still, I had reached the seldom trodden places of their hearts, and found the wellspring of their tears" (XI 279–80). As many scholars have noted, Hawthorne illustrates a distinction between truth and fiction in the two tales his narrator tells, and he gives the nod to truth telling, or history, when it comes to exerting a powerful effect on readers.[6] The invented gothic tale of incest and murder turns out to be less compelling than the historical narration of "real" events from the past. But this theoretical distinction tells only half the story, for Hawthorne still emphasizes the question of what will move ladies to tears. Arguably sexual in its sense of penetration, the narrator's "victory" fulfills a desire for power over women and women's emotions through the medium of storytelling. Mary Ventura even accuses the narrator of being a "sexual provocateur" and "rapist." The young women cry at the end of the story, she argues, "because they are tired, hungry, and frightened. And because they have been violated" (Ventura 1996, 29). Insofar as Hawthorne was testing author-audience relations, he emphasizes the goal of finding narrative ways to penetrate young women's hearts and release a flood of emotion and tears.

Hawthorne never collected "Alice Doane's Appeal." After being published in the *Token* in 1835, the tale was not reprinted in Hawthorne's lifetime. Perhaps, as Colacurcio hints, the tale reveals too clearly the connections between the "passionate young author who could not find a publisher for 'Alice Doane'" and the "disillusioned persona who takes a sort of vengeance on the audience those publishers imagined they were protecting" (Colacurcio 1984, 87). Perhaps the tale too obviously anatomizes the purpose and method Hawthorne was still using—the manipulative affective relationship he was still testing out with his audience.

None of Hawthorne's early tales fulfills the affective goal he marked out in "Alice Doane's Appeal" better than "Roger Malvin's Burial," for the tale shows Hawthorne ambushing the domestic project of women's fiction in the process of toying sadistically with women's maternal sympathies. The tale opens, however, in a manner that recalls one of James Fenimore Cooper's Leatherstocking Tales—as a frontier romance of Indian warfare. The story seems designed—metafictionally—to mark out the terms and conditions of manhood not only for its protagonist, but also for its author. In the complicated discussion of ethical responsibility with which the tale begins, Hawthorne limns the terms of a manly alternative to an emerging sentimental model of witness and emotional response. Leaving Roger Malvin to die alone in the wilderness, Reuben Bourne gets on with the business of life—a business that includes, even subsumes, the domestic order. So, too, does Hawthorne in denying his readers the death scene and the chance to mourn and memorialize Malvin emotionally. He saves the death scene for later—with a twist that brings the domestic sphere into violent emotional collision with the manly forest world with which he begins. "Roger Malvin's Burial" is a brilliant tale of moral quandaries—one of Hawthorne's best examinations of ethical complexities, as Colacurcio brilliantly demonstrates, rooted in the recognition that we cannot be sure of our own motives (ibid., 109). But the tale's hard-headed elucidation of mixed and mysterious motives belies one of its aims. To be sure, Roger Malvin employs an emotional, even sentimental, appeal in his efforts to convince Reuben to leave him. We do not imagine that Hawthorne is setting us up for a violent intervention—the annihilation of domestic tranquility and order. As Reuben discusses his options with Roger Malvin, both men remain aware of how Reuben's decisions will affect Dorcas. We little suspect the experience Dorcas has in store for her.

Reuben finally leaves Malvin, Hawthorne says, because the "desire of existence and the hope of happiness had strengthened in his heart, and he was unable to resist them" (X 345). Reuben's compromised heroism circulates (ironically) through Dorcas. His understanding with the paternal Malvin is already compromised at its inception because of their appeal to Dorcas and to the prospect of domestic happiness associated with her. Hawthorne then wages a subtle campaign, more subtle than Washington Irving's in "Rip Van Winkle," against domestic happiness as he describes the slow but steady deterioration of the farm Reuben has inherited with his marriage. Like Rip, Reuben becomes a "neglectful husbandman" and winds up a "ruined man" (X 350, 351).

The young Cyrus Bourne, as Ann Ronald notes, embodies the promise of frontier manhood in the manner of Cooper's Natty Bumppo, who had appeared in three of the five Leatherstocking Tales by the time Hawthorne wrote "Roger Malvin's Burial." Reuben loves his son precisely because he embodies those qualities and way of life that Reuben himself surrendered when he married Dorcas. Arguably, Hawthorne occupies a similar position as he domesticates his writing, and he idealizes Cyrus's thoughts of the "adventurous pleasures of the untrodden forest":

> In youth, his free and exulting step would know no barrier but the rolling ocean or the snow-topt mountains; calmer manhood would choose a home, where Nature had strewn a double wealth, in the vale of some transparent stream; and when hoary age, after long, long years of that pure life, stole on and found him there, it would find him the father of a race, the patriarch of a people, the founder of a mighty nation yet to be. (X 352)

Hawthorne even suggests that "the men of future generations would call him godlike" (X 352). At the same time, the "supernatural voice" that directs Reuben's actions in the moments before he kills his godlike son suggests, metafictionally, the author's superior hand. Indeed, Hawthorne's language ironically comments upon his character's inability to direct his own actions—his dependency upon external agency: "Unable to penetrate to the secret place of his soul, where his motives lay hidden, he believed that a supernatural voice had called him onward, and that a supernatural power had obstructed his retreat" (X 356). Hawthorne arrogates to himself that god-like power, snuffing out Cyrus's fantasy of "godhood" with his own "supernatural" power.

Meanwhile, back at the camp. In a perverse shift in point of view, the jump cut with which I began this essay, Hawthorne arrests his own narrative movement and thus postpones our discovery of Cyrus's body. By bringing Dorcas center stage, Hawthorne carries the story forward to his female readers—as if clicking (in contemporary terms) on the window he has opened but minimized in favor of his male narrative. In a lengthy paragraph describing her "preparations for their evening repast," he writes an apostrophe to domestic ideals—a veritable fairy tale of domesticity transported to the heart of the wilderness. The "snow-white cloth" and "bright pewter vessels" make this "one little spot of homely comfort, in the desolate heart of Nature." Dorcas even sings while she works. Her "voice danced through the gloomy forest" (X 357), while Hawthorne emphasizes that "four continually-recurring lines shone out from the rest, like the blaze of the hearth whose joys they celebrated. Into them, working magic with a few simple words, the poet had instilled the very essence of domestic love and household happiness, and they were poetry and picture joined in one" (X 358).

This excerpt from a lengthy passage illustrates the rhetorical lengths to which Hawthorne went in interpolating a spirit of domestic security and harmony. But I want to emphasize again that this paragraph occupies a space between the moment when Reuben fires his gun and Dorcas hears the shot. Hawthorne follows the passage I quoted with the following sentence: "She was aroused by the report of a gun, in the vicinity of the encampment; and either the sudden sound, or her loneliness by the glowing fire, caused her to tremble violently. The next moment, she laughed in the pride of a mother's heart." "My beautiful young hunter!" she exclaims; "my boy has slain a deer!" (X 358).

With that ironic line, Hawthorne keeps up the suspense and feeds—sadistically, it seems to me—the hope that Cyrus really has killed a deer, despite the violent trembling that the shot evokes in Dorcas. That is, Hawthorne deliberately plays with Dorcas's subjectivity—her fantasies and emotions—by allowing her to feel pride in Cyrus even as he lies dead on the ground just out of view. The emotional "high" of her mother's pride sets Dorcas (and the female reader) up for an even greater emotional "fall." Hawthorne then follows Dorcas into the woods and, from her point of view, finally shows the expectant reader the result of Reuben's shot:

> Oh! there lay the boy, asleep, but dreamless, upon the fallen forest-leaves! his cheek rested upon his arm, his curled locks were thrown back from his brow, his limbs were slightly relaxed. Had a sudden weariness overcome the youthful hunter? Would his mother's voice arouse him? She knew that it was death. (X 360)

Even at this moment, Hawthorne mocks sentimental tropes of death as sleep—raising the brief hope that Cyrus only sleeps before confirming his death and mocking, with his rhetorical question, the impotence of the "mother's voice." Dorcas's subjectivity can express itself only in a "wild shriek" (X 360). It has no other power. In interrupting his frontier narrative with the gunshot and extended domestic scene, Hawthorne might seem to be making a concession to female readers. Dorcas's scene, however, is little more than a commercial interruption—frontier narrative featuring violence and filicide, brought to us by *Woman's Day* magazine. Hawthorne's intuition—creating suspense with a gunshot and then filling the interval with a scene of homemaking—at once advertises his sentimental powers and turns them against the readers whose attention he has captured. Dorcas's homemaking enables more than it interrupts Hawthorne's frontier plot-making. She leaves her frontier hearth and home ready for a homecoming she will never enjoy.[7]

We can better understand Hawthorne's strategies and the relationship he establishes with female readers in "Roger Malvin's Burial" by examining "The Gentle Boy," a tale that he revised for the 1837 *Twice-Told Tales.* Like "Roger Malvin's Burial," "The Gentle Boy" features bad or careless parenting that leads to a child's death, but Hawthorne's treatments of the death scenes differ dramatically.

In January 1839, at the beginning of his courtship of Sophia Peabody and at virtually the same moment he accepted his first real job as measurer at the Boston Custom-House, Hawthorne published "The Gentle Boy" by itself as a "Thrice Told Tale"—with "An Original Illustration" by Sophia. One of Hawthorne's most popular tales during his lifetime, "The Gentle Boy" also epitomized his "feminine" qualities. Margaret Fuller praised the tale for having "so much grace and delicacy of feeling, that I am desirous to know the author, whom I take to be a lady" (Fuller [1834] 1983, 198). Longfellow cited the "strength and beauty of a mother's love" that Hawthorne had "poured over" the story and concluded that his "genius" was "characterized by a large proportion of feminine elements" (Longfellow 1842, 10). Sophia's presence on the title page—a deft courtship gesture—might also have helped Hawthorne enhance the tale's appeal to women. This thrice-published tale served as a sounding board on which he could negotiate the gendered terms of his relationship with Sophia and mark out the parameters of his male identity. It also represented another opportunity to come to terms with his female readers.

While Ilbrahim's Quaker mother (Catharine) exemplifies the bad or careless parenting Hawthorne had described in such tales as "Young Goodman Brown" and "The Hollow of the Three Hills," Tobias and Dorothy Pearson represent a more positive model. As initially depicted, Tobias is a failed husband and father, who has "found it difficult to provide for a wife and increasing family." All his children have died. "They had left their native country blooming like roses," Hawthorne notes, "and like roses they had perished in a foreign soil" (IX 76). Adopting Ilbrahim, however, offers Pearson a second chance at successful manhood and fatherhood. For an author still struggling to prove his manhood—on the verge of employment and romance—representing such a second chance must have resonated powerfully. In effect, Hawthorne could put a man in the role and in the home the fanatical Catharine had vacated. And with Sophia as his most important reader-collaborator, he was offering up an exemplar of fatherhood, as if auditioning for the role he himself might one day play.

Treated gently by his new parents, Ilbrahim's demeanor "lost a premature manliness" (IX 88), and he becomes a "domesticated sunbeam" (IX 89), but his re-education as a gentle—feminized—boy has unfortunate consequences. Befriending a boy who was injured near the Pearson home, he has "seized upon" and "clung" to the other boy in a strong homosocial bond (IX 90). Nothing could "arrest" the progress of Ilbrahim's affection, Hawthorne notes, "and there were many proofs that it met with a response from the dark and stubborn nature on which it was lavished" (IX 91). But when Ilbrahim attempts to lavish his affection upon the other Puritan children, "all at once the devil of their fathers entered into the unbreeched fanatics," who, like "a brood of baby-fiends," beat him with sticks and stones with "an instinct of destruction, far more loathsome than the bloodthirstiness of manhood." The very boy Ilbrahim befriended leads the charge and strikes Ilbrahim on the mouth "so forcibly that the blood issued in a stream" (IX 92). Frederick Crews argues that in "this surprisingly lurid scene—a sado-masochistic nightmare if there ever was one—Hawthorne has heaped on Ilbrahim all the accumulated cruelty of his plot. For the reader who has accepted the implied invitation to put himself in Ilbrahim's place, the episode is calculated to trigger a helpless rage against the unearned malice of mankind" (Crews 1966, 69). This psychoanalytic (Oedipal) reading of the tale works partly because Crews characterizes "the reader" as male ("himself"). He downplays the emotional opportunity that Ilbrahim's suffering and death afford an author interested in engaging his female readers.

If the attack on Ilbrahim is bloodier and more violent than Cyrus Bourne's death off stage in "Roger Malvin's Burial," Hawthorne's treatment of the two deaths illustrates the different relationships he established with his audience. He may still manipulate reader responses, but the use of suspense and shock, coupled with the sadistic apostrophe to domestic bliss, gives way in "The Gentle Boy" to straightforward sentimentality in which author and reader are on the same emotional page. Staging Ilbrahim's death as an occasion for emotional witness and sympathy anticipates the way Harriet Beecher Stowe uses Eva's death in *Uncle Tom's Cabin* (1852) or the way Charles Dickens depicts Nelly Trent's death in *The Old Curiosity Shop* (1841). Like those later divine children, Ilbrahim takes center stage on his deathbed and brings characters and readers alike into his emotional orbit. Indeed, Hawthorne doubles the pleasure this deathbed scene affords by bringing not one, but two mothers into the room. First he focuses on Dorothy Pearson's feelings, as the dying Ilbrahim takes her hand. She "almost imagined that she could discern the near, though dim delightfulness, of the home he was about to reach; she would not have enticed the little wanderer back, though she bemoaned herself that she must leave him and return" (IX 103). Heaven as superior to earth, a martyr's death superior to life in a demonic Puritan stronghold—these are the same terms that Stowe employs in *Uncle Tom's Cabin,* and they are designed to bring author, characters, and readers into a state of emotional communion, to make sure that, in Stowe's terms, *"they feel right"* (Stowe 1994, 385). Then, when Catharine enters the room, "she drew Ilbrahim to her bosom, and he nestled there, with no violence of joy, but contentedly as if he were hushing himself to sleep. He looked into her face, and reading its agony, said, with feeble earnestness, 'Mourn not, dearest mother. I am happy now.' And with these words, the gentle boy was dead" (IX 103–4). Restoring the estranged Catharine to her role as his "dear mother," Ilbrahim heals and blesses fractured family relationships. The happiness of his death contrasts with the perverse catharsis that attends Cyrus Bourne's—catharsis for his father, if not for his mother, whose "wild shriek" registers emotional violence far exceeding the quiet "agony" that Ilbrahim assuages.

"The Gentle Boy," even in its thrice-told form, did not fully assuage the doubts that Hawthorne had about the manly persona he was presenting to his readers. The promise of gentle manhood that collaborative republication of the tale seemed to inaugurate went by the wayside after the wedding. Some two years into the marriage, Sophia confided to her sister Mary: "He cannot bear to have woman come out of the shade, far less his wife, & never has forgiven himself for dedicating his Gentle Boy to me" (qtd. in Miller 1991, 213). Hawthorne also fretted about himself and about the public persona tales like "The Gentle Boy" presented to their readers—readers like Fuller and Longfellow and Sophia. Although he notes at the beginning of his Preface to the 1851 edition of *Twice-Told Tales* that the stories were written during the ten- or twelve-year period of his "young manhood" (IX 3), he worries that the author of those 1837 *Tales* has come "to be regarded as a mild, shy, gentle, melancholic, exceedingly sensitive, and not very forcible man, hiding his blushes under an assumed name." He cannot be sure, he admits, that he hasn't filled up "so amiable an outline or

acted in "consonance with the character assigned to him" (IX 7). In other
words, he worries, even at the age of forty-seven, that "The Gentle Boy" has
inscribed a gentle man.

The 1828–37 decade of Hawthorne's career produced many of the tales
we now consider his best and most characteristic work, so in setting them
aside in favor of sunnier tales and sketches for *Twice-Told Tales,* Hawthorne
was taking a break like the one he creates in the narrative of "Roger
Malvin's Burial"—interrupting the darker, more masculine story line of his
career in order to publish a more domestically friendly collection of his
brighter work. Hawthorne's selections, and especially his exclusions, for
Twice-Told Tales represent the subtlest manipulation of all, as if he were
clicking on the domestic window he had framed in "Roger Malvin's Burial," while keeping some of his most domestically violent tales in the background. Once he had his audience hooked—trapped within the domestic
sphere of fiction—he could introduce the violence he had waiting in the
wings. With help from Longfellow, of course, who had brought Hawthorne
out of his closet—as a writer of "womanly knowledge" (Longfellow 1842,
10)—both editions of *Twice-Told Tales* began to establish Hawthorne as a
public writer. If pleased to come before the public in the guise that Longfellow recognized, Hawthorne also saw himself in a different, antithetical way.
He had surprises in store for those who wanted more feminine touches
from his hand. Those readers would be like Dorcas Bourne, singing while
they worked away within the blissful home, going to see the result of the
gunshot they heard just outside the door. If they still didn't get it after comparing Hawthorne's twice-told tales with those he had published only
once, they could wait for Melville's review of *Mosses from an Old Manse,*
which of course included "Roger Malvin's Burial."

NOTES

1. Crews argues that Reuben identifies with Cyrus and the "sacrificial murder"
is "dictated by Reuben's unconscious charge of patricide and by his inability to
bring the charge directly against himself" (Crews 1966, 88).

2. The 1837 *Twice-Told Tales* included the following eighteen tales and
sketches: "The Gray Champion," "Sunday at Home," "The Wedding Knell," "The
Minister's Black Veil," "The May-Pole of Merry Mount," "The Gentle Boy," "Mr.
Higginbotham's Catastrophe," "Little Annie's Ramble," "Wakefield," "A Rill from
the Town-Pump," "The Great Carbuncle," "The Prophetic Pictures," "David Swan,"
"Sights from a Steeple," "The Hollow of the Three Hills," "The Vision of the Fountain," "Fancy's Show Box," and "Dr. Heidegger's Experiment."

3. Excluded tales and sketches include many we now consider Hawthorne's best—"Roger Malvin's Burial," "Young Goodman Brown," "Alice Doane's Appeal," and "My Kinsman, Major Molineux." Hawthorne also excluded "Sir William Phips," "Mrs. Hutchinson," "An Old Woman's Tale," "Dr. Bullivant," "The Haunted Quack," "The Wives of the Dead," "The Seven Vagabonds," "The Canterbury Pilgrims," "Sir William Pepperell," "Passages from a Relinquished Work," "The Haunted Mind," "The Village Uncle," "My Visit to Niagara," "Old News," "The Ambitious Guest," "The White Old Maid," "The Devil in Manuscript," "Sketches from Memory," "Old Ticonderoga," "A Visit to the Clerk of the Weather," "Monsieur du Miroir," "Mrs. Bullfrog," "The Man of Adamant," "A Bell's Biography," "Fragments from the Journal of a Solitary Man," "Edward Fane's Rosebud," and "The Toll-Gatherer's Day."

4. Famously in his review of *Mosses from an Old Manse,* Melville would declare that "the world is mistaken in this Nathaniel Hawthorne" ("Hawthorne and His Mosses," IX 243–44). "For spite of all the Indian-summer sunlight on the hither side of Hawthorne's soul, the other side—like the dark half of the physical sphere—is shrouded in a blackness, ten times black" (IX 243).

5. David S. Reynolds links "Young Goodman Brown" to nineteenth-century "dark reform" literature. When Hawthorne "mentions outwardly good women who kill their babies or husbands," Reynolds concludes, "he is tapping ironies that surrounded fallen women and women criminals in several popular works of the 1830s" (Reynolds 1989, 369).

6. G. Richard Thompson analyzes the narrative as a "remarkable nineteenth-century metafictional treatment, part tale, part sketch, of authorship and the relation between the created fictive world and the historical record of the 'real' world" (Thompson 1993, 160). Colacurcio, on the other hand, points out that the "narrator is not so much substituting a true story for a wild romance as he is merely literalizing psychohistory for an audience which obviously lacks the literary sophistication to discern the historical truth of a metaphorical fiction" (Colacurcio 1984, 87).

7. Hawthorne destroys another happy home in "The Ambitious Guest" (1835). He extols the virtue of hearth and home before annihilating the family that exemplifies that domestic ideal. In a cruel parodic twist, moreover, he has the family flee the home to seek shelter—only to have the avalanche destroy the shelter and leave the house intact. The fire on the hearth continues to burn with no family to be warmed by it, "as if the inhabitants had but gone forth to view the devastation of the Slide, and would shortly return, to thank Heaven for their miraculous escape" (IX 333).

8

Working Women and Creative Doubles: Getting to *The Marble Faun*

David Leverenz

I
n all of Hawthorne's tales and sketches, almost no respectable female characters work outside the home. For an antebellum writer, male or female, that's not surprising. Yet *The Marble Faun* (1860) features two young women who work enthusiastically as artists, far from their families, and seemingly without much narrative recrimination until near the end of the narrative. Here, as in many of his earlier writings, Hawthorne uses moral allegory and occasional demonizations to contain his anxious fascination with independent women, particularly with Miriam's volatile energies. His allegorical restraints don't quite work, in part because Miriam remains Hawthorne's most sustained creative double.

This essay sketches various representations of strong women in Hawthorne's stories and *The Marble Faun*. These characterizations sometimes express male constructedness and often challenge male control, even narrative control in the later texts. Throughout, Hawthorne struggles with contemporary norms of manhood, especially his shame at not being a provider for his family in the 1840s and his fear of his daughter's independence in the 1850s. Perhaps his greater receptivity to Miriam's creativity responds to the public women he encountered in the 1840s and 1850s. More profoundly, it signals a yearning to recapture the artistic energy that he knew he was losing. *The Marble Faun* is suffused with a quietly bilious sense of aging, sometimes projected onto Rome's oppressive fragmentation and decay.

The skimpy spectrum of working women in Hawthorne's tales shows his early and very conventional assiduousness in restricting women's activities to the home. As Brenda Wineapple (2003) notes in her fine recent biography, the women in his tales usually function as "cardboard props[.]"[1] Nonetheless, from the beginning of his career, a few of his writings betray his ambivalent fascination with vigorously public women. Hawthorne's first major sketch, "Mrs. Hutchinson" (1830), admires Anne Hutchinson's complexity and courage even as it dismisses her unseemly ambition. With more dramatic tension between mothering and public ambition, "The Gentle Boy" introduces a muffled woman who ascends to a Puritan pulpit, where she passionately denounces her audience. An abandoned little boy, Ilbrahim, then identifies her as his mother, who has been banished to the wilderness after a long European and American career as an inspired public speaker. Born in Turkey, her child was given that strange oriental name in gratitude for the Sultan's favor. At the end, Catherine suddenly appears again at her son's deathbed. Though the narrative takes considerable pains to disparage her public appearance and angry words, her despairing yearning to love her child helps to give the story its sympathetic climax.

The only early tale that depicts an American woman working respectably outside the home, even peripherally, is "Mr. Higginbotham's Catastrophe" (1834). Here the trader's niece provides the one element of calm good sense in a grotesquely racist and anti–Irish story. While countering rumors that her uncle has been murdered and that she has had hysterical fainting fits, she mentions that "I contribute to my own support by teaching a school" (IX 115). Yet at the end, after the murder story turns out to have been true but anticipatory, Miss Higginbotham shrinks into the expected role of wife and mother, and her "pretty school-mistress" identity (116, 120) recedes to a momentary blip. In the last sentence, which gives her husband all the agency for the family's move, she becomes a *feme couvert*.

Otherwise, Hawthorne's tales tend to group women as domestic angels or, more rarely, prostitutes, along the lines of "the lady of the scarlet petticoat" (XI 217, 229) in "My Kinsman, Major Molineux" (1831–1832). The taints of business and darkness, the fraudulence of the young woman's praise for Robin's worn clothes, and the ambiguity of her claim that his kinsman "dwells" rather than "lives" here suggest that Major Molineux has already enjoyed her sexual services. In a later tale, "John Inglefield's Thanksgiving" (1840), a young woman returns from the "many months of her absence in guilt and infamy" (XI 180) to regain temporary innocence at her family's Thanksgiving dinner before she departs again, presumably to resume her life of prostitution. Neither of these tales presents women's outside work as more than an immoral foil to enhance or enforce the sanctity of women in the home.

The missing third term in Hawthorne's stereotypical dichotomy of domestic angel versus prostitute is men's fears of women's independence and ambition. Most memorably, in "Rappaccini's Daughter" (1844), Professor Baglioni sees Beatrice as a professional threat. But his fear of Beatrice's scientific ambition turns out to be a male hallucination. As her spirit at last escapes patriarchal controls, the ending presents Baglioni, Giovanni, and Rappaccini as equally complicit in the male rivalry that has doomed her body. Another, less well-known story touches with heavy-handed comedy on a domesticated version of women's resourceful independence. In "Mrs. Bullfrog" (1837), the narrator mournfully recounts that he married a woman who turns out to be what a coach driver calls "a witch" and "a she-tiger" (X 134). To his horror, he learns that she has already sued another man for breach of promise. When he discovers that she has been awarded $5,000, Mr. Bullfrog is suddenly content with his wife's strength of temper.

A surprising association of artistic creativity with an angry, talented woman occurs in "Edward Randolph's Portrait" (1838), the second of the "Legends of the Province-House." Alice Vane, an "ethereal" young woman who has learned to paint in Italy, has "genius" as an artist (IX 259), and anticipates Miriam in *The Marble Faun*. At the story's climax, to confront Lieutenant-Governor Hutchinson, she unveils a portrait that she has retouched to display the evil in a former governor's actions against the American people. When Hutchinson dies, "choking with the blood of the Boston Massacre" (IX 269), his face resembles that portrait's horror. The narrative makes Alice an allegorical embodiment of New England's spirit of rebellion as well as a more generalized figure for the spiritualized artist.

That exhausts the possibilities for independent women as creative doubles in Hawthorne's tales. In "Edward Fane's Rosebud" (1837), the Widow Toothaker is "a nurse of great repute" (IX 464), but only because she nursed her sick husband, whom she married for revenge and came to love, and even nurses the former lover who jilted her. Vanished with the Indians is the possibility of a woman with power in the public sphere. "Main-Street" (1849) begins its procession of historical figures with "the great Squaw Sachem, whose rule, with that of her sons, extends from Mystic to Agawam" (XI 51). She has disappeared as completely as the "bold" Quaker woman who dared to challenge male authority (69).

More intriguingly, before his romances, Hawthorne contains the threat of strong, autonomous women by casting them as witches, particularly in his first and last tales, "The Hollow of the Three Hills" (1830) and "Feathertop" (1852). These oddly comic stories gain some measure of complexity because the manipulative old crones also function as demonized creative doubles. In these tales Hawthorne begins to reach beyond the bounds of his own conflicted allegiances to conventions of middle-class American manhood.

"The Hollow of the Three Hills" introduces a woman insistently described as old and ugly as well as malicious. She ostensibly counsels a young woman who has sharply deviated from her expected roles of dutiful daughter, wife, and mother. As a daughter, she had brought "dishonor" and "shame" to her parents (IX 202); as a wife, she had committed adultery; as a mother, she had "left her child to die" (IX 204). Now the witch conjures up the voices of the young woman's parents and her now insane husband, and makes the lady hear the funeral of the child she had abandoned. As the ghostly sounds recede, the witch discovers that the kneeling lady is dead. "'Here has been a sweet hour's sport!' said the withered crone, chuckling to herself" (204). Both sides of Hawthorne's dichotomy between young lady and old witch indict women who deviate from the norms of true womanhood. Yet the witch's malevolent power bears some analogy to the artist's potentially destructive power in conjuring up visions. Only Hawthorne's early sketch of "Mrs. Hutchinson" flirts with similar possibilities.

"Feathertop" explores that creative doubling with more bite and dash. Here Mother Rigby creates a lifelike scarecrow out of a pumpkin, a broomstick, a flail, a hoe-handle, and a stick, and stuffs it with straw. Once she has clothed and bewigged the figure, she gazes at it "with almost motherly affection" (X 226) and decides, "I'll make a man of my scarecrow, were it only for the joke's sake!" (X 227). Curiously, at the moment that Feathertop comes to life, the narrator inserts himself: "Shall I confess the truth? At its present point of vivification, the scarecrow reminds me of some of the lukewarm and abortive characters, composed of heterogeneous materials, used for the thousandth time, and never worth using, with which romance-writers (and myself, no doubt, among the rest) have so over-peopled the world of fiction." The explicit creative doubling of himself with a "strong-willed old beldam" seems oddly comfortable to this narrator, whose self-reflectiveness slides easily back into the "diabolic nature" of the "fierce old hag" (X 229–30).

The rest of the story plays out Feathertop's human progress as a fashionable, foppish gentleman who impresses almost everyone in the village with his pipe-smoking, his aristocratic clothes, and his mysterious reserve. Only a dog's howl, a child's cry, and a merchant's private skepticism dissent from his enthusiastic reception. Eventually Feathertop's appearance charms the merchant's young and pretty daughter, Polly Gookin, whose attentions to herself in the mirror make her almost "as complete an artifice as the illustrious Feathertop himself" (X 240). At last, as Polly happens to see him in the mirror, she too shrieks. If "Polly" evokes a parrot, Feathertop's "scarecrow" features can scare a human bird.

More fatally, when he looks in the mirror, Feathertop sees "a picture of the sordid patchwork of his real composition, stript of all witchcraft" (X 244). The emphasis on "composition" at that climactic moment links the narrator and Mother Rigby, who has "rigged" the whole affair. Her name connotes artistry as well as a somewhat ludicrous attire, a carriage, or a playful trick. Despairing at his own emptiness under the artifice, Feathertop returns home. There Mother Rigby decides to make a scarecrow of him after all, since her creation "seems to have too much heart to bustle for his own advantage, in such an empty and heartless world" (X 246).

Hawthorne's farewell to the short story genre inverts the drama of Poe's "The Man That Was Used Up" (1839), which similarly satirizes society's adulation of manly surfaces but reverses the process. Where Feathertop disintegrates into disparate, lifeless elements, Poe's story ends with a truculent black servant building Brevet Brigadier General John A. B. C. Smith out of artificial parts. Previously, various adoring onlookers have built up Smith's reputation by repeating his passing remarks about the age of invention, and by rhapsodizing about his alleged courage in the Bugaboo and Kickapoo Indian Wars, which gave him his wounds. He exists almost entirely through rumors about him. "He's the man," almost everyone says, including the narrator, until he finally finds the great man at home and sees him being put together.

Both stories expose manliness as a social performance that depends on the audience's gaze to cover its emptiness.[2] In that respect they anticipate Judith Butler's *Gender Trouble* (1990b) by 140 years or more. Poe goes further in his satire of manhood as a social construction, by dramatizing how this generic man—"John Smith" plus "A. B. C."—appeals to onlookers because he can be recirculated as public fragments, from his incomplete sound bites to his image as a former warrior. The story also satirizes consumerism through the mechanical man's inventory of the name-brand products that constitute his legs, eyes, shoulders, teeth, palate, and the rest of what enables his social identity.

Yet one moment in "Feathertop" goes further than Poe in evoking a man's sudden consciousness of his constructedness, and the author's self-consciousness about the fraudulence of his fictions. "The wretched simulacrum!" the narrator muses. "We almost pity him. . . . For perchance the only time, since this so often empty and deceptive life of mortals began its course, an Illusion had seen and fully recognized itself" (X 244). The story's relatively easy satire of the emptiness inherent in formulaic social behavior yields momentarily to a more unsettling self-reflection. Just as Mother Rigby's created gentleman sees his own illusoriness, so Hawthorne's created story sees its own fictionality, as if it too had a temporary life of its own. Though his creative double remains complacent about her powers, Hawthorne leaves his readers uneasy about whether the illusion can be contained in fictions of manhood, or whether it extends to his and our own selves.

Perhaps in mid-life, Hawthorne had found a little distance from the emptiness of what we now would call performative manhood. In any case, some degree of self-reflection helped to spring loose his major romances of the 1850s, in ways that I can't do more than touch on here. Not coincidentally, these romances explore the threat of women's potential independence with much more capacious ambivalence. *The Scarlet Letter* (1850) presents Hester literalizing "cottage industry" by working for pay as a seamstress at home, before she also becomes an unpaid counselor to unhappy Puritan women. *The House of the Seven Gables* (1851) opens with a patronizing account of Hepzibah gaining the courage to open a cent shop in her home. More flamboyantly, *The Blithedale Romance* (1852) depicts several possibilities for women in the public sphere. Yet the story ultimately reclaims Priscilla, a working-class seamstress, from Westervelt's mesmeric exhibitions of her as a spiritualist, while drowning Zenobia, a formidably complex feminist reformer.

The onset of what might be called Hawthorne's censorious receptivity might have been prompted by his various relations with ambitious public women. Throughout the 1840s and 1850s, Hawthorne not only encountered many vigorously independent women, but made some of them his friends, especially Elizabeth Peabody, Margaret Fuller—with whom Sophia studied—and more privately his forceful sister Ebe. Then, even while fulminating against women writers and trying to prevent his daughters from writing, he expressed admiration for Fanny Fern, whose *Ruth Hall* (1855) audaciously narrates the trials and triumph of a woman writer. He had cordial relations with other women writers, including Elizabeth Barrett Browning in Florence and, with private disdain, Grace Greenwood. In England in the early 1850s, he inexplicably took up the cause of Delia Bacon, an American writer who had written a book arguing that Francis Bacon (no relation) had actually written the plays attributed to Shakespeare. Even though he disagreed with her, Hawthorne got her a publisher, wrote a preface, and admiringly called her a "prophetess," in part because what he called her "Bedlamite" behavior gave him a role as protector. Eventually he arranged passage for her back to America. Even after she was put in a private sanitarium, Hawthorne praised her "sensitive and tumultuous character."[3]

In Rome, Hawthorne's circle included Maria Mitchell, an astronomer; Harriet Hosmer, a sculptor who liked to wear men's clothing; and more notoriously, Louisa Lander, who sculpted a fine bust of Hawthorne, then was cut socially when the Hawthornes heard rumors that she had posed nude as a model and perhaps lived with a man. Their oldest daughter, Una, who dismayed the Hawthornes by hoping to be a writer or artist, caught Roman Fever when sketching in the Coliseum with her governess. Sophia also sketched in public, and was astonished to find Italians congregating to admire her work.[4] The variety of these relationships probably helped Hawthorne gain more creative access to the ambivalences about strong women that flourish in his romances.

Reverberating with Hawthorne's Italian experiences, *The Marble Faun* (1860) develops working women as creative doubles with the most sustained complexity. In this romance, two young women painters in Rome don't consider their self-employment as an interim period between home and marriage, or as a detour in a young woman's conventional passage from daughter to wife and mother. Miriam, from an ambiguously Italian and English background, and her American friend Hilda have moved to Rome to further their dreams of artistic success. To contain their threat as potential career women, Hawthorne insistently frames Miriam and Hilda with a traditional moral allegory. Yet Miriam's passionate subjectivity exceeds the bounds of Hawthorne's moral critique.

With an initial bow to convention, the romance presents Miriam and Hilda as classically light and dark women. Whereas Hilda is a blonde Protestant New Englander "not overflowing with animal spirits" (IV 63), Miriam is a foreigner of seemingly cosmopolitan European origins, Italian and Catholic, with hints of Jewish antecedents. Only near the end do readers learn that Miriam's mother was an Englishwoman with a "vein . . . of Jewish blood," who died when Miriam was a child, while her father is a "princely" southern Italian with a name that remains hidden (IV 429–30).[5] Hawthorne's Gothic variation on the father-daughter theme portrays Miriam as enraged and enthralled by her "Model," whose pursuit traps her in a mysterious family history she is trying to escape. Until the end, readers know only that Miriam's mother died when she was young, leaving her father and this mysteriously father-like pursuer. Readers know even less about Hilda, who seems to have had no childhood at all. Once, glancingly, the narrator mentions her mother (IV 357). Emerging from these skimpy and contrasting backgrounds, each woman has chosen a life of "liberty" and artistic ambition, without "the shackles of our present conventional rules" about female propriety (IV 54–55).

Hawthorne's narration first constrains their threat by tilting the moral scales toward Hilda. Early in the romance, Hilda gives up the dangerously unfeminine dreams of originality that impel Miriam's creativity. Instead, she becomes "the best copyist in Rome" through her capacity for "sacrificing herself" as she "religiously" reproduces the paintings of the Old Masters (IV 59–60). More complexly, Hawthorne repeatedly contrasts Hilda's calm and virginal purity of soul with Miriam's eruptively changeable intensities, while intimating ambiguous taints in Miriam's background. When the two contemplate Hilda's copy of what was then thought to be Guido Reni's portrait of Beatrice Cenci, the woman in Renaissance Rome who allegedly killed her father after he raped her, Hilda sees "character" while Miriam sees "history," perhaps her own (IV 66).[6] As Miriam contemplates the possibility of sin and evil in herself, she wonders if Hilda's character will remain so pure that the Catholics would "make a Saint of you, like your namesake of old" (IV 53). At the end, after the American sculptor Kenyon does it instead, she returns to America, where she is "worshipped as a household Saint, in the light of her husband's fireside" (IV 461).

Miriam's creative ambitions can't be contained so easily. Alive with fancies, Miriam frequently seems "between" states of feeling, much as the faun-man Donatello wavers between animal and human. The allure of her embodied ethnic amalgamation makes people conjecture various fictions about her background. Is she Jewish? Does she have "one burning drop of African blood" (IV 23)? Is she an English lady? Whatever her mixture is, it gives her "magnetism" (IV 36) as well as mutability. As Hawthorne's creative shadow, Miriam gains a considerable degree of narrative empathy, before she is finally scapegoated, called a "hysteric" (IV 429), and imprisoned for murder. "[T]here was something in Miriam's blood, in her mixed race, . . . which had given her freedom of thought, and force of will" (IV 430) to resist a life like her mother's. Even Hilda doesn't remain immune from Miriam's influence. While copying a portrait of Beatrice Cenci, she sees Beatrice in her own face (IV 205), and she, too, has a "hysteric" flirtation with Catholicism (IV 357).

Miriam's art and life enact a contradictory fusion of anti-patriarchal rage and involuntary patriarchal submission. The rage first manifests itself as an internalized preoccupation with her guilt and sin. More directly, if ambivalently, her rage and yearning surface in her contradictory relation to the Model. In one aspect he seems to be a slavish follower, like Donatello; in another aspect he seems to be an enslaver. It's disappointing when the mystery fades into the light of common patriarchal day: Miriam has fled from the prospect of an arranged marriage, only to be shadowed by the man her father has chosen for her husband. Despite his death, he becomes the primary narrative device for chaining her subjectivity to her mysterious history.

Until then, the narrative invites speculations that the Model is Miriam's father, perhaps an incestuous father such as Dr. Rappaccini may well have been. Or he might be an allegorical embodiment of generic maleness. Or he might be a male version of Miriam's in-betweenness, half man and half demon, even her demon-lover. After Miriam's gaze induces Donatello to kill the Model, the corpse undergoes still another transformation to become the corpse of a Capuchin monk. Beyond or because of his oscillating identities, the Model holds her in some kind of "thraldom" from her girlhood onwards (IV 93). He is Miriam's constant "Shadow." Yet he is also her double, as she is Hawthorne's "model" of the original artist. As she says to him, "I am your evil genius, as you mine!" (IV 95).

Hawthorne's narration shares that contradictory energy. Throughout, the novel simultaneously attempts to impose and resist patriarchal closures. The patriarchal turns are rather obvious, particularly the progress of Donatello and Miriam toward the statue of Pope Julius III, where they confess their guilty bond. Later Hilda seeks out a father-confessor, and at the end, by voluntarily relinquishing her artistic ambitions to become Kenyon's wife, she accepts the traditional expectations that Miriam tries to resist. But Miriam's fate is more complex. After inducing the Model's fall from the Tarpeian Rock, Miriam continues to be shadowed, this time by several kinds of guilt. Not only has she failed to fulfill her family's traditional expectation that she will marry her betrothed, but she has murdered him instead. She is also shadowed by her narrator's insistent expectations for a woman's proper domestic role. In Hawthorne's allegory at least, a woman can't escape that historical fate, nor should she try, however strong her character. Yet what's best in his narrative returns again and again to Miriam's contradictory passions of in-betweenness, like an allegorical moth to a psychological flame.

To stabilize his narrative, Hawthorne tries to move Miriam and Hilda toward male-identified subjectivities. The second half of the romance arrests their friendship as well as their independence, though with ongoing sympathy for how women get imprisoned by men. Even Kenyon, who serves as a tame and tepid male double for Hawthorne, resolves to take Hilda "captive, and imprison her in his heart" (IV 395). Wavering between sympathy and censure, the narrator half endorses and half recoils from young women's rage against oppressive, incestuous fathers, figured in the recurrent motif of the Beatrice Cenci painting. Not coincidentally, Hawthorne began writing *The Marble Faun* just after his daughter Una became desperately sick, in part because of her conflicts between asserting and submitting. Tensions between a controlling father and a sexually maturing daughter seeking achievement and autonomy pervade this romance.[7]

As in *The Scarlet Letter* and *The Blithedale Romance,* Hawthorne is fascinated with dangerously transgressive heroines. Though Hawthorne can be gratuitously snide about other working women, Miriam remains his most complex artistic shadow, except perhaps for Hester Prynne. But Hawthorne is also shadowed by Spenserian thoughts of his own death in the offing, the ultimate loss of control. Hawthorne usually displaces his nervousness about mutability into snorts of disgust—at Rome, beggars, trickeries, Jewish tenement dwellers, laboring women, even Italian towns and frescoes. Yet the hysteria he occasionally lodges in Hilda and Miriam more appropriately describes his own sudden outbursts. As Hawthorne's rages erupt with no clear object, Italy's aging becomes an unwanted mirror.

Sometimes the narrator can be quite funny, as when his characters look at "the yellow Tiber, a mud-puddle in strenuous motion" (IV 370). More frequently, he inveighs against Italy, seemingly in his own voice, with barely controlled anger. Aging has not been good for Italy, he says in a great many ways. Ubiquitous yellow bricks show that the country "has done its best to ruin the very ruins" (IV 165). He fulminates against Jewish "maggots" that "overpopulate a decaying cheese" (IV 388). He sees Italy's decline from glory and greatness in the washerwomen who typify Rome's decay (IV 6), or the "manlike" women laboring in the fields (IV 290). The ridiculous modern spectacle of "feminine achievements in literature" (IV 61) also suggests cultural decay and decline. Sometimes Hawthorne melodramatically exaggerates his disgust, as when he rails against Italy's countryside towns and old frescoes. All towns should be burned every fifty years, he says (IV 301), and ruined frescoes should be covered with "white-wash!" (IV 303).

Hawthorne's biliousness against a great culture in decline climaxes in his lengthy tirade against modern Rome. The city is "a long decaying corpse . . . with accumulated dust and a fungous growth overspreading all its more admirable features . . . indescribably ugly[.]" Moreover, every night he meets with "a ravenous little populace" of bugs "feasting with our own substance" as he tries to sleep in a Roman bed. And yet, "hating her with all our might," cursing her "crimes" and trickeries, he finds himself "attached . . . to the Eternal City" despite himself (IV 325–26). Much as he felt about Salem, one might say. And, I suggest, much as he felt about his own mutable body. At these points, thoughts of young working women as creative doubles or dangers seem far away. A preoccupation with aging begins to overwhelm the wary receptivity to vivid and public women that generated much of Hawthorne's best writing in the 1850s.

As I've been arguing, *The Marble Faun* gains much of its narrative energy from covertly doubling a dangerously creative female character and the not quite controlling male narrator. In depicting young women's complex mixtures of accommodation and resistance to fathers and father-figures, Hawthorne intimates the discontents and the precariousness in middle-aged men's desires. From Spenser's Mutability Cantos through *The Marble Faun,* Anglo-American male writers have tried to use allegory to bring their representations of independent women toward patriarchal closure. Yet their attempts at containment betray male instability and lack.[8] These issues raise larger questions, both biographically and culturally. What has been so threatening to American middle-class men about the specter of respectable women working?

Biographically, we can trace some of Hawthorne's anxieties to his precarious financial condition as a short story writer. He wasn't measuring up to the manly norm of successful businessman and domestic provider. Put more bluntly, as his letters toward the end of the 1840s suggest, he hadn't made it, and he was broke. If mad Ireland hurt Yeats into poetry, as W. H. Auden said in his elegy, the New England marketplace hurt Hawthorne into romances. But not before he fled writing almost entirely for $1,200 a year in the Salem Custom-House. The 1842–1845 period "marks his last sustained creativity in short fiction," John Crowley concludes in his excellent notes to the Centenary Edition of *Mosses from an Old Manse* (X 504). Thereafter, Hawthorne wrote and published only five other short pieces, the last of which was "Feathertop."

"I have written with pretty commendable diligence, averaging from two to four hours a day," Hawthorne wrote in his journal for March 31, 1843 (X 504). But for what? A year later he writes to George Hillard, "It will never do for me to continue merely a writer of stories for the magazines—the most unprofitable business in the world; . . . If I am to support myself by literature, it must be by what is called drudgery, but which is incomparably less irksome, as a business, than imaginative writing" (X 509). The key word is his twice-emphasized "business." Hawthorne thinks of himself as a man now, not the adolescent boy-man who wants to match "the scribbling sons of John Bull," as he says in an 1821 letter to his mother.[9] He is married, with family responsibilities, and his "diligence" hasn't born fruit. Worse, he has had to borrow money, and he will again. Economic dependence for Hawthorne signifies "failure," he repeats in a letter of gratitude to Hillard for a loan that made *The Scarlet Letter* possible. And "ill-success in life is really and justly a matter of shame."[10]

Equally shameful to his manhood, as Edwin Miller (1991) notes, Sophia had to work "at least three hours a day" as a lampshade decorator while her husband was writing *The Scarlet Letter.* "My Hyperion is cook & maid," Sophia wrote to a friend.[11] During the Old Manse years Hawthorne sued

George Ripley for evicting his family, borrowed $150 from Horatio Bridge, and had to wait ages for a $100 check from John O'Sullivan, the editor of the *Democratic Review* and Una's godfather. A letter from Hawthorne to Evert Duyckinck concludes that his writing "turns out a sad business indeed" (X 516), and in another letter to Duyckinck he metaphorically condemns himself as an unfruitful father as well as a failed businessman. "I . . . will set about collecting my vagrant progeny forthwith," Hawthorne agrees. But

> I never mean to write any more stories (the one now in embryo excepted). . . .
> As the first essays and tentatives of a young author, they would be well
> enough—but it seems to me absurd to look upon them as conveying any claim
> to a settled literary reputation. . . . If they were merely spring blossoms, we
> might look for good fruit hereafter; but I have done nothing but blossom all
> through the summer. I am ashamed—and there's an end. (X 517)

He has been birthing his "vagrant progeny," "embryo," and "spring blossoms" while Sophia has been miscarrying and then birthing Una. Yet they have not brought him the manliness of "a settled literary reputation."

The subtext of these letters could be paraphrased as envious domestic rivalry: *my* creativity has not fathered a reputation, while Sophia's creativity has made her a full woman and mother. And worse, she has to work to support his authorship, too. As with many middle-class American men, until at least the 1970s, a wife working outside the home shows the husband's inadequacy as a man, especially to the husband. If the immediate context for Hawthorne's preoccupation with independent women in *The Marble Faun* was his daughter's mercurial temperament, her severe sickness, and her wish to develop her artistic skills, two more long-running issues impel his complex mix of feelings about seemingly willful young women. In the 1840s he had lived a felt lack of manliness, in trying to make it as an author in America. Now, in the late 1850s, he was living that lack in a different way: he was a famous author who couldn't quite live up to his fame.[12] Already he felt the onset of failing powers, domestically as well as in his writing. Imagining a vividly artistic young woman may have restored a vicarious sense of his own creativity, whereas subduing a wayward daughter or a wayward female character helped to explore and alleviate his sense of once and future lack.

These biographical issues have a cultural context that hasn't been sufficiently emphasized, at least for antebellum New England writers. The pressures of honor and shame helped to shape middle-class norms of American manhood, and women remained prime signifiers of honor for male-dominated families. In Harriet Beecher Stowe's *Uncle Tom's Cabin* (1852), for instance, Tom's wife Chloe asks Mrs. Shelby if she can leave home and her children to work for four years in Louisville, so that she can earn enough money to buy Tom back. Mrs. Shelby immediately assents. But they also agree that Mrs. Shelby shouldn't go to work. "I wouldn't hear to Missis' givin lessons nor nothing[,]" Chloe says. "Mas'r's quite right in dat ar;—'t wouldn't do, no ways. I hope none our family ever be brought to dat ar, while I's got hands." Mrs. Shelby translates that into white terms of honor and shame: "Don't fear, Chloe; I'll take care of the honor of the family" (X 238). Ironically, after Mr. Shelby dies, she proves to be much more adept at handling his business affairs. But a leisured white wife must symbolize the honor of the extended "family," including their slaves, at least while her husband is the prime provider.

The term hovering here is honor, manifested through control of one's women, and intertwined with the "feme couvert" common law implied in the disappearance of young Miss Higginbotham at the end of "Mr. Higginbotham's Catastrophe." Along with contemporary New England expectations that manhood should be demonstrated through self-reliance, success in business, moral character, and property ownership, the honor of a white middle-class man such as Mr. Shelby or Hawthorne depends on the widely shared presumption that a wife's or daughter's identity should be subsumed in the husband's paternal authority.

By recurrently turning to the specter and prospect of independent women, Hawthorne exposes the growing fragility of that traditional code. As "Feathertop" briefly suggests, and as *The Marble Faun* explores at length, without women to provide for and take care of and control, men may start to see honor and manhood as illusions, or self-delusions. Hawthorne's romances take fire when that prospect partially escapes his narrative controls. Confronted with the new prospect of his aging, he lets the fire die.

NOTES

1. Brenda Wineapple, *Hawthorne* (2003), 79.

2. On the fabrication of masculinity in "Feathertop," see Monika Elbert, "Hawthorne's 'Hollow' Men" (1991). Elbert emphasizes Feathertop's anachronistic gentlemanliness or foppishness and his inability to succeed in the marketplace world of Polly's skeptical merchant father. Poe's story also satirizes Richard M. Johnson, Martin Van Buren's vice president, who was badly wounded in fighting Tecumseh and walked on crutches. On its satire of mass culture, celebrity, and consumption, see Jonathan Elmer, *Reading at the Social Limit* (1995), 47–56.

3. Wineapple, *Hawthorne*, 289–95, quotations 293, 295. On Hawthorne and Grace Greenwood, a popular feminist writer, see Mellow, *Nathaniel Hawthorne in His Times* (1980), 407, 491, and 388 for his private disdain.

4. On Harriet Hosmer, see Herbert, *Dearest Beloved* (1993), 218; Wineapple, *Hawthorne*, 302; Mellow, *Nathaniel Hawthorne* (1980), 491. On Louisa Lander, see Herbert (1993), 227–34, who speculates that she represented Hawthorne's lost youthfulness and impulsive freedom, once shared with Sophia (230); also Wineapple, 302, 312–13. On Una's sketching in the Coliseum, see Herbert, 235 and 217 for Sophia's sketching.

5. The romance was first published in England as *The Transformation*, a week before its American publication (Wineapple 318). As Millicent Bell notes in "*The Marble Faun* and the Waste of History," it was the only one of Hawthorne's romances to sell well during his lifetime. Though Miriam's card prints "Schaefer" as her last name (Bell 1999, 39), the narrator always calls both young women only by their first names, either patronizingly or intimately, or both.

6. According to Richard Brodhead's note in the Penguin ed., Beatrice Cenci probably lied about the incest, Guido Reni didn't paint the portrait, and Beatrice is probably not its subject (Brodhead 1990, 473).

7. On Hawthorne's conflicts about Una's physical and emotional breakdown as the context for beginning *The Marble Faun*, see Herbert, *Dearest Beloved* (1993), 218–19, 235–38, 252–59, also 152–54, 175–87, 218–24, 234–83; also Wineapple, *Hawthorne*, 313–16, 319, also 9–12, 336–37. Against her parents' wishes, Una wanted to be an artist or writer, yet despised emancipated women (Wineapple, 284, 303, 330). As Herbert notes, Hawthorne began *The Marble Faun* on the day after Una's Roman Fever first appeared (Herbert 1993, 259). See also Herbert's "Erotics of Purity," which contextualizes the novel's sexually charged issues.

Recent criticism has focused on tourism, class contexts, and religious contexts. On tourism, see Brodhead's introduction to the Penguin ed.; also Richard Millington's "Where is Hawthorne's Rome" (1992) and William Stowe's *Going Abroad* (1994). Robert Levine's "'Antebellum Rome' in *The Marble Faun*" suggests that Miriam and the Model may have participated in a political assassination (Levine 1990, 27). Critics who focus on Miriam and Hilda include Frederick C. Crews, whose *Sins of the Fathers* presents Miriam as a "scapegoat for a sexual nausea" (Crews 1966, 222). Nina Baym's *Shape of Hawthorne's Career*, surprisingly sympathetic to Kenyon, sees Miriam as "less developed" than the others (Baym 1976, 235). In *Roads to Rome*, 350–58, Jenny Franchot emphasizes the unintegrated and evasive narration; for her, Hilda centers the romance's failed Protestant effort to comprehend Catholicism (Franchot 1994, 350). Richard Millington's *Practicing Romance*, 177–206, finds Miriam's romance of transgression slowly yielding to Hilda's sentimental fiction of conscience and suppression, with a fatigued and disaffected voice speaking from the margins (Millington 1992, 178–80, 195, 203). A "careful" reader will become Miriam's uncomfortable partisan (Millington 1992, 201). Millicent Bell's "*The Marble Faun* and the Waste of History" argues that the narrative identifies with Miriam's sense of history as a meaningless composite of fragments and debris. Drawing on Bell's essay, Wineapple notes that the narrative's fragmentation is "like the body parts strewn throughout the novel" (Wineapple, 327, also 319–21).

8. For a more ample analysis of these historical tensions, see David Leverenz, *Paternalism Incorporated* (2003), ch. 2.

9. Hawthorne's letter of 13 March 1821 to his mother is reprinted in *Nathaniel Hawthorne's Tales,* ed. James McIntosh (1987), 295–96. See David Leverenz, "Historicizing Hell in Hawthorne's Tales" (1993), 101–4.

10. For Hawthorne's response to Hillard's letter of 17 January 1850, see Edwin Haviland Miller, *Salem Is My Dwelling Place,* 275–76. As Miller notes, the letter evokes Dimmesdale's painful ending, which Hawthorne was writing at the time (Miller 1991, 276).

11. Miller, *Salem,* 275; Sophia qtd. in Herbert, *Dearest Beloved,* 153. Cf. Wineapple, *Nathaniel Hawthorne,* 183, also 189–90, 207–8 on the Hawthornes' poverty.

12. In *School of Hawthorne,* Richard Brodhead astutely suggests that Hawthorne was the first victim of his own anxiety of influence (Brodhead 1986, 70; also 72–81 on Hilda as an enforcer of reverence for the newly emerging cultural category of high culture).

9

Estranged Allegiances in Hawthorne's Unfinished Romances

Rita K. Gollin

Back Home

The Hawthornes "do not want to leave exactly, at least they don't know what they want," Annie Fields—the wife of Boston's major literary publisher and Hawthorne's old friend James T. Fields—wrote to her mother from London in May 1860 (Gollin 2002, 30). On June 28, the Hawthornes and the Fieldses arrived in Boston harbor on the Cunard liner *Niagara*. After seven years abroad, the first four as American Consul to Liverpool, Hawthorne uneasily returned to a far more troubled country than he had left.

He moved back into the house he called the Wayside, in Concord, the only house he had ever owned. While living in rented lodgings and hotels in England and on the Continent, Hawthorne had fantasized about setting down new roots—in Siena, perhaps, or in an English manor house. But he returned to the Wayside. His neighbor Ralph Waldo Emerson gave a party in his honor the next day; the following day he attended the monthly dinner meeting of the elite Saturday Club (which had elected him to membership while he was abroad); and two days later his publishers William D. Ticknor and James T. Fields honored him with a banquet. Yet as Hawthorne later told his English friend John Bright, he had stayed abroad too long and lost his "home-feelings" (XVIII 356). He had lost even more. As he more plaintively told another English friend, Francis Bennoch, "I lose England without gaining America" (XVIII 352).

When Hawthorne bought the Wayside in 1852, its chief attractions were the hillside behind it and its moderate price, and it had easily accommodated the family whose three children then "bundled together in one room" (XVIII 263). But Una and Julian now required separate "apartments" and Hawthorne wanted a study. He therefore contracted for an addition capped by a third floor "sky-parlor," accepted the carpenters' $500 estimate, and anticipated swift completion. His household was disrupted for months, however, and the final costs exceeded $2000.

Hawthorne had gone to Liverpool anticipating that savings from his consular salary and fees would make him financially secure for the rest of his life, and he had lived frugally in England and on the Continent. But his income turned out to be lower and his consular costs higher than anticipated; and he had made loans to a few old friends, given small sums to destitute Americans and European exiles, paid his sister a monthly allowance, and underwritten Delia Bacon's polemic about the "true" authorship of Shakespeare's plays. The unexpectedly high cost of remodeling the Wayside required him to resume writing even before his "sky-parlor" was finished. Drawing on his English notebooks in July, Hawthorne prepared "Some of the Haunts of Robert Burns" for the *Atlantic Monthly*, which his publishers had recently acquired. Soon afterward, he resumed work on a romance that he had conceived in England and sketched in Rome.

Meanwhile, the Civil War was looming. Even before sailing for England, Hawthorne had been out of step with his abolitionist friends and neighbors. Like them, he had opposed the Fugitive Slave Law and signed a Free Soil petition. Yet his 1852 campaign biography of the Democrats' presidential candidate Franklin Pierce had praised the steadfastness of Pierce's conviction that Southern slavery was protected by the Constitution. It had also presented the "view" that slavery was "one of those evils, which Divine Providence does not leave to be remedied by human contrivances" but eventually "causes to vanish like a dream" (XXIII 352).

What Hawthorne had told his friend Horatio Bridge in January 1857— that he loved New England but felt "no kindred with nor leaning towards the Abolitionists" (XVIII 8)—remained true. Therefore, in November 1860, two days before Lincoln was elected President, he declined to attend a Saturday Club dinner honoring the strongly abolitionist Republican governor of Massachusetts, Nathaniel Banks. As he explained, "In the ruin and dismemberment of the party to which I have been attached, it might behove [*sic*] me to show a somewhat stronger political feeling than heretofore"(XVIII 336).

Hawthorne's political feeling was still relatively tepid in December, when South Carolina was on the point of seceding from the union. If Henry Bright came to America, Hawthorne told him, he would have the pleasure . . . of seeing the Union in its death-throes, and of triumphing over me in revenge for all the uncivil things I used to say about England and her institutions.

He was "ashamed to say how little" he cared about "the matter":

New England will still have her rocks and ice, and I should not wonder if we become a better and a nobler people than ever heretofore. As to the South, I never loved it. We do not belong together; the Union is unnatural . . . ; and as long as it continues, no American of either section will ever feel a genuine thrill of patriotism, such as you Englishmen feel at every breath you draw.

He even ventured a comical suggestion: England "might be induced to receive the New England States back again"(XVIII 354–56).

Such professions continued even after the Confederate States of America was formed in February 1861. "Perhaps . . . I shall have a new Romance ready by the time New-England becomes a separate nation," Hawthorne told Ticknor, "—a consummation I rather hope for than otherwise" (XVIII 363). By then he was working steadily on a new version of the romance he had first drafted in Rome, centered on a young American who contemplates claiming his ancestral English heritage, calculated to "illustrate the sympathy and the difference between Americans & Englishmen" (XII 485).

In Hawthorne's English notebooks, most assessments of that difference "assert American superiority" (XXI 342). As a curious example, Hawthorne thought his "excellent" Oxford host Richard J. Spiers, a former town mayor who purportedly "began life as a hairdresser, . . . would be altogether more at home, and more in keeping with the society around him, in America, than here" (XXII 149–50). And "only America could have produced" the "vicissitudinous" seventy-year-old Kentucky man Philip Richardson, who called at the consulate, a former mine owner and ships' captain. Richardson had "fought through the whole war of 1812" and killed dozens of Englishmen at the Battle of New Orleans, including a handsome officer who died with "the sweetest and happiest smile over his face that could be conceived" (an image Hawthorne would put to good use) (XXII 170–73).Richardson's antitype was a seventy-year-old Liverpool "Inspector of Nuisances" Hawthorne encountered on a train, a "puffy" and "insipid" man who was "odorous of his office," but whose greatest contrast with "the American lies in the narrower circuit of his ideas" (XXII 173–74).Yet many of his countrymen also seemed ridiculous. They included the many callers at the consulate who cherished claims to English estates.

In a sense, Hawthorne was one of them. Though he had found little to admire in Liverpool, entering its harbor had been a form of homecoming to his ancestral birthplace. This was the country whose language and literature were also his, where his books had been published and praised. "What a wonderful land! It is our forefathers' land; our land; for I will not give up such a precious inheritance," he later exclaimed (XXII 260). Not even "bloody wars and vindictive animosities" could eradicate Americans' "unspeakable yearning towards England" (V 18).

In his autobiographical preface to *The Scarlet Letter* (1850), Hawthorne had crossed "the gulf of time" to revivify a seventeenth-century Puritan ancestor and his Puritan son, imagining how they would scorn their "story-writing descendant," yet affirming that "strong traits of their nature have intertwined themselves with mine" (I 9–10). Soon after arriving in England, Hawthorne explored that linkage further:

> My ancestor left England in 1630. I return in 1853. I sometimes feel as if I myself had been absent these two hundred and eighteen years [*sic*]—leaving England just emerging from the feudal system, and finding it on the verge of Republicanism. It brings the two far separated points of time very closely together, to view the matter thus. (XXI 138)

This energized his imagination. "In my romance," he wrote in his journal in April 1855, "the original emigrant to America may have carried away with him a family-secret, whereby it was in his power . . . to have brought about the ruin of the family. . . . At last, the hero of the Romance comes to England, and finds that . . . he still has it in his power to procure the downfal [*sic*] of the family" (XXI 162).

During his first spring in England, while dining at Smithell's Hall, "one of the oldest residences in England," Hawthorne acquired a "good legend" about a "bloody footstep" in the entrance hall. "The tradition is that a certain martyr, . . . being examined before the then occupant of the Hall, and committed to prison, stamped his foot in earnest protest against the injustice with which he was treated" (XXI 160). A variant attributed the footstep to a man wounded by his brother.

To visit Smithell's Hall was to visit the distant yet persistent past. Hawthorne spent a night in an old oak-lined chamber, explored the mansion and its grounds, and inspected the "miraculous footstep." Although he mocked the John Bulls and their "females" who were also house guests, and although he attributed the putative footstep to "a darker vein cropping up through the grey flag-stone" (XXI 290–99), he had acquired the setting for his "American Claimant" romance and its central symbol.

THE AMERICAN CLAIMANT

What is now called The American Claimant Manuscripts includes three distinct attempts to write a romance interrogating Americans' attraction to England ("our old home," Hawthorne later called it) through a particular American's claim to an English estate. The first, written in Rome in 1858, is called "The Ancestral Footstep" (XII 3–89). The second and third drafts, written in Concord between 1860 and 1861 on the eve of the Civil War, are entitled "Etherege" and "Grimshawe" (90–342 and 343–471). The manuscripts include notes to himself, plot sketches, and meditations on emergent themes and motifs. No draft is complete. Yet even Hawthorne's hoary gothic motifs—an old key the hero carries without knowing what it might unlock, an ancient house that is perhaps "his," an antagonist who tries to kill him, and the legendary bloody footstep—display the intertwined continuities of England and America.

Hawthorne never settled on a single back story for the bloody footstep. Perhaps one brother had killed or perhaps merely wounded another, perhaps during England's Civil War, and perhaps the woman they both loved eloped to America with her bloodstained sweetheart. Or, a rebellious brother not only opposed the King during England's Civil War but also beheaded him, and thereafter left a bloody footprint wherever he went. Or, a Quaker tormented by his papist brothers escaped to America, bleeding as he went, then suffered "persecution likewise from the Puritans." In each variant, the footstep signifies "brotherly hatred and attempted murder." All are glosses on America's ties to and severance from England, the archetypal fratricide of Cain, and the inherent fratricide of all civil wars.

Hawthorne's protagonist is a young American with a lively curiosity and an anglocentric cultural perspective who has come to England in search of his ancestral roots. He hopes to bridge the spatial and temporal gulf between his Puritan ancestors' land of origin and his own. That hope—which Hawthorne shared—is the inverse of the Puritans' dream: the hero hopes to reclaim what his ancestors had forfeited.

In the fragmentary "Ancestral Footstep," written in Rome, the names of people and places sometimes change, but the hero's character remains stable. Usually called Middleton, he is a lawyer who, like Franklin Pierce, had fought in the Mexican-American War and served in Congress, and who, like Hawthorne, had been scarred by party politics. But he is now on vacation and on a pursuit that might altogether change his life. An unattached bachelor, he embodies the American ideal of Adamic opportunity.

The story opens as he is strolling in the verdant English countryside, venturing into the domain that he has long dreamed of possessing. We learn his name and national identity only after he is defined as a man of "ready sensibility" who enjoys interacting with everyone he meets; his flexibility "was perhaps a variety of his American nature" (4). During his political career he had "acquired something of the faculty (good or evil, as might be), of making himself all things to all men" (36). But his basic "fineness" remains intact.

In each disjunctive plot variant, Middleton enters into dialogues about England and America—initially with an old man he met on his walking tour, later with the incumbent of the ancestral estate, and repeatedly with a spirited young woman. The old man thinks the differences between the two countries cannot and should not be bridged:

> England will never understand America, for England never does understand a foreign country, and whatever you may say about kindred, America is as much a foreign country as France itself. These two hundred years of a different climate and circumstance . . . have created a new and decidedly original type of national character.

Middleton replies that the English and Americans are "in any event two noble breeds of men, and ought to appreciate one another," and thinks "America has the breadth of idea to do this for England, whether reciprocated or not" (32–33).

A more disputatious dialogue occurs after Middleton has entered the grounds of the ancestral estate and encountered its incumbent. Because that Englishman disdains "Yankees, whose democracy has demoralized them to the perception of what is due to the antiquity of descent," he is nonplussed by the Yankee's confident rejoinder. "'Yes,' said Middleton quietly, 'we have sympathy with what is strong and vivacious to-day; none with what was so yesterday'" (67).

More central to the plot are his discussions with a vivacious young woman called Alice. Now that Middleton has gratified his "natural yearning" to see his forefathers' country, she argues, he should

> return, and cast in your lot with your own people, let it be what it will. I fully believe that it is such a lot as the world has never yet seen, and that the faults, the weaknesses, the errors of your countrymen will vanish away. . . . (56)

Hawthorne himself was never that optimistic. But Alice's faith in America's future and her conviction that claiming the ancestral estate would lead to catastrophe turn Middleton's thoughts to "the life that he ought to be leading in America, the struggles in which he ought to take part" (70–73).

That sense of obligation underlies a plot resolution that Hawthorne entertained: Middleton decides to abandon his claim and return to America, with Alice at his side. "Thus he and his wife become the Adam and Eve of a new epoch and the fitting missionaries of a new social faith," one plot summary concludes (58); and another ends as the new Adam and Eve "depart, lofty and poor, out of the home which might be their own, if they would stoop to make it so" (85).

The plural pronoun is consistent with Middleton's feminist sympathies. Advocates of women's rights favor "yielding the whole sphere of human effort to be shared equally with women," he informs Alice, then praises his countrywomen's "courage, patience, energy," and boldness in "every good cause." Alice's reply is a tease rather than a dissent, a rare bit of Hawthornean burlesque: "I think I see one of those paragons now, in a Bloomer, I think you call it, swaggering along with a Bowie knife at her girdle, smoking a cigar, no doubt, and tippling sherry cobblers and mint-juleps'" (71).

Earlier, Hawthorne had mocked the incumbent of the ancient estate, who wondered whether Middleton "came from the State of New England, and whether Mr. Webster was still President of the United States" (45). Yet despite such mockery and despite Hawthorne's note to himself that "The Ancestral Footstep" "must be a humorous work, or nothing"(58), most of it is solemn. When he set it aside in May 1858, it was primarily because his imagination had become more engaged by the ideas and images that would eventuate in *The Marble Faun.* He had two romances in progress, he told Fields that September, one or both of which he could complete "in a few months if I were either in England or America" (XVIII 151). He completed *The Marble Faun* in England the following autumn. The other lay fallow until he returned to America.

By the time Hawthorne resumed work on his American Claimant romance at the end of 1860, almost everything that had seemed stable in his own life and his country's had become unmoored. That may be why he decided to begin his next attempt, "Etherege," and then its variant, "Grimshawe," with the orphaned hero's childhood in post-revolutionary America, the time of his own childhood. The house where the boy lives with a little girl and their guardian adjoins a cemetery whose soil contains the dust of seventeenth-century Puritans (including Hawthorne's witch-persecuting ancestor). "I have a terrible repugnance against spending any time in Salem or even passing through, if I can help it," Hawthorne told his sister Elizabeth (XVII 311). Yet he reentered it by setting the American sections of his resumed romance in the "town with which I used to be familiarly acquainted" (XII 343).

In Salem's old cemetery, the children discover a key with which the boy will eventually try to unlock a presumably rich treasure in England. Their dark old house (based on the one where Sophia Hawthorne was reared) is "overlaid with dead men's dust" and covered inside with cobwebs. In it, they are "singularly insulated from the rest of the world"(XII 117), as Hawthorne felt he had been in his own family's house. "I have . . . put me into a dungeon," he had told Longfellow in 1837, a dozen years after their graduation from Bowdoin College, "and now I cannot find the key to let myself out . . ." (XV 251).

In a particularly severe indictment of Salem in "Grimshawe," the "hereditary growth of the frame of public mind which produced the witch-craft delusion" generates an attack on the English-born Grimshawe by a mob, "off-scourings of the recently finished war, old soldiers, rusty, wooden-legged; [and] sailors, ripe for any kind of mischief" who shout "'Tar and feather the infernal Tory. . . . Kill him! Kill him!'" while the "respectable" men of the town merely look on (XII 382–85). More bitterly than in "My Kinsman, Major Molineux," Hawthorne deplored mob violence, scapegoating, indifference to suffering, and the ravages of war while challenging the myth that America is the land of "liberty and justice for all." The deep divisions in the country he had returned to were taking their toll.

Although Hawthorne never decided whether the beleaguered Grimshawe was essentially a benevolent nurturer of the boy he had "rescued" from an almshouse, or a conniver who molds the boy as his instrument of revenge against a noble English family, his stories of an ancestral English estate fuel the boy's imagination. "He shall have imaginative and poetic tendencies," Hawthorne told himself; "but yet young America shall show a promising blossom in him—there shall be a freedom of thought, a carelessness of the forms of things. . ." (XII 123).

Revisiting his own youth, Hawthorne acknowledged the "rudiments of a poetic and singular mind within the boy . . . ; a brooding habit [of] taking outward things into itself, and imbuing them within its own essence, until, after they had lain there awhile, they assumed a relation both to truth and to himself, and became mediums to affect other minds with the magnetism of his own." The boy "lived far too much an inward life for healthfulness" (XII 425). But the fatherless boy's guardian (like Hawthorne's uncle Robert Manning) gave him "the means of obtaining as complete an education as the country would afford, and of supporting himself, until his own exertions would be likely to give him the success which his abilities were calculated to win" (XII 437).

At that point in "Etherege" and then at the equivalent point in "Grimshawe," Hawthorne leaped in time and across the Atlantic to the

"The Ancestral Footstep"'s story of a young American who comes to England to seek out an ancestral estate, and to the project of comparing America and England. When the old man of "The Ancestral Footstep" reappears, he questions the protagonist's ability to "feel a heart's love" for anything beyond New England or "for a mere political arrangement, like your union," and expresses Hawthorne's own doubts about whether the American "experiment" could endure. The hero—now called Etherege—protests that he loves America and is proud of its institutions: "there is no man above me—for my ruler is only myself, in the person of another, whose office I impose upon him" (XII 161–62). Yet he remains torn between staying in England (the land of the past) and resuming the "tumultuous life" of his own country (XII 305).

As in the first American Claimant narrative, the protagonist is warned to "let the past alone" and is punished when he ignores that warning. In one variant, he is attacked as a trespasser by the gun-bearing incumbent of the noble English estate, who accidentally kills himself and leaves Etherege bloodstained. In another, Etherege himself is accidentally shot; and he is poisoned in yet another. But the starkest such warning is an allusion to a pit in which plague victims had been buried: when opened, it had released a deadly contagion.

Etherege nonetheless feels drawn to the country his forefathers had left, a country more beautiful and more civilized than his own, where primeval nature had been"redeemed" by centuries of cultivation, and where every inch could be known and loved. Among the virtues of England's defects, its stodginess promises sanctuary from the volatile American present, its class system offers the comforts of knowing one's place, and the populace is unified by allegiance to the Queen. Moreover, Etherege's mind is "full of English thoughts, his imagination of English poetry, his heart of English character and feeling" (XII 147).

His America is a "wild" country despite its limitless opportunities for success. He had learned the hard way that its wilderness is inherently dangerous, and that the flip side of opportunity is the risk of failure. He had lived in ramshackle houses, participated in the "quick violent struggles of his native country," and survived the"feverishness of active life." In "one of those fitful changes, to which American politics are peculiarly liable," his political success as a state legislator and then a Congressman had abruptly ended; and (like Hawthorne) he had endured "the virulence of party animosity, the abusiveness of the press" (XII 147). In a happier "fitful" change in the story's present, his party resumes power and the President offers him a diplomatic appointment (as Pierce had done for Hawthorne).

In neither "Etherege" nor "Grimshawe" did Hawthorne decide whether his protagonist was the rightful heir to the English estate, and (if so) whether he would renounce it and return to America. But as both a condition and a consequence of his immersion in the narrative during the winter of 1860–61 and into the spring, Hawthorne remained detached from American politics.

That detachment ended in mid-April 1861, when the Confederates fired on Fort Sumter and Lincoln declared war. Swept up by "the heroic sentiment of the time," Hawthorne was delighted to feel that at last he "had a country" (XVIII 380). As dozens of his young neighbors answered Lincoln's call for volunteers and younger ones, including Julian, practiced military drills, Hawthorne anticipated a quick Northern victory and even fantasized shouldering a musket himself. "The war, strange to say, has had a beneficial effect upon my spirits," he declared (XVIII 380).

He continued to insist that "We never were one people, and never really had a country since the Constitution was formed." At least provisionally, however, he now agreed with his abolitionist friends and neighbors: "If we are fighting for the annihilation of slavery . . . it may be a wise object, and offers a tangible result, and the only one which is consistent with a future Union between North and South" (XVIII 381).

As his identification with the Union cause increased, the problems of an American claimant to an English estate mattered less. "The war continues to interrupt my literary industry," Hawthorne admitted to Ticknor in mid-May, fearing it would "be long before Romances are in request again, even if I could write one" (XVIII 379). Then in mid-July came the rout at Bull Run, the first major battle of the war. This immediately dispelled Hawthorne's anticipation of a swift Union victory and even put eventual victory in doubt. If the news "puts all of us into the same grim and bloody humour that it does me," Hawthorne told his abolitionist friend James Russell Lowell, "the South had better have suffered ten defeats than won this victory" (XVIII 394). Everyone had relatives and neighbors in uniform and at risk. Lowell found himself in too grim a humor to write. Melville read news of catastrophic Union losses and grimly observed in "The March into Virginia, Ending in the First Manassas. (July, 1861)" that boys may enter battle in "blithe mood," but they "die experienced" soon after; and he later composed the scores of other sorrowful poems about his "country's ills" collected in *Battle-Pieces and Aspects of the War* (1866; ed. Kaplan 1972; see Garner 1993). Whitman started to accumulate the images of war-torn America that would recur in his correspondence (ed. Miller 1961) and would eventuate in *Drum-Taps* (1865–66) and *Memoranda during the War* (1876). Hawthorne's passionately pro-Union friend and editor Fields began including at least one poem, story, or personal account about the war in every issue of the *Atlantic*. And Hawthorne permanently abandoned his American Claimant romance, leaving the protagonist he called his "double ganger" in limbo. "I have little heart for anything," he told his old friend Bennoch (XVIII 387–88). The war was too much with him.

THE ELIXIR OF LIFE

During the spring and summer of 1861, while the Northern army was struggling to preserve the Union, Hawthorne's mind turned to his country's beginnings. Sometime that summer, he began formulating a work of fiction set in Concord at the onset of the American Revolution. He told Fields about it one September day while they were walking along the hill behind the Wayside. "In compliance with your exhortations, I have begun to think seriously of that story," Hawthorne reported in October, "not as yet with a pen in my hand, but trudging to-and-fro on my hill-top." It might "come to nothing," he warned, admitting he had seen "hopefuller plots fail utterly" (the American Claimant plot among them); but he promised to "give it a fair trial for I want to be doing something to earn my bread" (XVIII 408).

Hawthorne told Bright about it in November, though without going into specifics. "The war at first drew my thoughts wholly to itself," he said, "but latterly, I am meditating a Romance, and hope to have it finished by the time the public shall be ready for any other literature than the daily bulletin, or treatises on warlike strategy." Admitting that he felt "a good deal for my native land, since our troubles began," he defended the North's policies to Bright without expecting to persuade him, "for I know Englishmen too well, and know that every man of you wishes to see us both maimed and disgraced, and looks upon this whole trouble as a god-send—if only there were cotton enough at Liverpool and Manchester . . . " (XVIII 420–21). His new romance would attest to his increased distance from England and preoccupation with his native land.

Its seed was a legend about the Wayside Hawthorne had heard from Thoreau: a man had once lived there who believed he would never die. Hawthorne set a story about that man at the beginning of the Revolution, and on his own home grounds. He worked steadily on it for months. In mid-February of 1862, however, he admitted that he felt "mentally and physically languid" (XVIII 427). Then on March 6 he set off for Washington, hoping the change of scene would rekindle his energy, and eager to see something of the war for himself. At the White House, Hawthorne called on Lincoln—"the essential representative of all Yankees, and the veritable specimen, physically, of what all the world seems determined to regard as our characteristic qualities." At the Capitol, he watched Emanuel Leutze at work on his massive fresco "Westward the Course of Empire" and felt cheered by its augury of an "enduring national existence." His numerous excursions included tours of battlefields and army camps; he bemoaned Virginia's "amputated" woodlands, "barren esplanades," and abandoned houses; he praised the maligned General McClellan as a man of courage and integrity; he boarded the "new war-fiend" called the *Monitor;* and he scrutinized filthy Confederate prisoners, including one "wild beast of a man." Talking to a group of ragged and hungry fugitive slaves, he worried about their future and called them "our brethren." And he pondered the "anomaly of two allegiances" that had turned honest Southerners into traitors who considered themselves patriots—men who had drawn "their swords against the Constitution which they would once have died for . . . with a bitterness of animosity which is the only symptom of brotherhood (since brothers hate each other best) that any longer exists" (XXIII 403–42).

Returning from his month-long trip "sorry for the Southerners, and sorry, most of all, for ourselves," Hawthorne prepared the long, vividly detailed, pro-Union, but sometimes puzzlingly ironic account of his trip for the *Atlantic* entitled "Chiefly About War-Matters. By a Peaceable Man." Before submitting it, he removed "whole pages of freely expressed opinion . . . which I doubted whether the public would bear" (XVIII 457), and he subsequently changed others that consternated the "black Republican" Fields. But he also added footnotes—ostensibly written by his editor— which implicitly invited readers to challenge their own opinions as well as his.

The author states, for example, that John Brown was "justly hanged"— a judgment few (if any) *Atlantic* readers shared. The "editor" then asks, "Can it be a son of old Massachusetts who mutters this abominable sentiment? For shame!" (XXIII 427). The author declares about the war, "No human effort, on a grand scale, has ever yet resulted according to the purpose of its projectors." The "editor" asserts that "The counsels of wise and good man are often coincident with the purposes of Providence, and the present war promises to illustrate our remark" (XXIII 431). The author sympathizes with the Southerner whose primary allegiance is to his home State, "the altar and the hearth," rather than a distant and abstract "General Government." The "editor" has trouble understanding this passage, yet feels "inclined to think its tone reprehensible, and its tendency impolitic in the present stage of our national difficulties" (XXIII 417).

It has been said that Hawthorne was the "only notable writer or thinker who took a detached and critical view of the Union cause" (Frederickson 1965, 2), and that to many of his contemporaries, including Lowell and Emerson, his "alleged neutrality was incomprehensible" (Aaron 1975, 44). Yet his sympathy for the South in "Chiefly About War-Matters," like Melville and Whitman's sympathy for Southern soldiers, was not a form of neutrality. Moreover, the two-page piece that Hawthorne wrote for a short-lived Concord periodical—"Northern Volunteers—From a Journal"—was fervently partisan. Southern soldiers send their families Northerner's bones and skulls to use as trinkets and punchbowls, Hawthorne reports in disgust. By contrast, he celebrates the "manly" Union soldiers who had "choked up a bridge" en route to Alexandria but who open a path for the women traveling with him. "'My mother was a woman,'" one of them exclaims, expressing "what we felt to be true of those fifteen thousand volunteers. They carried their home in their hearts" (XXIII 445).

Soon after saying so, Hawthorne returned to the romance that opens on the eve of the Revolutionary War, when Americans fought Englishmen who might well have been their cousins. For months, he labored on the successive drafts known as "Septimius Felton" (XIII 3–194) and "Septimius Norton" (XIII 195–448). Yet he brought neither to completion. The issue of national identity emerges on the first page of "Septimius Felton," with two young men and a young woman sitting on a Concord hillside where "the first settlers of the village had burrowed in caverns," and where during the next century dwellings were erected and fertile meadows were cultivated— the very place where the war was about to erupt(XIII 3–4). "This country was on the eve of a great convulsion which shook the country, and was thence communicated over the world," Hawthorne added in "Septimius Norton," "whence its profound vibrations have not yet ceased to be felt"(XIII 209). In both Septimius narratives, he projected the traumas of the Civil War backward onto that founding convulsion. And in both, he seems uneasy that these"external events" intrude on his "history of a mind bewildered in certain errors" (XIII 16).

Septimius's chief error is that he wastes his life in an isolated and obsessive pursuit of earthly immortality. It is one more formulation of Hawthorne's lifelong conflicting imperatives: his need as a writer for isolation, but also for immersion in real life. A complex embodiment of multiple American identities, Septimius can trace his ancestry back to an English baron who had arrived well before the first Puritans, then married an Indian woman and succeeded her father as Sagamore. Their half-Indian son married a Puritan and begat two children—a son who became a zealous Puritan minister and scalped an Indian, and a daughter who was executed for witchcraft.

Septimius is their much later descendant. A graduate of Harvard College, "where the traditions of the great English Universities had lingered on, and had as yet been invigorated by no fresh life of thought, springing up in our own soil," he had taught school and studied for the ministry (XIII 195). But "bewildered" by his obsessive pursuit of an elixir of life in the story's present, Septimius "knew nothing, thought nothing, cared nothing about his country or his country's battles" (XIII 139), insulated "from all consciousness of the civil war that was going on" (XIII 393). As the term "civil war" suggests, Hawthorne conflated Septimius's predicament with his own.

Septimius's childhood friend Robert is a far simpler and more optimistic embodiment of an American identity. Robert assumes that the imminent war will prove that Americans have not lost the courage and strength their forefathers brought from England. A stalwart yeoman, he soon carries his grandfather's gun into battle "in hot blood, and for a good cause" (XIII 157). He matures in the course of inflicting death, surviving wounds on battlefields as far off as Quebec, and—in the narrative's only festive event—he marries the gentle schoolteacher named Rose, who is Septimius's half-sister.

The narrative gets under way on the Lexington Road leading to Concord, soon after the skirmish at Lexington and just before the Battle of Concord, then moves on to the British retreat along the ridge behind it. Bound by a single purpose, colonial America converts itself from peace to war. Curiously apologetic yet ironic in the "Septimius Felton" version, Hawthorne regrets that

> it is necessary that we should advert to the circumstances of the time in which [Septimius's] inward history was passing. We will say, therefore, that that night there was a cry of alarm passing all through the succession of country towns, rural communities, that lay around Boston, and dying away towards the coast, and the wilder forest borders. Horsemen galloped past the lone farm-house shouting alarm, alarm!—there were stories of marching troops, coming like dreams through the midnight. Around the little rude meeting-houses, there was here and there the beat of a drum, the assemblage of farmers, neighbors, with their weapons. So, all that night, there was marching, there was mustering, there was trouble; and on the road from Boston, a steady march of soldiers' feet onward, onward, into this land, whose last warlike disturbances had been when the red Indians trod it. (XIII 15–16)

When he rewrote that scene in "Septimius Norton," Hawthorne began with a more protracted apology:

If the course of the narrative . . . sometimes leads us amid historic events, . . . we accept the necessity for alluding to such, only because it is unavoidable; not really caring much about anything that took place outside of Septimius's brain. (XIII 210)

Then, instead of merely glancing at the "great historic incident," he expatiated on it. "Septimius Felton"'s undifferentiated group of horsemen "shouting alarm, alarm" is succeeded in "Septimius Norton" by a shirt-sleeved hatless "countryman, who had perhaps taken his horse from cart or plough, and . . . was now belaboring his panting sides with a whip of twisted cowhide," and shouting "'Alarm! Alarm! Alarm!'—trailing the sound behind him like a pennon." The dust and frenzy of this apparition anticipates the culminating observation of Hawthorne-as-spectator: "It seemed as if wars must follow helter-skelter after this messenger of dread" (XIII 215–16).

The scene is more vivid than the comparable one in "Paul Revere's Ride," the long poem Henry Wadsworth Longfellow wrote in the spring of 1860, which Hawthorne certainly saw when it appeared in the *Atlantic* in April 1861. At that time of dire threat to the nation, Longfellow, like Hawthorne, reviewed its beginnings. The poem ends,

> So through the night rode Paul Revere,
> And so through the night went his cry of alarm
> To every Middlesex village and farm,—
> A cry of defiance, and not of fear,—
> A voice in the darkness, a knock at the door,
> And a word that shall echo forevermore!
> For, borne on the night-wind of the Past,
> Through all our history, to the last,
> In the hour of darkness and peril and need,
> The people will waken and listen to hear
> The hurrying hoof-beat of that steed,
> And the midnight-message of Paul Revere.

Hawthorne's greater attention to historical specificity is evident in the list of weapons local farmers carry into battle in "Septimius Felton": "the old fowling piece of seven foot barrel, with which the Puritans had shot ducks on the river and Walden Pond, the heavy harqebuss, which perhaps had levelled one of King Philip's Indians, the old King's Arm that blazed away at the French of Louisburg or Quebec" (XIII 16–17). The cumulative effect Hawthorne achieves is of a country arming itself with its own past.

The similar list in "Septimius Norton" (written several Civil War battles later) ends more grimly with an "old rusty sword, the scythe, or whatever thing had the value (at that moment the chief one) of being adapted to shed blood" (XIII 216). The more Hawthorne contemplated the homely heroism of the provincial farmers, the more he was depressed that in April 1861, as in April 1775, the "Demon of War" had converted "the peaceful husbandman to a soldier thirsting for blood" (XIII 37).

"The experiences of our own day" enable us to know "what emotions were in the atmosphere of that April morning, nearly ninety years ago," Hawthorne declared (XIII 216).

> It was a good time, everybody felt, to be alive in; a nearer kindred, a closer sympathy from man to man, a sense of the goodness of the world, of the sacredness of country. . . . The ennobling of brute force, the feeling that it had its god-like side; the drawing of heroic breath amid the scenes of ordinary life. . . . We know something of that time now; we that have seen the muster of village soldiery on meeting-house greens, and at railway stations; and heard the drum and fife, and seen the farewells, seen the familiar faces that we hardly knew, now that we felt them to be heroes . . . felt how a great impulse lifts up a people, and every cold, passionless, indifferent spectator, lifts him up into religion, and makes him join in what becomes an act of devotion, a prayer, when perhaps he but half approves. (XIII 17)

That same divided attitude pervades Hawthorne's account of the Redcoats' march toward the village of Concord. It begins as they move "massively, with the tramp of a thousand feet" while fifes and drums play a quick step. Though obviously "wearied by their long night-march, their black gaiters bemuddled and bedraggled," sweat running down from their powdered hair, they seem "welded together, their crossbelts all aslant in one direction, their bright musket barrels all gleaming in a line." An hour's rest, a good breakfast, and a pot of beer would revivify them, the narrator-spectator believes, and their "kindly, homely, hearty, honest, obtuse" faces "made you remember they had mothers and homes . . . ; it seemed a pity to shoot them." Yet "any spectator" was also conscious of "a heavy, brutal element" which could transform these homely Englishmen into "atrocious ruffians" (XIII 221–22).

When the Redcoats retreat from the village, Septimius's Indian blood rises as he grabs his great-grandfather's gun and loads it; then a group of them come so close to where he "lurks" on the hillside that he can see their faces. He shoots their officer, neither of them aware that they are cousins. The possessions the dying officer bequeaths to Septimius include a musty old manuscript that will absorb and virtually destroy him—a cryptic formula for an elixir of life.

"'Scalp him,'" Septimius's aunt urges, "whatever of witch and Indian squaw there was in her . . . triumphing over what civilization & christianity had been trying for a century and a half to do towards taming her." Septimius rebukes her: "'Hush, witch! are you a woman at all! Look at the boy, and think that he had a mother!'" Her civilized self then quells her "savage strain" and she rebukes Septimius: "'it was a cruel thing to kill him, when the Indian has been tamed out of you so long'" (XIII 241–42).

Hawthorne seems to be exploring an atavistic component in the American character. Perhaps one reason Hawthorne made Septimius and his aunt part-Indian was that Thoreau, his source for the legend of a man who thought he would live forever, had often spoken about Indians as "our predecessors." In his romance, Hawthorne literalized that conception. But like most of his contemporaries, he conceived of Indians both as noble savages who lived in harmony with nature, and as brutal savages who had impeded the grand work of civilizing the wilderness. His summations of Septimius's "wild genealogy" incorporate but complicate those antitheses.

"It is not our purpose to tell a story of Indian warfare, the meanest kind of contest in which blood has ever been shed," he said in "Septimius Norton," "nor to illustrate another incident in the Red Man's struggle with the Whites; a struggle in which there is such a character of fate, that it almost precludes the ideas of wrong and pity" (XIII 260). Daily newspaper reports must have intensified Hawthorne's concern with the wrong and pity of such warfare.

Nor could issues of race have been far from his mind. His narrative contains more than one story about Septimius's Indian ancestors. In one rambling sketch, Puritans attack their peaceful village and slaughter the English-born Sagamore, his "dusky wife," and all but one of their "wild progeny." That infant is taken to the Puritan village and grows into an idle but "comely" young man addicted to drink, "a specimen of what the Indian has generally been, when in contact with the whites, all saving virtues blighted by civilized air . . ." (XIII 261–63). The fiercely righteous Puritan minister who is this half-breed's son not only hates his sister but testifies against her during "the witchcraft delusion . . . when the contagion of terrible suspicions was in the atmosphere" (XIII 263–66). "The mixture of race [is] a crime against nature, therefore pernicious," Hawthorne asserted (XIII 256). "Something in the mixture of bloods, first of Indian and civilized blood, then of this with the hostile blood of the Puritans, had not amalgamated well" (XIII 266).

The man who had interrogated national myths from the time of his earliest tales specifically condemned the colonists' mistreatment of Indians.

Most of those who survived pestilence and English guns had been "poisoned . . . with fire-water," he said, "and teazed [*sic*] . . . to death with catechisms" by settlers who "took their land, and are still ploughing and planting it . . ." (XIII 362). Hawthorne nonetheless believed that mankind has gradually evolved from savagery to civilization, and that—within each individual as within each society—the "civilized" is superior to the "savage" and should govern.

Therefore, he lamented that in the summer of 1775 as in the summer of 1861, war "filled the whole brain of the people, and enveloped the whole thought of men in a mist of gunpowder" (XIII 54). His bleakest anti-war statement is in his brief depiction of wartime Boston. When Septimius walks into the provincial metropolis, he enters a panorama of devastation, noting vacancies where houses had been torn down for fuel, hoofmarks on the doorstep of a church that had become a dragoons' riding school, broken cannons lying "idle" in the streets, maimed men limping along, young men training "to kill one another," boys hurling mud at an old man they called a Tory, and "forlorn, mateless" women standing in doorways. "War was in the ascendant," Hawthorne observed, "the early enthusiasm of the struggle having subsided, and its hard, heavy, dogged, sullen strain being now felt" (XIII 131–32).

Even so, the Americans who fought the English, implicitly the Union soldiers who fought the Confederates, were heroes. Hawthorne's chief example is Septimius's friend Robert, who bravely inflicts and survives wounds in one battle after another. But Hawthorne also makes the case for such heroism through Septimius himself, when he is tempted to leave his study and "go to the wars, which were now drawing into them the energy and courage of every spirited young man," and "die if he must, live if he might the full, free, generous life of humanity, the conditions of which are to share all the liabilities of his fellow men" (XIII 130).

In "Chiefly About War-Matters," implicitly explaining why he abandoned his own study for a trip to wartime Washington, Hawthorne said, "there is a kind of treason in insulating one's self from the universal fear and sorrow, and thinking one's idle thoughts in the dread time of civil war" (XXIII 403). However guiltily, Hawthorne returned to his study and to the romance of Septimius. In one conclusion he projected, Septimius anticipates seeing "the glory and the final event of the American Republic, which his contemporaries . . . are fighting to establish" (XIII 512). But Hawthorne abandoned the second and last draft of his romance at the moment when Septimius is tempted to join humanity and "die if he must."

Like Hawthorne, Septimius had "dreamed a life-like dream, most life-like in its force and vividness, most unlifelike by its inconsistency with all that really is, with men's purposes, fates, business." "I know well what his feeling was!" Hawthorne exclaimed. "I have had it oftentimes myself" (XIII 129–30). More deeply confessional is his statement that whenever Septimius felt "on the verge of some utterance that would illuminate the whole subject, and make all its obscurities . . . blaze out into vivid meaning," he encountered "a tract of dense, impenetrable darkness, on the other side of which appeared a disconnected radiance, which could not be brought into relation with what had gone before" (XIII 316). His own mortality was beginning to weigh on Hawthorne's mind. He was ill.

A more poignant confession is provoked by Septimius's feelings of despair:

> Perhaps none are more subject to it than Romance writers; they make them-
> selves at home among their characters and scenery, and know them better
> than they know anything actual . . . ; so that all seems a truer world than that
> they were born in; but sometimes, if they step beyond the limits of the spell,
> ah! the sad destruction, disturbance, incongruity that meets the eye. . . . Thus
> he that writes the strange story of [Septimius] may well sympathize with the
> emotion of that moment. (XIII 446–47)

When he wrote those words, Hawthorne was only a paragraph away from abandoning his "strange story" altogether.

His efforts to pursue it during "the dread time of civil war" included resuscitating some of the abandoned themes of the Ancestral Footstep narratives. Thus in "Septimius Felton," a Grimshawe-like Englishman who is aware of Septimius's genealogy says England could use an "infusion of fresh life" and urges Septimius to claim the "ancient hall where your forefathers have dwelt since the conquest." Septimius's "Indian blood" makes him reject "what you think so valuable," yet grants that it might suit him "for a time" (XIII 140–45). Then in the draft's last paragraph, Hawthorne-as-narrator offers a rumor that Septimius eventually claimed the ancestral estate and passed it on to his posterity. And in the penultimate sentence, Hawthorne's truthful statement that he had visited Smithell's Hall "while in England" is followed by a wholly fictional claim: his host had an American physique and "a certain Indian glitter of the eye and cast of feature" (XIII 194).

In October 1862, half a year after returning from Washington and before abandoning "Septimius," Hawthorne admitted that he found it "impossible to possess one's mind in the midst of a civil war to such a degree as to make thoughts assume life" (XVIII 501). Worse was to come. In early December—the time of the Union's devastating defeat at Fredericksburg, when Louisa May Alcott was nursing wounded soldiers in

Georgetown, when Whitman located his wounded brother at the front and then began his long ministry to wounded and dying soldiers in Washington—Hawthorne told Fields he had been "quite ill for some days past" (XVIII 508). Even before then, he had sometimes felt too weak to walk on his hillside or climb up to his study. Then or about then, he gave up on "Septimius" altogether.

During the next year, Hawthorne managed to support his family, meet Fields's request for manuscripts, and remain in the public eye by writing witty and thoughtful *Atlantic* essays based on material in his English notebooks. Fields's encouragements included glowing reports of readers' praise, an increased rate of pay, and the suggestion that he expand the series into what became a twelve-chapter book—*Our Old Home*. When it appeared in September 1863, many Northerners resented its dedication to the Confederate sympathizer Franklin Pierce (Emerson sliced it out of his copy, and Harriet Beecher Stowe called Hawthorne a traitor), and many English readers resented Hawthorne's jibes at their institutions, manners, and physiques. But *Our Old Home,* the only book Hawthorne would ever complete after returning from England, sold well on both sides of the Atlantic.

In the Preface to *Our Old Home*—written in July 1863, the time of the Union's hard-won victories at Gettysburg and Vicksburg, the violent draft riots in New York, and the horrific slaughter of Massachusetts' all-black 54th Volunteer Infantry—Hawthorne said he had hoped to draw on his English notebooks for a work of fiction that might "convey more of various modes of truth than I could have grasped by a direct effort." But as he poignantly explained,

> The Present, the Immediate, the Actual, has proved too potent for me. It takes away not only my scanty faculty, but even my desire for imaginative composition, and leaves me sadly content to scatter a thousand peaceful fantasies upon the hurricane that is sweeping us all along with it, possibly into a Limbo where our nation and its polity may be as literally the fragments of a shattered dream as my unwritten Romance. (V 4)

Hawthorne was telling the truth, though not the whole truth. Although he had not completed any work of fiction after returning to America, he had struggled with two.

Shortly afterward, he began planning yet another romance that he hoped would be "full of wisdom about matters of life and death" (XVIII 626)—"The Dolliver Romance." Its setting is the old house Sophia's family had occupied alongside Salem's Charter Street cemetery, which Hawthorne had previously appropriated for "Etherege" and "Grimshawe." Dolliver, who had been "breeched at the breaking out of King Philip's Indian War" (XIII 462), is an aged apothecary who (like Chillingworth as well as Grimshawe and Septimius) has mastered both the old world's pharma-copeia and Indian herbal lore (yet another allusion to America's cultural pluralism). As the story opens, he bestirs his "rusty joints" with less pain than usual, which he attributes to his first sip of a "certain cordial" con-cocted by his long-dead grandson. As the sole guardian of his three-year-old-great-granddaughter Pansie, he is "loth to leave her alone in the world" (XIII 546). Therefore he continues to dose himself with the remarkable elixir that turns out to reverse the entire process of aging.

Though Hawthorne began sketching the romance in the summer of 1863, he had only one chapter to show Fields in December. He would com-plete only one more installment for the *Atlantic* before admitting to Fields that his "literary faculty" had "broken down" ((XVIII 640–41). In one of Hawthorne's scenarios for the remainder, Dolliver leaves Salem after reach-ing middle age, then returns as a nameless toddler after Pansie has become a grandmother. Despite its inherent absurdity, this situation is autobio-graphical in its rueful acknowledgment of Hawthorne's infirmities and his concerns about his family's welfare. Sketching Dolliver as a happy toddler sitting on his great-granddaughter's lap was whimsical wish fulfillment bordering on the surreal. By contrast, in a brief scrap that darkly reprises an American Claimant motif, the middle-aged Dolliver commits "murders and wrongs," including one at Smithell's Hall, where he "treads in the Bloody Footstep and renews it" (XIII 544).

In all the Elixir of Life manuscripts, including this one, Hawthorne asserted that death should not only be accepted but welcomed. In one of his Septimius studies, for example, he wanted his reader "to see how all that is highest and holiest in life depend on death and the expectation of it"(XIII 511); the young officer Septimius kills dies with a "smile lingering on his lips" (XIII 239); and Hawthorne intended "The Dolliver Romance" to come out "in favor of that poor maligned individual, Death" (XIII 545).

During an overnight visit to the Fieldses in December1863, during which the editor enthusiastically praised what he had seen of "Dolliver," Hawthorne called England's empire a rambling squash vine that could be cut at the root and destroyed. By then he no longer harbored any hope of returning there, whether for pleasure or to secure the English copyright of a new romance. As for America, though he had previously avoided talking about the Civil War, he said he hoped the North would win "now" because that seemed "the only way to save the country from destruction" (Gollin 2002, 57).

Ten months earlier, after describing a tunnel under the Thames in *Our Old Home,* Hawthorne had fantasized about what might happen in one under the Hudson or the Potomac:

> It would be delightful to clap up all the enemies of our peace and union in the dark together, and there let them abide, listening to the monotonous roll of the river above their heads or perhaps in a state of miraculously sus- pended animation, until—be it after months, years, or centuries—when the turmoil shall be all over, the Wrong washed away in blood, (since that must needs be the cleansing fluid,) and the right firmly rooted in the soil which that blood will have enriched, they might crawl forth again and catch a sin- gle glimpse at their redeemed country, and feel it to be a better land than they deserve, and die! (V 250–51)

During his visit to the Fieldses in December 1863, he hoped for such a redemption, but none was forthcoming.

In February 1864, Hawthorne was asked for an "autograph, accompa- nied with a patriotic statement" for sale at a "Sanitary Fair." He replied with an admission of "ill-health" but also a terrible confession: "I can really express nothing at this time—except that an American, sick or well, ought to be ashamed (as I myself sincerely am) who can find nothing patriotic to do or say at the crisis of his country's fate" (XVIII 635).

Three weeks later, after months of illness during which he could rarely write or even read, Hawthorne told Fields he would never finish "Dolliver." Reverting to the bitter humor of his 1834 tale "The Devil in Manuscript," and using the imagery of warfare he had incorporated into his Septimius narrative, he said,

> if I make too great an effort to do so, it will be my death; not that I should care much for that, if I could fight the battle through and win it, thus end- ing a life of much smoulder and scanty fire in a blaze of glory. (641)

At no time during his last three months of life could he make that effort. Hawthorne died in New Hampshire on May 19, 1864, and he was buried in Concord four days later. It seems curiously appropriate that Fields placed the manuscript of "Dolliver" on Hawthorne's coffin, and equally appropri- ate that he then retrieved it.

10

Nathaniel Hawthorne, Writer; or, The Fleeing of the Biographied

Brenda Wineapple

> Facts, as we really find them, whatever poetry they may involve, are covered with a stony excrescence of prose, resembling the crust on a beautiful sea-shell, and they never show their most delicate and divinest colors, until we shall have dissolved away their grosser actualities by steeping them long in a powerful menstruum of thought. And, seeking to actualize them, we do but renew the crust.
>
> Nathaniel Hawthorne, *Our Old Home* (V 135–36)

Nathaniel Hawthorne is the dead white male we love. After all, more people read *The Scarlet Letter* than see the movie, any movie, based on it; and while other dead white male writers languish, their books largely untaught—John Dos Passos, William Dean Howells, or my favorite, Theodore Dreiser—Hawthorne soldiers on, a mainstay in high school and college curricula in spite of the changing canon. What's more, Hawthorne's correspondence, his journals, his fiction, his nonfiction, his children's tales, and his early bad poetry have been gathered together in twenty-three thick volumes, each well annotated, called the *Centenary Edition of the Works of Nathaniel Hawthorne*. If that weren't enough, there's so much critical ink spilled about Hawthorne that the annual called *American Literary Scholarship* devotes an entire chapter to him. As for biographies: mine (Wineapple 2003) is not the only one and certainly won't be the last; they've been appearing with regularity since the decade after his death in 1864.

But Nathaniel Hawthorne is also the dead white male we love to hate.

Though we set his stories to music and tiptoe through the *House of the Seven Gables* (which soon will contain a Hawthorne museum), we denigrate Hawthorne as a man and, often, even as an artist. Pitting him against his dead white canonical peers—our Manichean culture demanding invidious comparisons—Hawthorne frequently comes up the loser. Or at least that's what happened when T. S. Eliot set Hawthorne's novels next to Henry James's; and, more recently, when literary critics measure Hawthorne's personality against Herman Melville's: Hawthorne appears fastidious, withdrawn, remote; Melville, generous, seductive, bold—and the writer, unlike Hawthorne, for whom truth forever has its ragged edge.

Even deep-dyed Hawthorne fans tip their hats to Melville. "I just wanted to say that if anybody is lacking in the [Melville-Hawthorne] friendship, it's Hawthorne," a Hawthorne scholar not long ago claimed. "I don't think there's a Hawthornian that will not say that" (Bryant and Milder 1997, 247).[1] The issue here is not art but the two writers' truncated friendship. And the rub is not that a cold Hawthorne rejected an effusive Melville or even that the friendship ran its natural course during the fifteen months both men lived in the Berkshire hills. It's that Hawthorne committed the sin of remaining popular while Melville's literary stock plunged soon after he met his handsome neighbor. As a consequence, Hawthorne fails to get Melville's high grades not because Melville is an unruly artist lavishing talent on every object in his ken but because he's a victim of bad press, stupid readers, lousy sales, and his own nihilistic profligacy. Hawthorne, by contrast, becomes an "establishment writer" to Hershel Parker, Melville's most recent biographer. An author as popular as Longfellow (an offense), Hawthorne is simply not cut from the same apostate cloth as Walt Whitman or, patently, Melville himself (Parker 2002, 876).

Two years after Hawthorne and Melville met, Hawthorne's publisher, the irrepressible James T. Fields, judged Hawthorne's newest book, *The Blithedale Romance* (1852), a failure—let's hope we have no more of these, he wrote a friend—and then in 1860 *The Marble Faun,* Hawthorne's last completed novel, annoyed its share of readers (like Thoreau, who called the book mere mush). Regardless, Hawthorne's reputation soared. Henry James himself said he wept the day Hawthorne died. And Hawthorne's books, even if they didn't earn pots of money, continued to stay in print. When booksellers wisely interlarded the Tauchnitz edition of *The Marble Faun* with pictures of the sites Hawthorne described in the novel, even dubious Americans began to carry it abroad as if, enthusiasts would note, Dostoyevsky had written a guidebook.

Nor did Hawthorne's Anglophobic essays, collected in the volume *Our*

Old Home (1863), wreck his reputation. Fields understandably had worried that, if nothing else, Hawthorne's dedication of the book to Franklin Pierce, fourteenth president of the United States and Hawthorne's friend since college, would ruin sales. Discredited by the time *Our Old Home* was published, Pierce had presided over some of the most dubious federal policy in the nation's short history: namely, the enforcement of the Fugitive Slave Law, mandating that escaped slaves be returned to their masters, and the passage of the Kansas-Nebraska bill, which not only ensured violence, bloodshed, and slavery in the territories but augured the massacres that would become de rigueur in the Civil War. During that war, Pierce had been reckoned nothing more than a drunken traitor—the "hero of many a hard-fought bottle," critics laughed—who, it was later alleged, had urged his former secretary of war, Jefferson Davis, to secede.

Hawthorne held firm, his steadfastness endearing him—far more than Pierce—to posterity. In the dedication he praised his friend, declaring that "no man's loyalty is more steadfast, no man's hopes or apprehensions on behalf of our national existence more deeply heartfelt, or more closely intertwined with his possibilities of personal happiness, than those of FRANKLIN PIERCE" (V 5). (Disgusted, Emerson sliced the dedication out of his copy of the book.) But sixteen years later, in 1879, the matter still irksome, Henry James put it to rest with characteristic savoir-faire. Hawthorne "defended . . . [Pierce] manfully," James extemporized in his fine study of the elder writer, "without a grain of concession, and described the ex-President to the public (and to himself), if not as he was, then as he ought to be" (James 1984, 449). James then quoted in approbation Hawthorne's letter to Fields insisting he include the dedication despite his publisher's advice: "If he [Pierce] is so exceedingly unpopular that his name ought to sink the volume, there is so much the more need that an old friend should stand by him" (450).

Hawthorne's reputation was saved. But he *had* parted company with most of his literary peers—Thoreau, Emerson, Longfellow, the Alcotts, and Henry James Sr., for instance—on the matter of slavery, which is one reason, no doubt, why the literati who outlived him conveniently forgot, or wished to forget, his politics. His sister-in-law Elizabeth Peabody, a tireless Hawthorne booster, insisted Hawthorne "knew nothing about slavery . . . he knew nothing about contemporaneous history," adding "that he could not understand history until it was at least a hundred years old!"[2] Similarly, Hawthorne's friend George William Curtis, the anti-slavery editor of *Harper's Weekly,* rationalized Hawthorne's seeming detachment from the turmoil engulfing the country. "If you ask why this is so," wrote Curtis shortly after Hawthorne's death,

—how the tragedy of an old Italian garden, or the sin of a lonely Puritan
parish, or the crime of a provincial judge, should so stimulate this imagination with romantic appeals and harrowing allegories, while either it did not
see a Carolina slave-pen, or found in it only a tame prosperity,—you must
take your answer in the other question, why he did not weave into any of his
stories the black and bloody thread of the Inquisition. His genius obeyed its
law. (Curtis 1879, 354)

Which is to say that Curtis and others believed that Hawthorne's genius
obeyed a transcendental law, floating above the mire of petty politics even
when these politics had everything to do with the fate of an American
nation, the subject of much of Hawthorne's work. Obviously, some people
were troubled by Hawthorne's sentiments. "What a devil of a Copperhead
he was!" Walt Whitman remarked. Yet Whitman also forgave Hawthorne
his ways, as did many others, by adverting to his talent. "I always more or
less despise the Copperheads, irrespective of who they are, their fame—
what-not," Whitman declared, "but aside from that, all my tendencies
about Hawthorne are towards him—even affectionate, I may say—for his
work, what he represented"(Traubel 1982, 6:123).

When Henry James in 1879 portrayed the author as a benighted
provincial too callow to occupy the sophisticated drawing rooms of sex,
power, and money, his book set the tone for future Hawthorne biography
as well as a cottage industry investing Hawthorne with eremitic ingenu-
ousness and straining to minimize his political involvement and prove he
was nothing more than a consummate artist with an itchy conscience. It
had been fashionable, for instance, to ignore Hawthorne's unsavory political alliances, and as a result Hawthorne for many years came before the
public as a special sort of visionary delivered from the tawdry realities of
time and place or people, like Pierce, we don't much like. In 1872, Leslie
Stephen (who would soon publish James's *Daisy Miller* in his *Cornhill
Magazine*) highhandedly characterized Hawthorne as an "American,"
which, according to him, is a man confined "till middle age among the
bleak granite rocks and the half-baked civilization of New England"—a
romantic genius in the wilderness with no sense of political or cultural
realities (Idol 1994, 491). Then, following James, the early biographer
George Woodberry insisted in 1902 that Hawthorne "took the party view
of the slavery question, not with any energy, but placidly and stolidly, as far
as one can judge. In fact he took little or no interest in the matter"(Woodberry, 1902, 237).

F. O. Matthiessen himself perpetuated this sort of perspective in *American Renaissance* (1941), a brilliant and for many years standard book

about the personal style—or artistry—and public voice—or humanity—of five American writers, all devoted, as Matthiessen declared, "to the possibilities of democracy"(ix). Yet even for Matthiessen, Hawthorne was a problem. Describing the writer as taciturn and "tragically secluded" (329) in a chapter ostensibly about Hawthorne's politics (and so titled), Matthiessen insists that Hawthorne as writer seeks not to explain "the superficial and journalistic aberrations of the moment" but to illuminate "what is essentially human," delving into "the primary attributes of man, through grasping the similarities of his problems beneath different guises" (329, 320). Trust the tale, we're told, in modernist terms compatible with Matthiessen's.

And so we should, up to a point. For the biographer, however, it's not a viable point of view. One simply cannot ignore the maker of the tale who, in this case, was not an American rube, wide-eyed at malfeasance and heedless of current events—even if he's often associated with the Puritans and colonial New Englanders, the subject of many of his early stories. But no wonder: born in Salem, Massachusetts in 1804, Hawthorne grew up with civic history in his bones. Schoolchildren are still reminded, as was Hawthorne, that his notorious ancestors, among the oldest English settlers in America, were folk of iron, hard and mean: his great-great grandfather, the Puritan magistrate William Hathorne, was particularly intolerant of Quakers, and burning holes in the tongues of women who talked too much; William's son John, Hawthorne's great-grandfather, piously sought the death penalty for hundreds of the accused during the infamous witchcraft delusion of 1692.

These trusty tales helped form the teller.

And in a town like Salem—in a state like Massachusetts—the past is never dead. "One lived in the atmosphere of the Stamp Act, the tea tax, and the Boston Massacre," said Henry Adams, who, had he been from Salem, would have also added the atmosphere of the witch trials and Jefferson's embargo (Adams 1931, 43). The former leeched the town of its self-righteousness (though not its snobbery); the latter, of its prosperity. Said Hawthorne himself, Salem was the New England city over which an aristocratic class held firmest sway, although scorned by its own merchants and ship owners, and where a chill ocean wind blew through the old wooden houses, "few or none of which pretend to architectural beauty" (I 8).

The past, the present: Hawthorne was oblivious of neither. Nor was he unaware of the women and men reshaping his culture—contrary to Stephen, American culture did exist—and his world: Frederick Douglass, Abraham Lincoln, Henry Thoreau, Charles Sumner, Margaret Fuller, Sojourner Truth, Garrison, Greeley, Alcott, Stowe, Whittier, Walt Whitman,

P. T. Barnum, and of course Emerson, Longfellow, John Brown, and Eliza-beth Peabody. These were Hawthorne's contemporaries, mostly sprung from the same antebellum soil as he. Yet they are largely absent from the record partly because, early on, they were edited out. In this, Hawthorne's wife, Sophia, assisted; she, along with James T. Fields, who stoked the Hawthorne fires, shared the genteel premise that to countenance Hawthorne, warts and all, would belittle him. Thus, according to the dic-tates of the day, they discreetly sanitized Hawthorne's language, abjured any reference to politics or political unpleasantries, and refashioned Hawthorne as the lofty genius.

In subsequent years, Julian Hawthorne, the author's son, further domesticated his father in his own two-volume biography, *Hawthorne and His Wife* (1884). Narrating his father's life along the lines of a fulfilled mar-riage plot—mother and father reborn as the ideal couple—Julian retells his father's life as a composite story of success (an unknown Hawthorne takes world literature by storm); of romantic genius (complete with untimely death); of victimization (the genius cheated by unprincipled or negligent editors); and of crisis and recovery in which the eternally optimistic Sophia rescues Hawthorne from despair and dismal solitude.

In this fashion, Julian Hawthorne inducted the Hawthorne marriage into the Hawthorne saga, where it frequently remains: Sophia Hawthorne is the angel behind the artist, a muse releasing Nathaniel from his "dismal and squalid chamber" (Hawthorne's term) in which his stories—albeit some of his best—were first created (XXIII 152). Of course, there are gaps in the story, not just pertaining to Hawthorne's political cronies but to his early years, when Hawthorne was reared in a bustling household that included his mother, two sisters, at least one aunt, and two uncles along with a servant, several cats, and a steady stream of visiting relatives and friends. The years of Hawthorne's so-called seclusion (bachelorhood sans Sophia) have become a presumptive psychological conjecture based on the absence, rather than the presence, of evidence.

While Hawthorne, as unmarried adult, lived in Salem, he wrote to his family only when he traveled, if then; his family, meanwhile, had no occa-sion to write to one another. His friends, particularly those friends engaged in public service, evidently destroyed his letters, and he theirs. As a result, little documentary material from this period survives, which isn't the same as saying its paucity proves Hawthorne stayed at home, day and night, locked in his chamber. Rather, it being more useful to wonder about the purpose of this story, we discover without too much trouble that it com-plements the legend of the liberating marriage: Hawthorne reborn in Sophia's arms.

Similarly, the tale of Hawthorne's honeymoon years at the Old Manse accommodates the legend of the now happily married man—even though a crushing poverty gripped the new family and sent them back, humiliated, to Salem's dismal chamber. Still, Hawthorne's marriage was central to him and his work, although perhaps not in the way Sophia and Julian intended. For example, when the former soldier and political activist, Thomas Wentworth Higginson, reviewed Julian Hawthorne's biography, Higginson concluded that "both Mr. and Mrs. Hawthorne came to each from a life of seclusion; he had led it by peculiarity of nurture, she through illness; and when they were united, they simply admitted each other to that seclusion, leaving the world almost as far off as before" (Higginson 1884, 407). Reproving though it is, Higginson's observation nonetheless sustains the picture of the Hawthornes in retirement, shut away from the world. Hawthorne is a family man to be sure, but now sharing with his wife an ignorance about contemporary events. More recently, in *Dearest Beloved* (1993), his pellucid examination of Hawthorne's novels, T. Walter Herbert persuasively argues that the shelter, which did exist, had a creaking latch: the Hawthorne marriage was a partnership that depended, as collaborations do, on mutually fulfilling fantasies that run afoul of individual needs.

Doubtless, Nathaniel and Sophia Hawthorne devoted themselves to the making of a neat, even repressive, middle-class nuclear family, which also meant they worked hard to insulate and protect themselves from ideas and people they found threatening. Elizabeth Peabody tried in vain to supply her niece, the Hawthornes' elder daughter, Una, with pamphlets on slavery, while Sophia violently protested, "And you would display before her great, innocent eyes a naked slave girl on a block at auction!!! which I am sure is an exaggeration. I have read of those auctions often, and even the worst facts were never so bad as absolute nudity" (Wineapple 2003, 332).

The insights of Higginson and Herbert notwithstanding, if the don't ask/don't tell school of Victorian biography (still extant today) reassembles Hawthorne, by happenstance or design, in the death mask of the Romantic genius—a solitary figure (male) in a garret, inhibited and solipsistic, or just different from the whole damned bunch—their heirs frequently follow in the wake of Frederick Crews and his shrewd reading of Hawthorne's work. These critics deploy a psychological vocabulary which, again, deprives both Hawthorne and his work of the history they inhabit, to say nothing, in his case, of choices he consciously made. Instead, by plumbing his character for tics, indiscretions, such armchair psychologizing locates the origin of character, fiction, and even voting habits in supposed childhood trauma (alleged but never demonstrated), as if character remains, from murky childhood onward, static, unmoved—and independent of economic and political (or accidental) contingencies.

Take, for instance, that biographical canard, already mentioned, of Hawthorne's relationship with Melville. A conscientious Melville biographer, Laurie Robertson-Lorant, misidentifies Hawthorne's father—not a heinous crime—but then goes on to claim that Hawthorne's uncle "evidently transgressed [sexual] boundaries in ways that disturbed Nathaniel, as he was on guard against physically demonstrative men for the rest of his life" (Robertson-Lorant 1996, 255). Her source, a footnote in James Mellow's 1980 Hawthorne biography, is itself so shaky a supposition that the prudent Mellow himself avoided including it in his text. No matter. Though generally judicious, Robertson-Lorant cannot forgive Hawthorne's declining to write a review of *Moby-Dick* after Evert Duyckinck published his own slighting one. Hawthorne is therefore "self-centered and self-absorbed," Robertson-Lorant writes, a man suppressing his "hurt and angry inner child" (292, 269).

Nor is Robertson-Lorant alone in ascribing to Hawthorne an interior life in conformity with present-day fashion. At the hand of several contemporary critics, this inner child—the subject of Edwin Haviland Miller's 1991 biography—matures into a homophobe. Apparently, by refusing to accept Melville's proffered intimacy—whatever that was, wherever it may have occurred—Hawthorne suggests to the psychologically wishful literary community that he would not or could not deal with the lust in his heart. But what constitutes evidence in a situation like this? The evidence, again, is Mellow's speculation based on an enthusiastic reading of various texts as well as inspired fantasy. That no concrete evidence exists for Melville's overture or, obviously, for Hawthorne's refusal makes little difference to the fantasizer.

Besides, we must ask, do litterateurs bedevil only one another? Hawthorne may have disappointed Melville (or Melvilleans), but he did sustain lifelong friendships with a number of men lacking Melville's cachet—Horatio Bridge, Franklin Pierce, John O'Sullivan, or even William D. Ticknor and James T. Fields—men whose rugged entrepreneurship, miserable politics, or impressive lack of grandeur have kept them under the academic radar, where they will not complicate, or implicate, Hawthorne. Nor do Hawthorne's friendships with these men advance the myth of the writer as grand isolato or victim of his seething unconscious. Better, then, forget them although, again, this is not a wise biographical option.

But because the current climate, at least in the academy, is moralistic in tone and aim, despite pretensions to the contrary, critics less overtly psychoanalytic now travel a different and presumably "historical" road, upbraiding

Hawthorne for what he did not write rather than looking at whom he knew and what he did. Armed with the obsessions of the present, they hunt for signal failures: Did Hawthorne endorse Jackson's Indian policies? All of them? Any? Is the Missouri Compromise at stake in *The Scarlet Letter*? Committed to finding rot in every narrative joist, these critics accuse Hawthorne of what he didn't do and call it "cultural work." To take one case, consider the recent books that flay Hawthorne for *not* mentioning race in his stories or novels, even though race plays a part in such diverse writings as "Old News," "A Select Party," and "Sunday at Home," as well as *The House of the Seven Gables* and *The Marble Faun*. In truth, race was very much on Hawthorne's mind, early and late, particularly in his unfinished "Elixir of Life" manuscripts, where the main character, Septimius, is descended from both Indians and Africans. Septimius is a "hybrid" (CXIII 40): Hawthorne's term is not used in its current fashion as something salutary. "The mixture of race is a crime against nature," Hawthorne writes in his notes to himself, [and] "therefore pernicious" (XIII 40, 246).

That Hawthorne writes about racial issues directly, forcefully, or unpleasantly is no discovery—unless, like early Hawthorne critics, we accept the myth of the lonely author, swathed in an inky cape, silently striding through the darkened streets of Salem where he "gained companionship in dreams alone," as Edmund Clarence Stedman rhapsodized (Stedman 1908, 185), and then berate him for the so-called unconscious of his texts, from which his unreconstructed political views leap forth. But Hawthorne once referred to himself as "a thorough-going Democrat" ("Old Esther Dudley," [IX 290]) with only a modicum of irony who remained faithful to the political party that most people associate, then and now, with imperial expansion and, not coincidentally, slavery's extension into the territories. Moreover, Hawthorne wrote of racial issues not just in sketches and tales but in Horatio Bridge's *Journal of an African Cruiser* and, even more explicitly, in his 1852 campaign biography of Franklin Pierce. Here Hawthorne wasn't particularly cagey, plainly stating—hoping—that the institution of slavery, if let alone, would eventually disappear like a dream, "by some means impossible to be anticipated, but of the simplest and easiest operation" (XXIII 352).

The campaign biography "cost me hundreds of friends, here at the north, who had a purer regard for me than Frank Pierce ever gained, and who drop off from me like autumn leaves," Hawthorne vocally confided to Horatio Bridge after the book was published. "But they were my real sentiments," he added, "and I do not now regret that they are on record" (XVI 605).

Almost ten years later, Hawthorne's mind had not changed; if anything, his position was more entrenched. "We go all wrong, by too strenuous a resolution to go all right," he wrote in *The Marble Faun,* reiterating phrases from his Pierce biography, namely:

> There is no instance, in all history, of the human will and intellect having perfected any great moral reform by methods which it adapted to that end; but the progress of the world, at every step, leaves some evil or wrong on the path behind it, which the wisest of mankind, of their own set purpose, could never have found the way to rectify. (IV 239; XXIII 352)

He's alluding to the abolitionists, their methods and aims. And when Elizabeth Peabody sent him antislavery pamphlets, he paraded the same phrases past her. "Vengeance and beneficence are things that God claims for himself," Hawthorne scolded. "His instruments have no consciousness of His purpose; if they imagine they have, it is a pretty sure token that they are not His instruments" (XVIII 116). Always loyal, Peabody decided that Pierce, the knave, had led Hawthorne astray.

Long a thorn in the side of the Hawthorne myth, Elizabeth Peabody represents an alternative political voice that contrasts with that of Nathaniel and Sophia Hawthorne's, much to their discredit. This may be one reason why Peabody has been consistently belittled, the rumor of her engagement to Hawthorne summarily dismissed. For years Hawthorne scholars, all male, scoffed at the notion that someone as talented and sexy as Hawthorne might ever have toyed with someone so tiresome and, well, so earnest. Moreover, an engagement between Nathaniel and Elizabeth flies in the face of Hawthorne's inevitable marriage to Peabody's more quietistic sister. Regardless, the very hint of a liaison, even if spurious, with Peabody might explain why Hawthorne kept his engagement to Sophia a secret for so long. Perhaps he wanted to wait a suitable period of time before announcing to the world that he had jilted—or had seemed to jilt— the other Peabody sister. For whether he had proposed to Elizabeth Peabody or whether she thought he had, he would have been well aware of the stickiness of the situation, and a man of his scrupulous sensitivity would have pondered his moral obligation, if any, to an implied promise.

Whether or not Hawthorne proposed to Peabody (there is no definitive proof either way), my point is far simpler: the less information we gather, sift, and reconsider about Hawthorne, the more he will, over time, become merely a creature of our fancy. As Samuel Johnson observed, "Many things which are false are transmitted from book to book, and gain credit in the world" (Boswell 1986, 215). This is particularly true in Hawthorne's case, since his elegant prose, drenched in irony, is slippery, elusive, eminently ambiguous, and encourages all manner of speculation (itself of some bio-graphical interest).

As if goading the reader, Hawthorne cloaks himself in the kind of demurral that provokes conjecture, his writing a performance of a decid-edly self-conscious sort. Carefully selecting what to keep and what to give away, what to show and what to hide, he often concealed his identity with pseudonyms, at least in his early stories, as if he wanted to wrap himself in a fiction; and then he concocted stories—fictions—in which he takes a demonstrable part, as himself. He shunned publicity. Or said he did, declaring in his preface to *Mosses from an Old Manse* that he was not, "nor have ever been, one of those supremely hospitable people, who serve up their own hearts delicately fried, with brain-sauce, as a tidbit for their beloved public" (X 33). More famously, in "The Custom-House" essay that introduces *The Scarlet Letter,* Hawthorne writes, "it is scarcely decorous, however, to speak all, even where we speak impersonally," but he then also admits he will lift the veil, just a little, declaring that "it may be pardonable to imagine that a friend, a kind and apprehensive, though not the closest friend, is listening to our talk; and then, a native reserve being thawed by this genial consciousness, we may prate of the circumstances that lie around us, and even of ourself, but still keep the inmost Me behind its veil" (I 4).

Playing hide-and-seek with the reader, Hawthorne wrote ambivalence into his most prominent symbols, like the minister's creepy black veil, or the scarlet letter, which announces Hester Prynne's disgrace even as it dis-guises her inner life, to say nothing of the father of her child. Hawthorne refused, or so he said, to write unabashed autobiography—it's indecent exhibitionism, he suggests. But he was also willing to adopt a persona where he himself is the first-person narrator, as in his several sketches or in famous tales like "Rappaccini's Daughter," the story about a woman locked in a garden, in the prologue to which Hawthorne identifies himself as a voluminous though neglected French writer who "occupies an unfortunate position between the Transcendentalists (who, under one name or another, have their share in all the current literature of the world), and the great body of pen-and-ink men who address the intellect and sympathies of the multitude." High and low brow. And Hawthorne? A nowhere man who writes tales, he continues, "sometimes historical, sometimes of the present day, and sometimes, so far as can be discovered, that have little or no refer-ence either to time or space" (X 92). So once again he catapults himself above and beyond us all.

But in the everyday life of his own milieu, which is where, in the final analysis, a biographer looks for him, Hawthorne contemplates, as do we all, the superficial and journalistic aberrations of the moment, his moment, from the vantage point of his own needs, economic and social, his past, his present preoccupations and anxieties; his friends, travel, city of origin, and his political party; his failures, successes, and metaphors. And so in "The Custom-House," when he impersonates himself, Hawthorne adds an elaborate though typical conceit: pretending to be Custom-House surveyor, which he in fact was from 1847–49, he one day stumbles on an artifact, a red cloth embroidered as the letter A, among the personal effects of a former surveyor in the dusty attic of his workplace. Intrigued, he happens to place the letter on his chest, but it's so hot it burns him and he drops it to the floor. Thus Hawthorne becomes one more character in his own tale— and, by implication, the wearer of a scarlet symbol. Why? Because he's a writer. "What is he?" he imagines one of his Puritan forefathers scorning him. "A writer of story-books? What kind of business in life,—what mode of glorifying God, or being serviceable to mankind in his day and generation,—may that be? Why the degenerate fellow might as well have been a fiddler!" (I 10).

Though Hawthorne respected, even venerated, the writer's calling, the feminine and elitist sensibility he associated with writing placed him in a discomfiting and untenable position: taking pleasure in his growing reputation as eminent author, he could not sell enough of his work to support himself and his family. For much as he loved what he did and needed to do it, literature was an idler's sport—so say those imagined ancestors. Moreover, to be successful, Hawthorne had to be a kind of aristocratic huckster, like the shopkeeper Hepzibah Pyncheon in *The House of the Seven Gables,* proud woman of a pretentious family so far down on its luck that she must open a cent-shop to earn her keep like ordinary folk. Hawthorne preferred the narcotic of civil service. Government jobs allowed him to eat, to be sure, and to feed his family; but the very positions Hawthorne sought and accepted also reveal something of who he was and perceived himself to be. The world of politics—a man's world of dockworkers, lawyers, and old salts—was an asylum from literature and an affirmation of manhood.

This means, in his case, that the well-buckled Puritans still tenanting Hawthorne's inner world were able to join forces with the Jacksonians peopling his outer one, each reinforcing the other with the notion Hawthorne shrank from and half-believed: his profession, that of writing fiction, had no quantifiable social value. A pastime more than a vocation, it seemed a form of domestic work, underpaid, if paid at all, like woman's work; or, if paid well, polluted, like the work of that "damn'd mob of scribbling women," as he so memorably called them, who were, like pen and ink men, not beyond the reach of filthy lucre or popularity, and, like the annoying

Mrs. Stowe (XVII 304). But then that made writing, for him, a rich dilettante's hobby. "N. Hawthorn's reputation as a writer is a very pleasing fact," Emerson equivocated in his own journals, "because his writing is not good for anything, and this is a tribute to the man" (Emerson 1982, 288).

Forced to vacate the Custom-House (with the Democrats voted out of office), Hawthorne writes his departure as a tale of vengeful liberation, a fortunate fallout of the grind of civil service ("The Custom-House" essay). This too is part of an inveterate Hawthorne legend, concocted by himself and well-meaning relatives like Elizabeth Peabody, who announced as early as 1838 (eleven years earlier) that no Pegasus should be tethered to a dray-cart. Writers should live only on ambrosia and air.

Hence Hawthorne's conflict: "No Man can be a Poet & a Book-Keeper at the same time," Hawthorne postured to his sister when a boy of sixteen (XV 132). This did not mean he wished to give up bookkeeping or the cash—and the autonomy—associated with it any more than he wished to chuck writing poetry. Rather, he inhabited the world of poet and the world of bookkeeper in a culture that rewards only the latter. A place like the experimental commune Brook Farm might offer temporary refuge where he could live apart from the competitive world of Boston, defining himself as artist while at the same time expressing manliness in feats of hard, physical labor. By contrast, writing is unmuscular, dreamlike, invisible, womanly—and Hawthorne couldn't write, anyway, at Brook Farm.

That Hawthorne went to Brook Farm has seemed odd to readers who associate him more with grammars of sin—unpardonable ones—than pie-eyed utopia. But it makes sense. Among other reasons, Hawthorne went to Brook Farm expressly hoping to heal the rift between poet and bookkeeper, which the West Roxbury community purported to do. The commune, as might be expected, could do no such thing, and Hawthorne realized it in a matter of months. Civil service, once the Democrats returned to office in 1846, suited him better.

"'The little power you might once have possessed over the tribe of unrealities is gone!'" Hawthorne later told his tale of liberation; too long a stint in the Custom-House has stolen valuable writing time. "It was not merely during the three hours and a half which Uncle Sam claimed as his share of my daily life, that this wretched numbness held possession of me" (I 34; 35). The image of Hawthorne bartering his self-respect for Uncle Sam's gold is worth examining, for Hawthorne had chafed under the parental yoke of two uncles, Robert and Richard Manning, who served as surrogate fathers during his youth. Though attention has been given to Robert by biographers, Richard is perhaps the more important figure. Injured in a carriage accident, he exercised a considerable power over young Nathaniel who, for a few years, was stricken by a mysterious lameness—much like Richard's—that kept him housebound. No medical causes were found for Hawthorne's infirmity, but whatever the reason, one can assume this period of infirmity garnered much attention from the women in his life while at the same time it sheltered him from competitive interaction with other boys.

Figuratively, the lameness that Hawthorne experienced as a child returned in later life in his conceit of himself as a semi-invalid author. Refusing to compete with other males on their turf, he cast himself as the recluse in the attic to woo Sophia Peabody. In his well-known letter to her, he portrayed himself as sequestered, neglected, and in need of love's redemption: "Here sits thy husband in his old accustomed chamber," Hawthorne wrote from Salem to his fiancée,

> where he used to sit in years gone by. . . . Here I have written many tales— many that have been burned to ashes—. . . . If ever I should have a biographer, he ought to make great mention of this chamber in my memoirs, because so much of my lonely youth was wasted here, and here my mind and character were formed; and here I have been glad and hopeful, and here I have been despondent; and here I sat a long, long time, waiting patiently for the world to know me, . . . and sometimes wondering why it did not know me sooner, or whether it would ever know me at all—at least, till I were in my grave. (XV 494)

Although Poe called Hawthorne—in 1847—*the* example, par excellence, in this country, of the privately admired and publicly unappreciated man of genius, this passage is often quoted to give biographical heft to Hawthorne's sense of alienation or his pervasive, almost primitive, sense of isolation; but the graceful passage also speaks of overwhelming ambition, masked as humility; and it's the very ambition Henry James assured his audience that Hawthorne did not possess. Yet hypothesizing "if ever I should have a biographer," Hawthorne operated in the meantime as his own most consistent, most influential and deft chronicler, leaving something of himself—sometimes hidden, sometimes not—in his sketches, stories, essays, and correspondence.

In an early letter to Longfellow, to give another instance, Hawthorne characterized himself as dwelling in a dismal owl's nest, seldom venturing out till after dusk. For, protestations to the contrary, Hawthorne was no *ingénu.* Savvy enough to re-introduce himself to the well-established poet (Hawthorne's first collection of stories was soon to appear), he received, as he had hoped, the decisive review of *Twice-Told Tales* from Longfellow that helped to launch his career. Yet by the time Hawthorne was firmly entrenched in what we now regard as the literary pantheon, he was deemed a shy, quiet man, chary of public appearances, whose fame was thrust upon him by a literary meritocracy. In other words, Hawthorne's public (and biographers) fell for the ruse. This is one of the reasons Hawthorne now is the dead white male we love to hate. After Jane Tompkins launched her sharp, funny, and overstated investigation into the historical conditions—and machinery—that helped retail Hawthorne as a classic writer, scholars seem ready to construe both the man and his work as merchandise, which makes it easy to disparage one or the other.

Hawthorne, however, somewhat resented the image he'd helped to create, and in 1851 vented his irritation in the "Preface" to the second edition of *Twice-told Tales*, dryly and sardonically commenting that he,

> on the internal evidence of his sketches, came to be regarded as a mild, shy, gentle, melancholic, exceedingly sensitive, and not very forcible man, hiding his blushes under an assumed name, the quaintness of which was supposed, somehow or other, to symbolize his personal and literary traits. He is by no means certain, that some of his subsequent productions have not been influenced and modified by a natural desire to fill up so amiable an outline, and to act in consonance with the character assigned to him; nor, even now, could he forfeit it without a few tears of tender sensibility. (IX 7)

The multiple personae Hawthorne manufactured become him; a creature of his own making, he acknowledges that it forms as much a part of his biography as the external truths it may or may not represent. Significantly, Hawthorne contrives a narrative form that joins the personal essay with the ironic narrator, the sketch with the tale, history with fiction, the real world and faery-land in ways not easy to separate. In the sketch "A Book of Autographs," Hawthorne's narrator chances on a folio of letters supposedly written to a General Palmer, who just happens to be Sophia Hawthorne's grandfather. Were these letters real? Did Sophia Hawthorne or her mother or anyone in the Peabody family show them to her husband? I could not find them but believed in their existence enough to look.

I also believe Hawthorne wanted it both ways: actual and imaginary. The letters exist because they exist for the writer, who gives them meaning. An incipient postmodernist, Hawthorne blurs distinctions among genres, delighting in the myriad forms of representation available to him: history, satire, portraiture, sketch, story, essay, epistle, autobiography, even, eventually, daguerreotype and photography. But there he is: "He always put himself in his books," declared his sister-in-law Mary Mann; "he cannot help it" (Wineapple 2003, 59).

From this perspective and taken together, Hawthorne's work reads as a meditation on writing: the joy and sorrow of it, the pain, the loneliness, the uncertainty, and the great if fleeting sense of accomplishment. Early and late, Hawthorne countenances the difficulty of writing and quarters no excuse, though he provides his editors with many. Beset by a job in the Boston Custom-House, beset by requests for work, beset by distractions, he just can't get it right: "When we see how little we can express, it is a wonder that any man ever takes up a pen a second time" (VIII 250), he confided to his journals in 1844. Almost twenty years later, he sounded the same note in his last manuscript, "The Elixir of Life": "Various interruptions kept him from further examination of the manuscript, during the day," Hawthorne wrote of his title character, "for it may be observed, that a man no sooner sets his heart on any object, great or small, be it the lengthening out of his life interminably, or merely writing a romance about it, than his fellow beings, and fate and circumstance to back them, seem to conspire to hinder, to prevent, to throw in each his obstacle, great or small according to his power" (XIII 293).

Procrastination leads to doubt; doubt to dread: the writer whose work comes to nothing or, worse yet, the writer who fails himself. The plaint is a leitmotif in Hawthorne's work from the early storyteller series through his novels. "I am possessed, also, with the thought that I have never yet discovered the real secret of my powers," moans the narrator of "Journal of a Solitary Man" (XII 27); and in *The Marble Faun,* the copyist Hilda offers cold comfort to the artist Kenyon, telling him that "this final despair, and sense of shortcoming, must always be the reward and punishment of those who try to grapple with a great and beautiful idea. . . . The idea leaves you an imperfect image of itself, which you at first mistake for the real reality, but soon find that the latter has escaped out of your closest embrace" (VI 431).

Yet against all odds, and almost heroically, Hawthorne chose to write. And Emily Dickinson perhaps excepted, writers write in order to be published; the writer is not an introvert insofar as writing itself is, as Hawthorne knew, a form of exhibitionism even for the profoundly lonely man. Indeed, perhaps the lonely man, above everyone else, writes to an implied but almost palpable reader. "My theory is, that there is less indelicacy in speaking out your highest, deepest, tenderest emotions to the world at large, than to almost any individual," Hawthorne observed. "You may be mistaken in the individual; but you cannot be mistaken in thinking that, somewhere among your fellow-creatures, there is a heart that will receive yours into itself" (VI 324).

As Gertrude Stein would say, "I write for myself and strangers" (Stein 1971, 101).

Such contradictions need not be separated into two different Hawthornes: the isolato, in one instance, and the public man—writer or politician, or both—in another. "'May not one man have several voices, Robin, as well as two complexions?'" (XI 226). Hawthorne was sociable and reclusive—a man of intense privacy that he himself breached, over and over, by writing. This was never easy.

To me, then, Hawthorne's life is meaningful in the terms it was meaningful to him: a writer living in time, subject to its vicissitudes. "The biographer seeks what the subject's life meant *to the subject,* how the subject's experience registered on his or her consciousness, the satisfactions it supplied, dilemmas it produced," comments Kenneth Silverman (2003, 1; emphasis in original). A life of Hawthorne discovers Hawthorne in all that he wrote, he touched, he made, he left; it traces the patterns in the carpet, wondering all the while what it meant for him to be him: how, in other words, he came to see himself as he did; what, in other words, it meant to be a man, a writer, a descendant of illustrious forbears in a new country that touts democracy and equality; an artist and a politician, even at the same time; a Democrat among the Concord supporters of John Brown or in ever-fractious Salem.

His inner life inseparable from his outer life, they come together, perhaps, in his stories and tales and letters, but if he perceived inner or outer in conflict, or if others did, then that, too, is part of the story. So are his political views, for better or worse; the biographer is not a moralist. Imperfection is hot within us as well as the complications of being human, in history and of it. These are the stuff of biography, not canonization nor rectitude nor a prayer over the dead man's bones.

Nor is any biography complete. It can't be. "Biography first convinces us of the fleeing of the Biographied," Emily Dickinson wrote to Thomas Higginson (Dickinson 1986, 318). Hawthorne wrote the canonical novels of the nineteenth century, whose most striking characters—including himself—cast a very long shadow, even two hundred years after his birth. And along with everything that controls, confounds, and conditions them, they are all Nathaniel Hawthorne, the dead white Custom-House surveyor we love to hate, bookkeeper and poet, the man in the garret who loitered at the wharves. His vision was unremitting and, to be sure, often unsavory, as well as of his time and out of step with it and, in many ways, with ours. He saw the worst that we can do, not the best, which made him passive, ambitious, conservative, progressive, conflicted, compassionate, and cruel. And it gave force to his balanced, beautiful writing, which is not the writing of a languishing dilettante, as he feared, or of just another pen-and-ink hack marking time, and making money, on the Democratic payroll, but that of an unusual, not a simple man, dead and white to be sure and not easy even for himself to know—all at the very same time.

Notes

1.   During this discussion, Melville biographer Hershel Parker did note that he thought "that the friendship has been overemphasized," particularly in relation to the composition of *Moby-Dick*.

2.   Elizabeth Peabody to HB, June 4, 1887; Ronda 1984, 445.

Works Cited

Aaron, Daniel. *The Unwritten War: American Writers and the Civil War.* New York: Oxford University Press, 1975.

Adams, Henry. *The Education of Henry Adams.* New York: Modern Library, 1931.

Alam, Fakrul. *Bharati Mukherjee.* New York: Twayne, 1996.

Ammidon, Philip R. "Hawthorne's Last Sketch." *New England Magazine* 4 (June 1886): 516–27.

Anderson, Douglas. *A House Undivided: Domesticity and Community in American Literature.* New York: Cambridge University Press, 1990.

Anthony, David. "Class, Culture, and the Trouble with White Skin in Hawthorne's *The House of the Seven Gables.*" *Yale Journal of Criticism* 12 (1999): 249–68.

Arac, Jonathan. "The Politics of *The Scarlet Letter.*" In *Ideology and Classic American Literature.* Ed. Sacvan Bercovitch and Myra Jehlen, 247–66. New York: Cambridge University Press, 1986.

Balakian, Peter. "Two Lost Letters: Hawthorne at College; Longfellow and Hawthorne: The Beginning of a Friendship." *New England Quarterly* 56 (September 1983): 425–32.

"Balzac and his Writings." *Westminster Review* 60 (July and October 1853): 203, 212, 214.

Bancroft, George. *History of the United States from the Discovery of the American Continent.* Vol. 3. *History of the Colonization of the United States.* Boston: Little and Brown, 1840.

Bardes, Barbara, and Suzanne Gossett. *Declarations of Independence: Women and Political Power in Nineteenth-Century American Fiction.* New Brunswick, N.J.: Rutgers University Press, 1990.

Barlowe, Jamie. "Rereading Women: Hester Prynne-ism and the Scarlet Mob of Scribblers." *American Literary History* 9 (1997): 197–225.

———. *The Scarlet Mob of Scribblers: Rereading Hester Prynne.* Carbondale: Southern Illinois University Press, 2000.

Baym, Nina. "Passion and Authority in *The Scarlet Letter.*" *New England Quarterly* 43 (1970): 209–30.

———. "Hawthorne's Women: The Tyranny of Social Myths." *Centennial Review* 15 (1971): 250–72.

———. "The Romantic Malgré Lui: Hawthorne in the Custom-House." *ESQ* 19 (1973): 14–25.

———. *The Shape of Hawthorne's Career.* Ithaca,N.Y.: Cornell University Press, 1976.

———. "Melodramas of Beset Manhood: How Theories of American Fiction Exclude Women Authors." *American Quarterly* 33 (1981): 123–39.

———. "Thwarted Nature: Nathaniel Hawthorne as Feminist." In *American Novelists Revisited: Essays in Feminist Criticism.* Ed. Fritz Fleischmann, 58–77. Boston: G. K. Hall, 1982.

———. "Nathaniel Hawthorne and His Mother: A Biographical Speculation." *American Literature* 54 (1982): 1–27.

———. *The Scarlet Letter: A Reading.* Boston: Twayne, 1986.

Bell, Michael Davitt. *Hawthorne and the Historical Romance of New England.* Princeton, N.J.: Princeton University Press, 1971

———. *The Development of American Romance: The Sacrifice of Relation.* Chicago: University of Chicago Press, 1980.

Bell, Millicent. "Introduction." In *New Essays on Hawthorne's Major Tales.* Ed. Millicent Bell, 1–35. New York: Cambridge University Press, 1993.

———. "*The Marble Faun* and the Waste of History." *Southern Review* 35 (spring 1999): 354–70.

Ben-Joseph, Eli. *Aesthetic Persuasion: Henry James, the Jews, and Race.* Lanham, Md.: University Press of America, 1996.

Bentley, Nancy. "Slaves and Fauns: Hawthorne and the Uses of Primitivism." *ELH* 57 (1990): 901–37.

Bercovitch, Sacvan. *The Puritan Origins of the American Self.* New Haven, Conn.: Yale University Press, 1975.

———. *The Office of "The Scarlet Letter."* Baltimore, Md.: Johns Hopkins University Press, 1991.

———. *The Rites of Assent: Transformations in the Symbolic Construction of America.* New York: Routledge, 1993.

Berlant, Lauren. "Fantasies of Utopia in *The Blithedale Romance.*" *American Literary History* 1 (1989): 30–62.

———. *The Anatomy of National Fantasy: Hawthorne, Utopia, and Everyday Life.* Chicago: University of Chicago Press, 1991.

Bigsby, Christopher. *Hester: A Novel.* Hammondsworth: Penguin, 1994.

The Border Ruffian Code in Kansas. New York, 1855.

Boswell, James. *The Life of Samuel Johnson.* Ed. Christopher Hibbert. New York: Viking Penguin, 1986.

Brancaccio, Patrick. "'The Black Man's Paradise': Hawthorne's Editing of the *Journal of an African Cruiser.*" *New England Quarterly* 53 (1980): 23–41.

Breslaw, Elaine G. *Tituba, Reluctant Witch of Salem: Devilish Indians and Puritan Fantasies.* New York: New York University Press, 1996.

Brickhouse, Anna Campbell. "'I Do Abhor an Indian Story': Hawthorne and the Allegorization of Racial 'Commixture.'" *ESQ* 42, no. 4 (1996): 232–53.

———. "Hawthorne in the Americas: Frances Calderon de la Barca, Octavio Paz, and the Mexican Genealogy of 'Rappacini's Daughter.'" *PMLA* 113, no. 2 (1998): 227–42.

Bridge, Horatio. *Journal of an African Cruiser.* Ed. Nathaniel Hawthorne. New York: Wiley and Putnam, 1845.

Brodhead, Richard H. "Hawthorne and the Fate of Politics." *Essays in Literature* 11 (spring 1984): 95–103.

———. *The School of Hawthorne.* New York: Oxford University Press, 1986.

Brown, Gillian. *Domestic Individualism: Imagining Self in Nineteenth-Century America.* Berkeley: University of California Press, 1990.

Bryant, John, and Robert Milder, eds. *Melville's Evermoving Dawn: Centennial Essays.* Kent, Ohio: Kent State University Press, 1997.

Budick, Emily Miller. "The World as Specter: Hawthorne's Historical Art." *PMLA* 101 (1986): 218–32.

———. *Engendering Romance: Women Writers and the Hawthorne Tradition, 1850–1990.* New Haven, Conn.: Yale University Press, 1994.

Buell, Lawrence. *New England Literary Culture: From Revolution to Renaissance.* New York: Cambridge University Press, 1986.

Burr, George Lincoln, ed. *Original Narratives of Early American History: Narratives of the Witchcraft Cases, 1648–1706.* New York: Scribner's, 1914.

Butler, Judith. "Gender Trouble, Feminist Theory, and Psychoanalytic Discourse." In *Feminism/Postmodernism.* Ed. Linda J. Nicholson. New York: Routledge, 1990a.

———. *Gender Trouble: Feminism and the Subversion of Identity.* New York: Routledge, 1990b.

Calef, Robert, "More Wonders of the Invisible World." In *Original Narratives of Early American History: Narratives of the Witchcraft Cases, 1648–1706.* Ed. George Lincoln Burr, 289–393. New York: Scribner's, 1914.

Carpenter, Frederic I. "Scarlet A Minus." *College English* 5 (1944): 173–80.

Cash, W. J. *The Mind of the South.* 1941; reprint, New York: Vintage, 1991.

Charvat, William. *The Profession of Authorship in America, 1800–1870: The Papers of William Charvat.* Ed. Matthew J. Bruccoli. Columbus: The Ohio State University Press, 1968.

Chase, Richard. *The American Novel and Its Tradition.* Garden City, N. Y.: Doubleday and Co., Inc., 1957.

Cheyfitz, Eric. "The Irresistibleness of Great Literature: Reconstructing Hawthorne's Politics." *American Literary History* 6 (1994): 539–58.

Choate, Rufus. *The Works of Rufus Choate.* 2 vols. Ed. Samuel Gilman Brown. Boston: Little, Brown, 1852.

Clark, Elizabeth B. "Sacred Rights of the Weak: Pain and Sympathy in Antebellum America." *Journal of American History* 82 (September 1995): 463–93.

Colacurcio, Michael J. "Footsteps of Ann Hutchison: The Context of *The Scarlet Letter.*" *ELH* 39 (1972): 459–92.

———. *The Province of Piety: Moral History in Hawthorne's Early Tales.* Cambridge, Mass.: Harvard University Press, 1984

———. "The Woman's Own Choice": Sex, Metaphor, and the Puritan 'Sources' of *The Scarlet Letter.*" In *New Essays on* The Scarlet Letter. Ed. Michael J. Colacurcio, 101–36. New York: Cambridge University Press, 1985.

———. "Introduction." *Nathaniel Hawthorne, Selected Tales and Sketches.* Ed. Michael J. Colacurcio, vii–xxxv. New York: Penguin Books, 1987.

———. *The Province of Piety: Moral History in Hawthorne's Early Tales.* 1984; reprint, Durham, N.C.: Duke University Press, 1995.

Conway, Moncure Daniel. *Emerson, At Home and Abroad.* 1883; reprint, New York: Haskell House, 1968.

———. *Life of Nathaniel Hawthorne.* 1890; reprint, New York: Haskell House, 1968.

———. *Autobiography of Moncure Daniel Conway.* 2 vols. Boston: Houghton, Mifflin, 1904.

Cott, Nancy F. *The Bonds of Womanhood: "Woman's Sphere" in New England, 1780–1835.* New Haven, Conn.: Yale University Press, 1977.

Crane, Gregg D. *Race, Citizenship, and Law in American Literature.* Cambridge: Cambridge University Press, 2002.

Crenshaw, Ollinger. *The Slave States in the Presidential Election of 1860.* Baltimore. Md.: Johns Hopkins University Press, 1945.

Crews, Frederick. C. *The Sins of the Fathers: Hawthorne's Psychological Themes.* New York: Oxford University Press, 1966.

Crowley, J. Donald. *Hawthorne: The Critical Heritage.* New York: Barnes and Noble, 1970

———. "The Unity of Hawthorne's *Twice-Told Tales.*" *Studies in American Fiction* 1 (spring 1973): 35–61.

———. "Historical Commentary." In *The Centenary Edition of the Works of Nathaniel Hawthorne.* Vol. 9. *Twice-Told Tales.* Ed. William Charvat, Roy Harvey Pearce, and Claude Simpson, 458–533. Columbus: The Ohio State University Press, 1974.

Curtis, George W. "The Works of Nathaniel Hawthorne." *North American Review* 99 (October 1864): 539–57.

———. "Nathaniel Hawthorne." In *Essays from the* North American Review. Ed. Allen Thorndike Rice. New York: D. Appleton and Co, 1879.

Cutler, James Elbert. *Lynch-Law: An Investigation into the History of Lynching in the United States.* 1905; reprint, New York: Negro Universities Press, 1969.

Davidson, Cathy N., and Jessamyn Hatcher, eds. *No More Separate Spheres: A Next Wave American Studies Reader.* Durham, N.C.: Duke University Press, 2002.

DeForest, J. W. "The Great American Novel." *The Nation* 6 (9 January 1868): 27–29.

Dekker, George. *The American Historical Romance.* Cambridge: Cambridge University Press, 1987.

Demos, John. "The Antislavery Movement and the Problem of Violent 'Means.'" *New England Quarterly* 37 (December 1964): 501–26.

Derrick, Scott S. "'A Curious Subject of Observation and Inquiry': Homoeroticism, the Body, and Authorship in Hawthorne's *The Scarlet Letter.*" *Novel* 28 (1995): 308–26.

Desalvo, Louise. *Nathaniel Hawthorne.* Atlantic Highlands, N.J.: Humanities Press International, 1987.

Dickinson, Emily. *The Complete Poems of Emily Dickinson.* Ed. Thomas H. Johnson. Boston: Little, Brown and Co., 1960.

———. *Emily Dickinson Selected Letters.* Ed. Thomas H. Johnson. Cambridge, Mass.: Harvard University Press, 1986.

Egan, Ken. "The Adulteress in the Market-Place: Hawthorne and *The Scarlet Letter.*" *Studies in the Novel* 27 (1995): 26–41.

Elbert, Monika M. *Encoding the Letter "A": Gender and Authority in Hawthorne's Early Fiction.* Frankfurt: Haag & Herchen, 1990.

———. "Hawthorne's 'Hollow' Men: Fabricating Masculinity in 'Feathertop.'" *ATQ* 5 (September 1991): 169–82.

———, ed. Separate Spheres No More: Gender Convergence in American Literature, 1830–1930. Tuscaloosa: University of Alabama Press, 2000.

Eliot, George. *The George Eliot Letters.* 9 Vols. Ed. Gordon Haight. New Haven, Conn.: Yale University Press, 1954–78.

Elkins, Stanley M. *Slavery: A Problem in American Institutional and Intellectual Life.* 3rd ed., rev. Chicago: University of Chicago Press, 1976.

Elmer, Jonathan. *Reading at the Social Limit: Affect, Mass Culture, and Edgar Allan Poe.* Stanford, Calif.: Stanford University Press, 1995.

Emerson, Edward Waldo. "Notes." In *The Complete Works of Emerson.* 12 vols. Vol. 11. *Miscellanies by Ralph Waldo Emerson,* 547–648. 1903–04; reprint, New York: AMS Press, 1968.

———. *The Journals and Miscellaneous Notebooks of Ralph Waldo Emerson.* 16 Vols. Ed William H. Gilman et al. Cambridge, Mass.: Harvard University Press, 1960–1982.

———. *Emerson in his Journals.* Ed. Joel Porte. Cambridge, Mass.: Harvard University Press, 1982.

_____. *Collected Works.* 6 vols. to date. Ed. Robert E. Spiller et al. Cambridge, Mass.: Harvard University Press, 1971–.

_____. *Collected Poems and Translations.* New York: The Library of America, 1994.

Fetterley, Judith. *The Resisting Reader: A Feminist Approach to American Fiction.* Bloomington: Indiana University Press, 1978.

Fleischner, Jennifer. "Hawthorne and the Politics of Slavery." *Studies in the Novel* 4 (1991): 96–106.

Foner, Eric. *Free Soil, Free Labor, Free Man: The Ideology of the Republican Party before the Civil War.* New York: Oxford University Press, 1970.

Franchot, Jenny. *Roads to Rome: The Antebellum Protestant Encounter with Catholicism.* Berkeley: University of California Press, 1994.

Fredrickson, George M. *The Inner Civil War: Northern Intellectuals and the Crisis of the Union.* New York: Harper and Row, 1965.

Fryd, Vivien Green. *Art and Empire: The Politics of Ethnicity in the U.S. Capitol: 1815–1860.* New Haven, Conn.: Yale University Press, 1992.

Fuller, Margaret. *The Letters of Margaret Fuller.* Ed. Robert N. Hudspeth. 6 Vols. Ithaca, N.Y.: Cornell University Press, 1983–1994.

———. *"These Sad but Glorious Days": Dispatches from Europe, 1846–1850.* Ed. Larry J. Reynolds and Susan Belasco Smith. New Haven, Conn.: Yale University Press, 1991.

———. *Woman in the Nineteenth Century.* New York: Norton Critical Edition, 1998.

Gale, Robert L. *A Nathaniel Hawthorne Encyclopedia.* Westport, Conn.: Greenwood, 1991.

Garner, Stanton. *The Civil War World of Herman Melville.* Lawrence: University Press of Kansas, 1993.

Garrison, William Lloyd. *Selections from the Writings and Speeches of William Lloyd Garrison.* 1852; reprint, New York: Negro Universities Press, 1968.

Giles, Paul. *Transatlantic Insurrections: British Culture and the Formation of American Literature, 1730–1860.* Philadelphia: University of Pennsylvania Press, 1962.

Gilmore, Michael T. *Surface and Depth: The Quest for Legibility in American Culture.* New York: Oxford University Press, 2003.

Goddu, Teresa. "Letters Turned to Gold: Hawthorne, Authorship, and Slavery." *Studies in American Fiction* 29 (spring 2001): 49–76.

Gollin, Rita K. *Annie Adams Fields: Woman of Letters.* Amherst: University of Massachusetts Press, 2002.

Gougeon, Len. *Virtue's Hero: Emerson, Antislavery, and Reform.* Athens: University of Georgia Press, 1990.

Greeley, Horace. *Recollections of a Busy Life.* 1868; reprint, New York: Confucian Press, 1981.

Grimsted, David. *American Mobbing, 1828–1861: Toward Civil War.* New York: Oxford University Press, 1998.

Gross, Seymour. "Hawthorne's 'My Kinsman, Major Molyneux': History as Moral Adventure." *Nineteenth Century Fiction* 12 (September 1957): 97–109.

Grossman, Jay. "'A' is for Abolition?: Race, Authorship, *The Scarlet Letter.*" *Textual Practice* 7, no. 1 (spring 1993): 13–30.

Gupta, Akhil. "Reliving Childhood? The Temporality of Childhood and Narratives of Reincarnation." *Ethnos* 67, no. 1 (2002): 1–23.

Hall, Lawrence Sargent. *Hawthorne, Critic of Society.* 1944; reprint, Gloucester, Mass.: Peter Smith, 1966.

Hansen, Chadwick. "The Metamorphosis of Tituba, or Why American Intellectuals Can't Tell an Indian Witch from a Negro." *New England Quarterly* 47 (March 1974): 3–12.

Hawthorne, Julian. *Nathaniel Hawthorne and His Wife: A Biography.* 2 Vols. Boston: Houghton, 1884.

Hawthorne, Nathaniel. *The Scarlet Letter.* Vol. 1. *The Centenary Edition of the Works of Nathaniel Hawthorne.* Ed. William Charvat, Roy Harvey Pearce, and Claude M. Simpson. Columbus: The Ohio State University Press, 1962.

———. *The House of the Seven Gables.* Vol. 2. *The Centenary Edition of the Works of Nathaniel Hawthorne.* Ed. William Charvat, Roy Harvey Pearce, and Claude M. Simpson. Columbus: The Ohio State University Press, 1965.

———. *The Blithedale Romance.* Vol. 3. *The Centenary Edition of the Works of Nathaniel Hawthorne.* Ed. William Charvat, Roy Harvey Pearce, and Claude M. Simpson. Columbus: The Ohio State University Press, 1964.

———. *The Marble Faun.* Vol. 4. *The Centenary Edition of the Works of Nathaniel Hawthorne.* Ed. William Charvat, Roy Harvey Pearce, and Claude M. Simpson. Columbus: The Ohio State University Press, 1968.

———. *The Marble Faun: Or, the Romance of Monte Beni.* Ed. Richard Brodhead. New York: Penguin Books, 1990.

———. "The Ambitious Guest" (1835). In *Twice-Told Tales.* Vol. 9. *The Centenary Edition of the Works of Nathaniel Hawthorne.* Ed. William Charvat, Roy Harvey Pearce, and Claude M. Simpson, 324–33. Columbus: The Ohio State University Press, 1974.

———. "The Gentle Boy" (1832). In *Twice-Told Tales.* Vol. 9. *The Centenary Edition of the Works of Nathaniel Hawthorne.* Ed. William Charvat, Roy Harvey Pearce, and Claude M. Simpson, 68–105. Columbus: The Ohio State University Press, 1974.

———. "The Hollow of the Three Hills" (1830). In *Twice-Told Tales.* Vol. 9. *The Centenary Edition of the Works of Nathaniel Hawthorne.* Ed. William Charvat, Roy Harvey Pearce, and Claude M. Simpson, 199–204. Columbus: The Ohio State University Press, 1974.

———. *Mosses from an Old Manse*. Vol. 10. *The Centenary Edition of the Works of Nathaniel Hawthorne*. Ed. William Charvat, Roy Harvey Pearce, and Claude M. Simpson. Columbus: The Ohio State University Press, 1974.

———. "Roger Malvin's Burial" (1832). In *Mosses from an Old Manse*. Vol. 10. *The Centenary Edition of the Works of Nathaniel Hawthorne*. Ed. William Charvat, Roy Harvey Pearce, and Claude M. Simpson, 337–60. Columbus: The Ohio State University Press, 1974.

———. "Young Goodman Brown" (1835). In *Mosses from an Old Manse*. Vol. 10. *The Centenary Edition of the Works of Nathaniel Hawthorne*. Ed. William Charvat, Roy Harvey Pearce, and Claude M. Simpson, 74–90. Columbus: The Ohio State University Press, 1974.

———. "Alice Doane's Appeal" (1835). In *The Snow-Image and Uncollected Tales*. Vol. 11. *The Centenary Edition of the Works of Nathaniel Hawthorne*. Ed. William Charvat, Roy Harvey Pearce, and Claude M. Simpson, 266–80. Columbus: The Ohio State University Press, 1974.

———. "The Canterbury Pilgrims" (1833). In *The Snow-Image and Uncollected Tales*. Vol. 11. *The Centenary Edition of the Works of Nathaniel Hawthorne*. Ed. William Charvat, Roy Harvey Pearce, and Claude M. Simpson, 120–31. Columbus: The Ohio State University Press, 1974

———. *The Snow-Image and Uncollected Tales*. Vol. 11. *The Centenary Edition of the Works of Nathaniel Hawthorne*. Ed. William Charvat, Roy Harvey Pearce, and Claude M. Simpson. Columbus: The Ohio State University Press, 1974.

.———. "The Wives of the Dead" (1832). In *The Snow-Image and Uncollected Tales*. Vol. 11. *The Centenary Edition of the Works of Nathaniel Hawthorne*. Ed. William Charvat, Roy Harvey Pearce, and Claude M. Simpson, 192–99. Columbus: The Ohio State University Press, 1974.

———. *The French and Italian Notebooks*. Vol. 14. *The Centenary Edition of the Works of Nathaniel Hawthorne*. Ed. Thomas Woodson. Columbus: The Ohio State University Press, 1980.

———. *The Letters, 1813–1843*. Vol. 15. *The Centenary Edition of the Works of Nathaniel Hawthorne*. Ed. William Charvat, Roy Harvey Pearce, and Claude M. Simpson. Columbus: The Ohio State University Press, 1984.

———. *The Letters, 1843–1853*. Vol. 16. *The Centenary Edition of the Works of Nathaniel Hawthorne*. Ed. Thomas Woodson, L. Neal Smith, and Norman Holmes Pearson. Columbus: The Ohio State University Press, 1985.

———. "Mrs. Hutchinson" (1830). In *Miscellaneous Prose and Verse*. Vol. 23. *The Centenary Edition of the Works of Nathaniel Hawthorne*. Ed. Thomas Woodson, Claude M. Simpson, and L. Neal Smith, 66–74. Columbus: The Ohio State University Press, 1997.

———. *Nathaniel Hawthorne's Tales*. Ed. James McIntosh. New York: W. W. Norton & Co., 1987.

Herbert, T. Walter. "The Erotics of Purity: *The Marble Faun* and the Victorian Construction of Sexuality." *Representations* 36 (fall 1991): 114–32.

———. *Dearest Beloved: The Hawthornes and the Making of the Middle-Class Family.* Berkeley: University of California Press, 1993.

———. "Pornographic Manhood and *The Scarlet Letter.*" *Studies in the Novel* 29 (2001): 113–20.

Higginson, Thomas Wentworth. "Wedded Isolation." *Woman's Journal* (December 20, 1884): 407.

Idol, John, Jr., and Buford Jones. *Nathaniel Hawthorne: The Contemporary Reviews.* New York: Cambridge University Press, 1994.

James, Henry. *Literary Criticism: Essays on Literature, American Writers, English Writers.* 1878. Ed. Leon Edel. New York: Library of America, 1984.

———. *Nathaniel Hawthorne. English Men of Letters.* New York: Harper and Brothers Publishers, 1879; reprint, New York: Collier-Macmillan, 1966.

———. *William Wetmore Story and His Friends: From Letters, Diaries, and Recollections.* 2 vols. Boston: Houghton Mifflin Co., 1903.

———. *Literary Criticism: French Writers, Other European Writers. The Prefaces to the New York Edition.* Ed. Leon Edel. New York: Library of America, 1984.

Jefferson, Thomas. *Notes on the State of Virginia.* Ed. Merrill D. Petersen. New York: Library of America, 1984.

Jones, Catherine A. "Hawthorne's Scotland: Memory and Imagination," *Symbiosis* 4 (2000): 136.

Karcher, Carolyn L. *The First Woman in the Republic: A Cultural Biography of Lydia Maria Child.* Durham. N.C.: Duke University Press, 1994.

Kearns, Francis. "Margaret Fuller and the Abolition Movement." *Journal of the History of Ideas* 25 (1964): 120–27.

Kendall, Phebe Mitchell. *Life, Letters and Journal of Maria Mitchell.* Freeport, N.Y.:1896; reprint, Books for Libraries Press, 1971

Kilcup, Karen L. "'Ourself behind Ourself, Concealed': The Homoerotics of Reading in *The Scarlet Letter.*" *ESQ* 42 (1996): 1–28.

Klammer, Martin. *Whitman, Slavery, and the Emergence of "Leaves of Grass."* University Park: Pennsylvania State University Press, 1995.

Lang, Amy Schrager. *Prophetic Women: Anne Hutchinson and the Problem of Dissent in the Literature of New England.* Berkeley: University of California Press, 1987.

Lathrop, Rose Hawthorne. *Memories of Hawthorne.* 1897; reprint, New York: AMS Press, 1969.

Leavis, Q. D. "Hawthorne as Poet." *Sewanee Review* 59 (spring and summer 1951): Part I: 179–65; 198–205; Part II: 456–58.

Leverenz, David. "Mrs. Hawthorne's Headache: Reading *The Scarlet Letter.*" *Nineteenth-Century Fiction* 37 (1983): 552–75.

———. *Manhood and the American Renaissance.* Ithaca, N.Y.: Cornell University Press, 1989.

———. "Historicizing Hell in Hawthorne's Tales." In *New Essays on Hawthorne's Major Tales.* Ed. Millicent Bell, 101–32. Cambridge: Cambridge University Press, 1993.

———. *Paternalism Incorporated: Fables of American Fatherhood, 1865–1940.* Ithaca. N.Y.: Cornell University Press, 2003.

Levin, Harry. *The Power of Blackness: Hawthorne, Poe, Melville.* New York: Random House, 1958.

Levine, Robert S. "Antebellum Rome in *The Marble Faun.*" *American Literary History* 2 (spring 1990): 19–38.

Lewis, R. W. B. *The American Adam: Innocence, Tragedy, and Tradition in the Nineteenth Century.* Chicago: University of Chicago Press, 1955

Longfellow, Henry Wadsworth. Review of *Twice-Told Tales. North American Review* 45 (July 1837): 59–73.

———. Review of *Twice-Told Tales. North American Review* 54 (April 1842). Reprinted in *The Recognition of Nathaniel Hawthorne.* Ed. B. Bernard Cohen, 9–12. Ann Arbor: University of Michigan Press, 1969.

Luedtke, Luther S. *Nathaniel Hawthorne and the Romance of the Orient.* Bloomington: Indiana University Press, 1989.

Madsen, Deborah L. "'A is for Abolition': Hawthorne's Bond-servant and the Shadow of Slavery." *Journal of American Studies* 25 (1991): 255–59.

Mann, Horace. "Speech on the Institution of Slavery" (1852). Reprinted in *Against Slavery: An Abolitionist Reader.* Ed. Mason Lowance, 266–72. New York: Penguin Books, 2000.

Manning, Susan. *The Puritan-Provincial Vision: Scottish and American Literature in the Nineteenth Century.* Cambridge: Cambridge University Press, 1990.

Martin, Robert K. "Hester Prynne, C'est Moi: Nathaniel Hawthorne and the Anxieties of Gender." In *Engendering Men: The Question of Male Feminist Criticism.* Ed. Joseph A. Boone and Michael Cadden, 122–39, 304–6. New York: Routledge, 1990.

———, and Leland S. Person, eds. *Roman Holidays: American Writers and Artists in Nineteenth-Century Italy.* Iowa City: University of Iowa Press, 2002.

Marvell, Andrew. *The Poems and Letters of Andrew Marvell.* 2 vols. Ed. H. M. Margoliouth. Oxford: Clarendon Press, 1952.

Mather, Cotton. *The Wonders of the Invisible World.* 1693. Reprint Mount Vernon, N.Y.: The Peter Pauper Press, 1950.

Matthiessen, F. O. *America Renaissance: Art and Expression in the Age of Emerson and Whitman.* New York: Oxford University Press, 1941.

Mayer, Henry. *All on Fire: William Lloyd Garrison and the Abolition of Slavery.* New York: St. Martin's Press, 1998.

McPherson, James M. *Battle Cry of Freedom: The Civil War Era.* New York: Ballantine, 1989.

McWilliams, John P., Jr. "'Thorough-goin Democrat' and 'Modern Tory': Hawthorne and the Puritan Revolution of 1776." *Studies in Romanticism* 15 (1976): 549–71.

Melish, Joanne Pope. *Disowning Slavery: Gradual Emancipation and "Race" in New England, 1780–1860.* Ithaca, N.Y.: Cornell University Press, 1998.

Mellow, James R. *Nathaniel Hawthorne in His Times.* Boston: Houghton Mifflin, 1980.

Melville, Herman. *Battle-Pieces and Aspects of the War.* Ed. Sidney Kaplan. Amherst: University of Massachusetts Press, 1972.

———. "Hawthorne and His Mosses." In *The Writings of Herman Melville,* vol. 9. *The Pizza Tales and Other Prose Pieces, 1839–1860.* Ed. Harrison Hayford, Hershel Parker, and G. Thomas Tanselle, 239–53. Evanston, Ill.: Northwestern University Press, 1987.

Merish, Lori. *Sentimental Materialism: Gender, Commodity Culture, and Nineteenth-Century American Literature.* Durham, N.C.: Duke University Press, 2000.

Meyer, Michael. "Thoreau's Rescue of John Brown from History." In *Studies in the American Renaissance 1980.* Ed. Joel Myerson, 301–16. Charlottesville: University of Virginia Press, 1980.

Michaels, Walter Benn. "Romance and Real Estate." In *The American Renaissance Reconsidered: Selected Papers from the English Institute, 1982–83.* Ed. Walter Benn Michaels and Donald E. Pease, 156–82. Baltimore, Md.: Johns Hopkins University Press, 1985.

———, and Donald E. Pease. *The American Renaissance Reconsidered: Selected Papers from the English Institute, 1982–83.* Baltimore, Md.: Johns Hopkins University Press, 1985.

Miller, Edwin Haviland. *Salem Is My Dwelling Place: A Life of Nathaniel Hawthorne.* Iowa City: University of Iowa Press, 1991.

Miller, Perry. "Afterword." *The Sketchbook of Geoffrey Crayon, Gent.* New York: New American Library, 1961.

Miller, William Lee. *Arguing about Slavery: John Quincy Adams and the Great Battle in the United States Congress.* New York: Knopf, 1996.

Millington, Richard H. *Practicing Romance: Narrative Form and Cultural Engagement in Hawthorne's Fiction.* Princeton, N.J.: Princeton University Press, 1992.

———. "Where is Hawthorne's Rome?: *The Marble Faun* and the Cultural Space of Middle-Class Leisure." In *Roman Holidays: American Writers and Artists in Nineteenth-Century Italy.* Ed. Robert K. Martin and Leland S. Person, 9–27. Iowa City: University of Iowa Press, 2002.

Mitchell, Thomas R. *Hawthorne's Fuller Mystery.* Amherst: University of Massachusetts Press, 1998.

Moore, Margaret. "Nathaniel Hawthorne and 'Old John Brown.'" *Nathaniel Hawthorne Review* 26 (spring 2000): 25–32.

Morrison, Toni. *Playing in the Dark: Whiteness and the Literary Imagination.* Cambridge, Mass.: Harvard University Press, 1992.

Mukherjee, Bharati. *The Holder of the World.* New York: Knopf, 1993.

Myerson, Joel, ed. *Studies in the American Renaissance, 1996.* Charlottesville: The University Press of Virginia, 1996.

Newberry, Frederick. *Hawthorne's Divided Loyalties: England and America in His Works.* Rutherford, N.J.: Associated University Presses, 1987.

Newman, Judie. "Spaces In-Between: Hester Prynne as the Salem Bibi in Bharati Mukherjee's *The Holder of the World.*" In *Borderlands: Negotiating Boundaries in Post-Colonial Writing.* Ed. Monika Reif-Hülser, 69–87. Amsterdam: Rodopi, 1999.

Nudelman, Franny. "'Emblem and Product of Sin': The Poisoned Child in *The Scarlet Letter* and Domestic Advice Literature." *Yale Journal of Criticism* 10 (1997): 193–213.

Onderdonk, Todd. "'The Marble Mothers': Hawthorne's Iconographies of the Feminine." *Studies in American Fiction* 31 (2003): 73–100.

Packard, Christopher. "Who's Laughing Now? Sentimental Readers and Authorial Revenge in 'Alice Doane's Appeal.'" *Arizona Quarterly* 52 (1996): 1–20.

Parker, Hershel. *Herman Melville: A Biography,* vol. 2. *1851–1891.* Baltimore, Md.: Johns Hopkins University Press, 2002.

Parker, Theodore. "The Function and Place of Conscience in Relation to the Laws of Men." Ed. Dean Grodzins. In *Against Slavery: An Abolitionist Reader.* Ed. Mason Lowance, 273–85. New York: Penguin Books, 2000.

[Peabody, Elizabeth, A.] "Slavery in the United States: Its Evils, Alleviations and Remedies. *North American Review* 73 (October 1851): 347–86.

Pearson, Norman Holmes. *Hawthorne's Two Engagements.* Northampton, Mass.: Smith College, 1963.

Person, Leland S. *Aesthetic Headaches: Women and a Masculine Poetics in Poe, Melville, and Hawthorne.* Athens: University of Georgia Press, 1988.

———. "The Dark Labyrinth of Mind: Hawthorne, Hester, and the Ironies of Racial Mothering." *Studies in American Fiction* 29 (spring 2001): 33–47.

Pease, William H., and Jane H. Pease. "Antislavery Ambivalence: Immediatism, Expediency, Race." *American Quarterly* 17 (winter 1965): 682–95.

Pfister, Joel. *The Production of Personal Life: Class, Gender, and the Psychological in Hawthorne's Fiction.* Stanford, Calif.: Stanford University Press, 1991.

Phillips, Wendell. *The Philosophy of the Abolitionist Movement.* Anti-Slavery Tract no. 8. New York, 1860.

Poe, Edgar Allan. "The Man That Was Used Up" (1839). In *Edgar Allan Poe: Poetry, Tales, and Selected Essays.* Ed. Patrick F. Quinn and G. R. Thompson, 307–16. New York: Library of America, 1996.

Potter, David M. *The Impending Crisis, 1848–1861.* New York: Harper and Row, 1976.

Railton, Stephen. *Authorship and Audience: Literary Performance in the American Renaissance.* Princeton, N.J.: Princeton University Press, 1991.

Reynolds, David S. *Beneath the American Renaissance: The Subversive Imagination in the Age of Emerson and Melville.* New York: Alfred A. Knopf, 1988; Cambridge, Mass.: Harvard University Press, 1989.

Reynolds, Larry J. *European Revolutions and the American Literary Renaissance.* New Haven, Conn.: Yale University Press, 1988.

Richards, Leonard L. *"Gentlemen of Property and Standing": Anti-Abolition Mobs in Jacksonian America.* New York: Oxford University Press, 1970.

Robertson-Lorant, Laurie. *Herman Melville.* New York: Clarkson Potter, 1996.

Rogin, Michael. *"Ronald Reagan," the Movie: and Other Episodes in Political Demonology.* Berkeley: University of California Press, 1987.

Romero, Lora. *Home Fronts: Domesticity and Its Critics in the Antebellum United States.* Durham: Duke University Press, 1997.

Ronald, Ann. "Roger Malvin's Grandson." *Studies in American Fiction* 12 (1984): 71–77.

Ronda, Bruce. *The Letters of Elizabeth Palmer Peabody.* Wesleyan, Conn.: Wesleyan University Press, 1984.

Rosenwald, Lawrence A. "The Theory, Practice, and Influence of Thoreau's Civil Disobedience." In *A Historical Guide to Henry David Thoreau.* Ed. William E. Cain, 153–79. New York: Oxford University Press, 2000.

Rowe, John Carlos. *At Emerson's Tomb: The Politics of Classic American Literature.* New York: Columbia University Press, 1997.

———. *The Other Henry James.* Durham, N.C.: Duke University Press, 1998.

———. *The New American Studies.* Minneapolis: University of Minnesota Press, 2002.

———. "Nineteenth-Century United States Literary Culture and Transnationality." *PMLA* 118, no. 1 (January 2003): 78–89.

———, ed. *Selected Writings of Ralph Waldo Emerson and Margaret Fuller.* Boston: Houghton Mifflin Co., 2003.

Ryskamp, Charles. "The New England Sources of *The Scarlet Letter." American Literature* 31 (1959): 257–72.

Scott, Walter. *Waverley. The Edinburgh Waverley.* 48 Vols. Edinburgh: Constable, 1901.

Silverman, Kenneth. *The Life and Times of Cotton Mather.* New York: Harper and Row, 1984.

———. "Biography and Pseudo-Biography." *Common-place: The Interactive Journal of Early American Life* 3, no. 2 (January 2003): 1–3.

Smith, Henry Nash. *Virgin Land: The American West as Symbol and Myth.* Cambridge, Mass.: Harvard University Press, 1950.

Smith, R. McClure. "Void in the Narrative: The Seduction of the Reader in Nathaniel Hawthorne's 'Alice Doane's Appeal.'" *ATQ* 5 (1991): 73–82.

Stedman, Edmund Clarence. *The Poems of Edmund Clarence Stedman.* Boston: Houghton Mifflin, 1908.

Stein, Gertrude. *Everybody's Autobiography.* New York: Cooper Square Publishers, 1971.

Stowe, Harriet Beecher. *Uncle Tom's Cabin or, Life among the Lowly.* Introduction by Jeremy Larner. 1852; reprint, New York: Harper & Row, 1965.

———. *Uncle Tom's Cabin or, Life among the Lowly.* Ed. Ann Douglas. 1852; reprint, New York: Penguin Classics, 1986.

———. *Uncle Tom's Cabin: Authoritative Text, Backgrounds and Contexts.* Ed. Elizabeth Ammons. 1852; reprint, New York: W. W. Norton, 1994.

Stowe, William W. *Going Abroad: European Travel in Nineteenth-Century American Culture.* Princeton, N.J.: Princeton University Press, 1994.

Stryz, Jan. "The Other Ghost in *Beloved:* The Specter of *The Scarlet Letter.*" In *The New Romanticism: A Collection of Critical Essays.* Ed. Everhard Alsen, 137–57. New York: Garland, 2001.

Stubbs, John C. "A Note on the Source of Hawthorne's Heraldic Device in *The Scarlet Letter,*" *Notes and Queries* 15 (May 1868): 175–76.

Teichgraeber, Richard F., III. *Sublime Thoughts/Penny Wisdom: Situating Emerson and Thoreau in the American Market.* Baltimore, Md.: Johns Hopkins University Press, 1995.

Thomas, Brook. "Citizen Hester: *The Scarlet Letter* as Civic Myth." *American Literary History* 13 (2001): 181–211.

Thompson, G. R. *The Art of Authorial Presence: Hawthorne's Provincial Tales.* Durham, N.C.: Duke University Press, 1993.

———, and Eric Carl Link. *Neutral Ground: New Traditionalism and the American Romance Controversy.* Baton Rouge: Louisiana State University Press, 1999.

Thoreau, Henry David. *The Journal of Henry D. Thoreau.* Ed. Bradford Torrey and Francis H. Allen. Volume 6, December 1853–August 31, 1854. Boston: Houghton Mifflin, 1906.

———. *Reform Papers.* Ed. Wendell Glick. Princeton, N.J.: Princeton University Press, 1973.

———. *Journal. Volume 3: 1848–1851.* Ed. Robert Sattelmeyer, Mark R. Patterson, and William Rossi. Princeton, N.J.: Princeton University Press, 1990.

———. *Walden and Resistance to Civil Government.* 2nd ed. Ed. William Rossi. New York: Norton, 1992.

Ticknor, Caroline. *Hawthorne and His Publisher.* Boston: Houghton Mifflin Co., 1913.

Tomc, Sandra. "A Change of Art: Hester, Hawthorne, and the Service of Love." *Nineteenth-Century Literature* 56 (2002): 466–94.

Tompkins, Jane. *Sensational Designs: The Cultural Work of American Fiction, 1790–1860.* New York: Oxford University Press, 1985.

Traubel, Horace. *With Walt Whitman in Camden.* Vol. 6 (September 15, 1889–July 6, 1890). Carbondale: Southern Illinois University Press, 1982.

Trilling, Lionel. "Our Hawthorne." In *Hawthorne Centenary Essays.* Ed. Roy Harvey Pearce, 429–58. Columbus: The Ohio State University Press, 1964.

Turner, Arlin. *Nathaniel Hawthorne.* New York: Oxford University Press, 1980.

Upham, Charles. *Salem Witchcraft; with an Account of Salem Village, and a History of Opinions on Witchcraft and Kindred Subjects.* 2 Vols. 1867; reprint, Williamstown, Mass.: Corner House Publishers, 1971.

Ventura, Mary K. "'Alice Doane's Appeal': The Seducer Revealed." *ATQ* 10 (1996): 25–39.

Von Frank, Albert J. "Mrs. Brackett's Verdict: Magic and Means in Transcendental Antislavery Work." In *Transient and Permanent: The Transcendental Movement and Its Contexts.* Ed. Charles Capper and Conrad Edick Wright, 385–407. Boston: Massachusetts Historical Society, 1999.

Wallace, James D. "Hawthorne and the Scribbling Women Reconsidered." *American Literature* 62 (1990): 201–22.

Warren, Joyce W. *The American Narcissus: Individualism and Women in Nineteenth-Century American Fiction.* New Brunswick, N.J.: Rutgers University Press, 1984.

Weinauer, Ellen. "Considering Possession in *The Scarlet Letter.*" *Studies in American Fiction* 29 (2001): 93–112.

Welter, Barbara. *Dimity Convictions: The American Woman in the Nineteenth Century.* Athens: Ohio University Press, 1976.

Whipple, Edwin Percy. Review of *The Scarlet Letter. Graham's Magazine* 36 (May 1850): 345–46.

Whitman, Walt. *The Correspondence.* Vol. 1. *1842–1867.* Ed. Edwin Haviland Miller. New York: New York University Press, 1961.

Wineapple, Brenda. *Nathaniel Hawthorne: A Life.* New York: Alfred A. Knopf, 2003.

Woodberry, George. *Nathaniel Hawthorne.* Boston: Houghton Mifflin, 1902.

Wright, Nathalia. "Hawthorne and the Praslin Murder." *New England Quarterly* 15 (March 1942): 5–14.

Wyatt-Brown, Bertram. *Yankee Saints and Southern Sinners.* Baton Rouge: Louisiana State University Press, 1985.

Yellin, Jean Fagan. *Women and Sisters: The Antislavery Feminists in American Culture.* New Haven, Conn.: Yale University Press, 1989.

———. "Hawthorne and the Slavery Question." In *A Historical Guide to Nathaniel Hawthorne.* Ed. Larry J. Reynolds, 135–64. New York: Oxford University Press, 2001.

Zinn, Howard. *A People's History of the United States.* New York. Harper Collins, 1999.

Index

Printed in Great Britain
by Amazon

37859322R00137